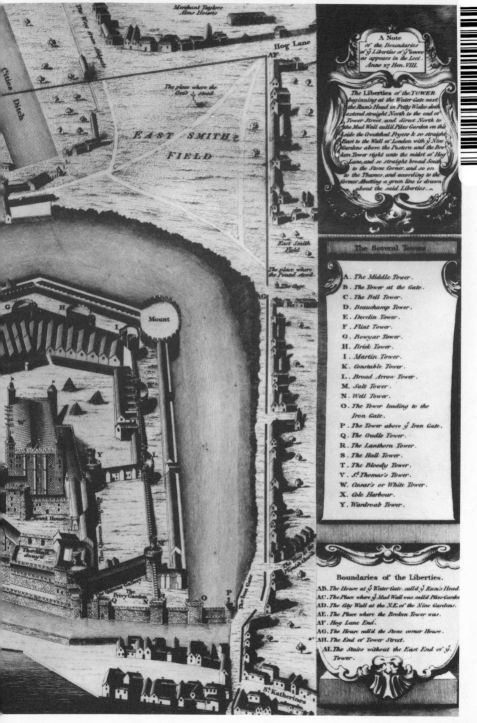

THE CHALLENGE OF ANNE BOLEYN

By Hester W. Chapman

The Challenge
of
ANNE BOLEYN

Hester W. Chapman

Coward, McCann & Geoghegan, Inc.

New York

TO ALLEN DRURY

End paper illustration, a contemporary drawing of The Tower of London in the reign of Henry VIII, British Crown copyright, reproduced with the permission of the Controller of Her Brittanic Majesty's Stationery Office.

First American Edition 1974

SBN: 698-10612-1

Library of Congress Catalog Card Number: 74-79681

PRINTED IN THE UNITED STATES OF AMERICA

Contents

Illustrations follow page 132

Acknowledgments

THE author's grateful thanks are due to Her Majesty Queen Elizabeth II for her gracious permission to reproduce the Holbein drawings of Sir Thomas Wyatt and Sir Thomas Boleyn, and the portrait of the Duke of Norfolk. Thanks are also due to His Grace the Duke of Northumberland for leave to reproduce the medallion of Henry Percy, Sixth Earl of Northumberland; to the Earl of Bradford for the Holbein drawing of Anne Boleyn; and to Lord Astor for a picture of Hever Castle and the falcon emblem of Anne, Marquess of Pembroke. The Master and Fellows of Corpus Christi College, Cambridge, kindly granted permission to show Anne Boleyn's letter written to her father, and the Warden of New College, Oxford, furnished the portrait of Henry VIII and the Pope (the latter upside down). Henry's letter to Anne is from the Vatican Library. The National Portrait Gallery supplied the portraits of Katherine of Aragon, Anne Boleyn, Cardinal Wolsey, Thomas Cromwell, Archbishop Cranmer, Jane Seymour and the Princess Mary. The portraits of Francis I and Pope Clement VII are the property of the gallery of the Louvre. Especial thanks are due to Miss Rosamond Lehmann and Mr George Rylands for invaluable criticism and advice, and to Miss Kate Chapman for editorial help.

Anne the quene

History to the defeated
May say Alas but cannot help or pardon
                    W. H. AUDEN

Foreword

SEVERAL lives of Anne Boleyn have been published, most of which are pejorative, when not condemnatory; and, indeed, she can hardly be described as an elevated or sympathetic character. One of the reasons for this is that her background, gorgeously appointed though it was, might be compared to a snake-pit, of which nearly all the occupants were venomous, not least the gigantic and terrible *magnifico* who ruled it, and over whom she achieved partial domination for some nine years. In such circumstances she inevitably acquired the reputation of an unscrupulous and predatory siren; she was reviled by the English people, feared even by her allies, but also adored, first by a feeble-spirited aspirant, later by the husband who struck her down, then by a poet of genius, and perhaps even by those five young men destroyed with and through her.

Anne Boleyn became one of the principal figures in a hideous melodrama, a corrupt and involute series of intrigues, in which the *mores* of her contemporaries are now difficult to assess. For in that world, compassion and honesty had no place, and no meaning; if it had been otherwise, she would have acquired neither power nor notoriety. Less than a century after her death, the presentation of Iago's fiendish wizardry, the gouging out of Gloucester's eyes and the torments of the Duchess of Malfi was calmly received by six-teenth- and seventeenth-century audiences: while we now incline to see the characters in such scenes as archaic examples of wickedness. At the Court of Henry VIII their prototypes not only existed, but surpassed, in evil, the villains of the Elizabethan and Jacobean playwrights. Briefly flourishing and often applauded, they expected to find treason in high places, and coolly accepted the spectacle of Justice and Law contemplating, well pleased, the persecution and putting to death of the innocent, the high-principled or the merely foolish. In these conditions, of capricious hatred and undeviating ruthlessness, Anne Boleyn lived, triumphed — and perished. Her qualities — courage, intelligence and energy — were thereby infected; yet they sustained her to the end.

Finally, it must be emphasized that her story is not for the squeamish. The fastidious reader has been warned. For the others — those attracted by the bizarre and the macabre, and armed to meet a glittering concourse of doomed and degraded personages — 'Non ragionam di lor: ma guarda, e passa ...'

PART I

Lady-in-Waiting

A wightly wanton with a velvet brow,
With two pitch balls stuck in her face for eyes;

*　　*　　*

And therefore is she born to make black fair.
Her favour turns the fashion of the days ...

Love's Labour's Lost

I

Blickling Hall and Hever Castle

IN the autumn of 1457 Sir Geoffrey Boleyn, having concluded his term of office as Lord Mayor of London, retired to his manor of Blickling Hall in Norfolk. Partly through business acumen, and also because he had effected several successful negotiations between the rival parties of Lancaster and York, he had preserved this and his other properties from depredations in the Wars of the Roses, and was now a rich man; furthermore, he had married an heiress, the daughter of Lord Hoo and Hastings. Fourteen years later he died, and was succeeded by his eldest son, William, who became a courtier under Edward IV, a Knight of the Bath and husband of an Ormonde heiress, Lady Margaret Butler.

Their successor, Thomas, who received his Garter from Henry VII in 1505, made an even greater match; his bride was Elizabeth Howard, eldest daughter of the Duke of Norfolk; and as her brother, Lord Thomas, was the husband of Lady Anne Plantagenet, Henry VII's sister-in-law, the Boleyns were now affiliated, although remotely, with the royal house. When Henry VIII succeeded in 1509, Sir Thomas Boleyn became a Gentleman of the Bedchamber. Lady Boleyn, gay, charming and witty, was one of the beauties at the court of the eighteen-year-old King.

This wealthy and successful couple spent part of their time on their country estates, one of which was Hever Castle in Kent; but in these early years they seem to have preferred Blickling as a residence (this house was entirely rebuilt a century later), where all their children were born. Every year, until her death from puerperal fever in 1512, Lady Boleyn had a baby; of these, three survived—Anne, Mary and George.[1]

Anne was born in 1503–4—the exact date is not recorded—and spent the first part of her childhood at Blickling.* Some years later,

* The *Encyclopaedia Britannica* and the *Dictionary of National Biography* give the date of Anne's birth, as do several historians, as 1507. For information on the correct date, see Friedmann, Vol. II, p. 315.

the family moved to Hever, and her father married again; his second wife was a local lady whose name and origin have not survived, and she had little or nothing to do with the education of her step-children. Sir Thomas saw to it that all three should acquire the learning and accomplishments which would prepare them for Court life. Until their teens they remained in Kent, in the care of tutors and governesses.

Hever Castle provided the perfect setting for a small family; then, as now, it had a fairy-tale beauty. Originally a stronghold, later a moated farm and finally a luxurious hunting-lodge, it had been restored, altered and enlarged since the thirteenth century. Yet this variegated treatment, culminating in Sir Thomas Boleyn's incorporation of a manor-house within the walls of a fortress, was, perhaps inadvertently, harmonious, resulting in a finely evolved example of domestic architecture. Remote, elegant and unique, Hever was also self-contained and unpretentious: rather a pleasure-dome than a mansion, surrounded by water and yew hedges and ringed by a deer forest. Its colouring, red-brown, cream and greyish-white, was that of the inside of a shell; the outer walls rose, solid and cool, above the amber encirclement of the moat; the drawbridge was guarded by four saints in niches above the gateway. The courtyard, with its gabled roofs and latticed windows, was rather dark, but neither gloomy nor forbidding.

The interior decoration was elaborately rich. Current fashion forbade the slightest hint of austerity; walls, ceilings, furniture and floors were covered, to the last inch, with patterns of great intricacy. Yet the effect was not stifling or vulgar, because an overall design controlled the mass, so that the general impression was processional and co-ordinated; technique and invention were combined in glowing splendour; saints, flowers, fruits, strapwork, cherubs, pendants, tapestries and fabulous beasts were dominated by an orderliness and a sense of proportion that achieved magnificence without strain. The rooms were not large; even the long gallery, the council chamber and the banqueting-hall were planned for privacy.

Informality therefore prevailed over stateliness, so that a comparatively small indoor staff—not more than fifty, if as many—served the Boleyns in these early days, before Sir Thomas was in a position to entertain the King and his retinue. Meanwhile, his and the children's daily routine was invariable and strenuous. Breakfast, of ale, bread and beef, was at seven; dinner, consisting of some fifteen to twenty dishes, at twelve; and supper, a slightly less lavish feast, at five in winter and between six and seven at other seasons.

This schedule was subordinated to the hunting and hawking expeditions which continued all the year round, and enabled the Boleyns to meet and entertain the neighbouring families; of these, the most important was that of Sir Henry and Lady Wyatt, distant cousins, whose eldest son, Thomas, a handsome and spirited boy, was exactly Anne's age and became her earliest admirer. But her father's plans for the future did not include an alliance for either her or Mary with the Wyatts; he looked higher, and was justified in doing so, for all his children were remarkably attractive and intelligent. Mary, the elder girl, was better-looking than Anne, whose appearance, although striking and unusual, was neither then nor later that of a fashionable beauty, for she was slender, dark and rather sallow, and had the beginning of a second nail on one finger; also, her huge black eyes protruded a little; her hair reached below her waist and was her chief asset. Her possibilities called for every advantage, and these were under consideration before she reached her teens.

While George Boleyn's lessons in Italian, Latin, theology and mathematics were given by tutors, with the aid of a writing-master, he and the girls learned French from a Mademoiselle Semmonet; all three practised dancing together; then Anne and Mary rode out or walked in the garden and their brother worked with his fencing-master. Music was the most important accomplishment, comprising the practice of lute, harp, viol and virginals, and, in George's case, composition; it was at about this time that he began to write poetry, and to make free translations from Petrarch and Dante. His sisters' French was fluent at an early age, as may be seen from Anne's only surviving letter to her father in that language. Formal but unsupervised, it is a sixteenth-century version of the modern *devoir*, and follows the pattern of the Latin letters composed by most upper-class or royal children to parents, tutors and one another.

Anne, hearing that Sir Thomas has arranged for her to appear at Court, 'and that the Queen will condescend to enter into conversation with me', rejoices at this news and promises to work hard at her French, adding that her spelling — which is highly eccentric —

has not been corrected by Semmonet, so that 'nobody may know what I am writing to you'. She concludes with the assurance of leading 'as holy a life as you may please to desire', and of her dutiful love, 'after having very humbly craved your goodwill and affection'.[2]

This letter was sent from Hever. It indicates that the writer was to be presented, not only to Queen Katherine, but also to Henry VIII's younger sister Mary, who, having just been married by proxy to Louis XII of France, was about to leave for that country, attended by a large suite; of these, Anne was to be one, provided she made a good impression on the eighteen-year-old bride.

This break in her life, made in October 1514 between the ages of eleven and twelve, was the first step in the 'finishing' period of her education. Her father, who had sent his elder daughter to the Court of the Hapsburg Archduchess Margaret in Brussels, intended Anne to remain in France until he had arranged her marriage: for she had not, in the conventional sense, her sister's assets, and would therefore be more difficult to place. In addition to the malformation of a finger, she had several moles, one on the front of her neck and others on different parts of her body; so it seemed best to keep her out of England until a suitable husband had been chosen and contracted.[3] Suitable, in Sir Thomas's circle, meant of course wealthy and aristocratic; his ambition and avarice were combined with total indifference to his children's happiness and morals.

It was then a commonplace among visiting foreigners, not only that English people were cold and sometimes cruel to both sons and daughters, but that there were those who actually hated them. Such a generalization, although in many cases misleading, was true of the Boleyns. Sir Thomas was incapable of affection. Grasping, acute, cunning and ruthless, he saw his children simply as means to greater riches and power. They must therefore be trained to excel; and he came to hate and work against them when they failed — as they all did, eventually — to do so.

This aspect of his character was not apparent till much later, and had little or no effect on the course of their development. None of them expected or desired closer contact than that provided by his commands and plans; and they came to share his ambitions at an early age. When Anne and Mary left England, George, already established at the University, was being trained for diplo-

macy; eight years were to pass before they all met again, and by
that time the whole pattern of their lives had changed, with Mary
in the ascendant. Meanwhile Anne, leaving her home without
regret, was nearly drowned in the process. If this obscure twelve-
year-old had perished in that crossing, the course of the Reformation might have been delayed, and the greatest monarch ever to sit
on the English throne would not have been born.

Anne Boleyn's training for this, her first employment, had been
carried out on conventional lines. Her religious orthodoxy was
beyond dispute — with the household, she attended Mass every
day, and several times on holy days and Sundays — her knowledge
of French was above the average, and her dancing and singing
were of a higher standard than that of her contemporaries. Nothing
more was required of her. The study of Greek, Latin and patristic
literature was not practised by upper-class girls till the next
generation; and it is unlikely that, even given the chance, she would
have taken to the scholarship for which a selected few, including
her own daughter, were to become celebrated. That she was
livelier and more attractive than Mary Tudor's other ladies was not
then apparent; but she seems to have pleased the young Queen
and to have been on friendly terms, not only with her companions,
but also with the rather formidable Lady Guilford, Mary's
Mistress of the Robes.

The bridal party, numbering some three hundred persons, left
London for Dover escorted by Sir Thomas Boleyn and the second
Duke of Norfolk, Anne's maternal grandfather. Henry and Queen
Katherine accompanied them, and they were all established in the
Castle. Here they had to wait for a fortnight, while storms raged,
the wind continued contrary and Queen Mary became more and
more depressed: for she had hoped to be allowed to marry Charles
Brandon, Duke of Suffolk, with whom she had privately exchanged
vows, and was appalled at the thought of being bedded with the
'feeble and pocky' Louis XII. When the wind changed and she
went down to the shore, she extracted a promise from the King
that her next husband should be chosen by herself, and, weeping,
embarked, while Anne, Lady Guilford and some of her other
ladies boarded a different galleon.[4] Then the wind changed again,
the storm rose and the vessels were separated, struggling against
the tempest for four days and nights. Finally, Mary's ship landed
on a sand-bank near Boulogne, and that containing her suite

entered the harbour, while the rain continued to stream down. Soaked, faint with seasickness and in terror of being submerged in the surf, they were carried ashore and conducted to the Castle. There they were given time to rest and recover before moving on to Abbeville. In these unpropitious circumstances Anne Boleyn's new life began.

She had been rescued from death by the skill, devotion and courage of the men set to guard and protect her — and was none the worse. Such an experience may well have inspired the cool dauntlessness and bold optimism which were to become part of her character.

NOTES

1. Ellis, *Original Letters Illustrative of English History*, Third Series, Vol. III, p. 22.
2. Corpus Christi MSS.
3. Wyatt, *Extracts from the Life of the Virtuous, Christian and Renowned Queen Anne Boleyn* (hereafter cited as *Anne Boleyn*), p. 2.
4. Chapman, *The Sisters of Henry VIII*, p. 171.

II

From Paris to London

QUEEN MARY'S party reached Abbeville on October 6th, 1514. Some miles from the city they were met by the future Francis I, Louis's cousin and son-in-law, who, with his nobles, drew back when the King, dressed for hawking—i.e. for a semi-private, impromptu meeting with his bride—was seen approaching. Accompanied by two hundred ladies and his daughter, Madame Claude, Francis's wife, who was to become a major influence in Anne's life during her teens, Louis spurred forward to embrace Mary, knocking her red velvet hat on one side as he did so.[1]

The rain, which had ceased during the first part of her progress, then came down again, so heavily that all were drenched before they reached Abbeville. Here, Mary and her ladies were escorted to a house next to the King's; and at seven o'clock the next morning her attendants walked about the garden while she and Louis talked alone; then they rode through the city to the Cathedral for the marriage ceremony. The Queen's beauty—'She is a Paradise,' the Venetian Ambassador reported[2]—entranced the spectators, who had eyes for no one else, least of all for Anne. She remained unobserved during the ensuing celebrations: banquets, parades—and a ball, at which the poor old King insisted on taking the floor, very nearly incapacitating himself in the process, with the result that departure for Paris was delayed for three weeks.

Then, four days after the consummation of his marriage, Louis asserted himself. To the horror of his wife, he announced his intention of dismissing her Mistress of the Robes and her eighty ladies, but was persuaded to allow Anne and her contemporaries, Elizabeth and Anne Grey, to remain, presumably on the grounds that they were too young to be of any importance. Lady Guilford, he said, had interfered with his courtship of Mary, and she must go. Ignoring his bride's tears and protests, he also dismissed the Duke of Norfolk and Sir Thomas Boleyn.[3]

So Anne and the Grey sisters were left with only their waiting-women to look after them until they reached Paris, where Madame

Claude took them over. Some time ago, she had set up what would now be described as a finishing school for young ladies, supervised by an elderly governess, and held her own Court within that of her father. This arrangement, approved by Sir Thomas, ensured his daughter's being educated and chaperoned as became her station. Officially, Anne was still in attendance on the Queen; in fact, her days were subordinated to an almost conventual routine; for Madame Claude, although only seventeen, was puritanically strict and strongly opposed to the easy-going gallantry and idle habits of Francis and his favourite sister, the poetess and novelist Marguérite de Valois. There was no question, either then or later, of his remaining faithful to his wife; they led separate lives, although he treated her courteously during their public appearances. So Anne became accustomed to the spectacle of a husband whose position as heir-presumptive enabled him to ignore the proprieties and indulge his caprices.

Francis had not long to wait for his inheritance. Louis XII died on January 1st, 1515, and some weeks later his widow secretly married the Duke of Suffolk, who had come to Paris on an embassy of condolence. In May they left for England. Through Cardinal Wolsey, with whom he was now temporarily allied, Sir Thomas Boleyn arranged that Anne should be transferred to the service of Queen Claude until he had contracted her in marriage to an Ormonde cousin, Sir James Butler. But Lord Ormonde's insistence on a large dowry held up the negotiations, so that, using the Cardinal as an intermediary, Sir Thomas asked Henry VIII to exert his powers. Henry, who then had no knowledge of or interest in Anne, approved the match, and desired his minister, through Anne's uncle, Lord Surrey (later the third Duke of Norfolk), to forward it.[4]

As Sir Thomas and Lord Ormonde continued to haggle, Anne stayed on in Paris. She was now a Court lady, and beginning to attract a certain amount of attention. But Queen Claude's supervision prevailed, and she continued under the discipline ordained by her mistress; at tournaments, hunting parties and receptions she was still one of a number of background figures.

Some ten years later, when it became public news that, on dynastic grounds and at the dictates of his conscience, Henry VIII intended to put aside the wife of eighteen years' standing in order to marry again, and that his choice was set on a lady-in-waiting, those who had frequented the Tuileries and the Louvre at Francis I's accession began to search their memories for reminiscences of Queen Katherine's supplanter. And nine years after that, when Anne Boleyn was the first Queen of England to be charged with and executed for adultery and high treason (and, in her case, incest as well), many, including a few who had never seen her, rushed to record — one in verse — all they had heard of her capacity to allure and seduce. Some of these descriptions — of her blue velvet gowns, her leaps and pirouettes in the dance, her jewelled brodequins, her gauze head-dresses and her long hair — may be authentic;[5] they must, however, be taken cautiously and with reservation, in view of the fact that the most celebrated of these memoirists, Brantôme, was not born until four years after her death. By then, what would now be called her aspect as a *femme fatale* had become a legend; and, then as now, she was seen as the dark siren, the evil creature whose enticements had furthered England's separation from the Papacy, and who perished as she deserved. That the break with Rome would have been brought about in any case was not, for several centuries, admitted. Henry's divorce and his assumption of Supremacy over the English Catholic Church were inextricably confused, as they still sometimes are in the public mind, with the sorceries of the woman continental Ambassadors described as 'the Concubine', and with whom they considered him to have committed bigamy three years before he sent her to the block.

In these, the first years of Francis's reign, Anne's daily routine, alternating between public appearances and private entertainment, formed her tastes and helped to develop the strength of character which was to sustain her against the attacks of enemies and the advances of admirers when she reached maturity. The restrictions of family life in a rustic setting had now given way to the customs of a fantastically luxurious Court ruled by a twenty-year-old Maecenas, in whom self-indulgence and display were intermittently combined. The portraits of this unpleasant Roi-Chevalier, Titian's and Clouet's especially, show him, not only as evil and conceited, but also as rather silly. It is as if those great artists were unable to conceal their contempt for the ineffable frivolity, the monstrous arrogance of an Italianate virtuoso, a patron whose discrimination and open-handedness were merely another means of self-glorification.

In 1515, for instance, Anne Boleyn's part in the parade organized by Francis for a provincial tour, although no doubt enjoyable, thrust her — with twenty-six other girl attendants on the Queen — into a procession of small open sailing-boats drawn by white harts through the waters of the Saône as a means of entry into the city of Lyons. This absurd and pretentious exhibition, amusingly recorded in a series of drawings,[6] enforced discomfort without dignity, and was typical of many similar efforts produced by Francis's masters of ceremony. That Queen Claude's suite should be squashed together, with fatal effect on their gowns and head-dresses, was a foretaste of the King's love of horseplay, which developed into violence and brutality as he grew older.

Anne's existence therefore became one of disturbing contrasts. While Francis encouraged and headed the licence of his courtiers, and the exhibitionism of his mistresses, the Queen's prudery was intensified and her rules were more strictly applied. Plain, stout, dull and dowdy, she made no attempt to emulate her brilliant sister-in-law, Marguérite; and here her influence on Anne prevailed; for neither then nor later did that young lady care for poetry (though she inspired it), or romances, or for literature of any kind. Picture-books seem to have appealed to her,[7] but she was no reader. At this time, her performances as a singer and dancer were perfected; and concern for her disabilities resulted in her wearing a narrow jewelled band round her neck, and sleeves that concealed her hands. The current fashion of halo caps enhanced her sculpturally set head and the streams of black hair falling below the veil attached to a coif set with semi-precious stones.

Meanwhile, the restless atmosphere and headlong pace of the French Court suited her energetic temperament. Also, the settings created by the patron of Leonardo da Vinci, Primaticcio and Cellini developed her visual sense as she became one of the performers in a masque of exquisite beauty. The delicate richness, the extravagant elaboration of her surroundings, were partly the cause of the elegance for which she was to become famous in her own country.

At this time she was moving towards a group who ignored when they did not mock Queen Claude's insistence on modest behaviour ('maintien décent'), while exercising their gifts of 'préciosité et plaisanterie gauloise'.[8] Acquiring these, Anne may have come to accept the varied dissipations of a circle in which the rumours

(probably false) of the King's incestuous relations with Marguérite
de Valois were freely circulated. Meanwhile, Anne's love of rich
food is more likely to have been formed in these early, luxurious
years than her later, rather superficial interest in Erasmian criticisms of religious orthodoxy. Francis, that most Christian King,
tolerated this revolutionary cell, while taking pleasure in watching
the torture of heretics; this was one of his distractions in the intervals of hunting, jousting and the composition of music and verse.
(The rhyme with which he is now associated, 'Souvent femme
varie, Bien fol est qui s'y fie', was not his; and none of his poetry
has survived.) Much praised for these talents, and for his generosity
and gaiety, he saw to it that the ladies of the Maison du Roi were
well paid, so that Anne's standard of expenditure became very
high. There is no record of Francis being attracted to her; she may
have been too closely guarded, not only by the Queen, but also by
the King's mother, Louise of Savoy, the only person able to control
him. Thus Anne began to acquire an instinctive caution; no hint
of scandal was attached to her name during her years in France.

One admirer, whose name has not survived, wrote some verses
about her, which are now in the Bibliothèque Nationale; and in
1817 Georges Crapelet attached them to his edition of Henry
VIII's love-letters to Anne.[9] This anonymous courtier mentions
her arrival with Mary Tudor and her being retained by Queen
Claude when Mary left for England. He then describes the dancing,
singing and huge black eyes of 'Mademoiselle Anne Boullant', and
adds that she was generally able to make people do what she
wanted. In very indifferent rhyme he gives the impression that
this then unknown girl became conspicuous, although she does not
seem to have flouted the conventions. One of Anne's first biographers has attributed these verses to Clément Marot; they show
no sign of that poet's quality, and do not appear in his collected
works.[10]

Anne was about sixteen when her father, visiting the French
Court, decided that she should remain there, his plans for the
Butler alliance having failed to materialize, although he had not
given up hope of Lord Ormonde's accepting his offer. At about
this time, he removed Mary Boleyn from the Archduchess
Margaret's service and placed her in Queen Katherine's entourage.
She then became the mistress of Henry VIII, supplanting
Elizabeth Blount, by whom he had had a son in 1519. This

connection did not much benefit Sir Thomas, and lasted over a year. With the conclusion of his embassy to France, he renewed his negotiations for Anne's marriage to James Butler, but still without success; neither the King nor Wolsey was able to persuade the Ormondes to meet his terms, and they ceased to trouble about the matter. By the time Anne accompanied Queen Claude to the Field of Cloth of Gold she was seventeen, and should long since have been married; but nobody seemed to want her, perhaps because her dowry was not sufficiently tempting.

At that meeting, as pointless as it was extravagant — both Kings arrived accompanied by some five thousand persons — Anne Boleyn's attendance on Queen Claude gave her a privileged position among the spectators. With her companions, she moved into one of the pavilions especially built for the occasion — and had to move out again when it was blown down by a high wind.[11] She watched Henry and Francis, each heading their troops, pause to gaze at one another across the Val d'Or; when the trumpets sounded, they advanced and embraced.

In his twenty-ninth year, Henry, who had begun to put on weight, was still a magnificent spectacle, towering, majestic, superb. Francis, equally tall, but slighter and more lightly moving, appeared as the epitome of French elegance and grace. For a fortnight, banquets, balls and jousts ensured a surface geniality. Then, on the last day, when the wind was too high for tilting, Henry proposed a wrestling match with Francis — and was thrown. Furious, he sprang up and flung himself upon his good friend and brother for another bout: but both Queens rushed down from their stands to intervene.[12] Gallantry and courtesy prevailed; and so it was that Anne saw her future husband publicly humiliated, and then restored to good humour through feminine persuasion.

On June 23rd, 1520, after attending High Mass and hearing a sermon on the blessings of peace, the monarchs parted. A year later, they were again in angry disagreement ('These sovereigns', observed the Venetian Ambassador, 'are not at peace ... they hate each other'[13]), and a few months after that were preparing for war — Francis against Katherine's nephew, Charles V, and Henry, with Pope Leo X, in support of the Emperor. Wolsey, conferring with Charles at the English colony of Calais, was pursued by Henry's letters urging the recovering of his 'rightful inheritance' of the French territories acquired by Henry V.

In the following year France and England were at war for the second time since Henry's accession, and early in 1522 Sir Thomas Boleyn arranged for Anne's return home. After a short stay at Hever, he placed her in Queen Katherine's household.[14]

And now she came to a crossroads. For the first —and last — time in her life, she fell in love, passionately, desperately, and in fierce revolt against all the rules and customs of the day.

NOTES

1. Chapman, *The Sisters of Henry VIII*, pp. 172-4.
2. Ibid.
3. Ibid.
4. Friedmann, *Anne Boleyn*, Vol. I, p. 42.
5. Strickland, *Lives of the Queens of England*, Vol. II, p. 182; Bourgueville, *Recherches et Antiquités*, p. 29.
6. *Génies et Réalitiés*, p. 20.
7. See p. 91.
8. *Génies et Réalités*, p. 120.
9. Crapelet, *Lettres de Henry VIII à Anne Boleyn*, p. 169; Bourgueville, op. cit., p. 29.
10. Friedmann, op. cit., Vol. II, p. 317.
11. *Calendar of Venetian State Papers* (*hereafter cited as Ven. Cal. P.*), Vol. III, pp. 68-9.
12. Ibid., p. 95.
13. Ibid.
14. *Letters and Papers, Foreign and Domestic, of the Reign of Henry VIII* (hereafter cited as *L. & P.*), Vol. III, pt. 2, p. 856.

III

Henry Percy

THE circle of which Anne Boleyn became a member at the age of
nineteen bore only a superficial resemblance to that of Francis I.
A papal representative who had attended both, described Henry
VIII's Court as possessing the riches and civilization of the world;[1]
and he did not exaggerate; for although Henry and his nobles
were unable to employ the great Italian artists patronized by
Francis, their care for learning had made the English Court a
centre of intellectual activity in a setting of solid magnificence,
enhanced by a dignity of bearing and an outward observance of the
proprieties which could not have existed under Francis's rule.

But while admiring this display, many visiting envoys recorded
their dislike of English insincerity and frivolity. Charming and
hospitable, these eccentric islanders could not be relied on for a
moment, and were expert liars. Their extravagance was deplorable, and their levity, boasting and gluttony horrified those
foreigners they condescended to entertain. Also, their women
thought nothing of showing their legs, kissed strangers of both
sexes on introduction and dined unchaperoned with their husbands' friends. And having no idea of 'the point of honour', these
husbands often drew their daggers on one another, exchanged
stabs, and would be seen a few hours later drinking together.[2]

Yet his critics had to admit that Henry's Court was perfectly
organized. Its splendours provided many kinds of pleasure,
especially that of appearing in fancy dress for what would now be
described as the private theatricals in which Anne Boleyn became
one of the principal performers; for long before Henry realized
that he was in love with her, he made her his leading lady in a
series of masques of immense elaboration. These entertainments,
inspired by both the King and Cardinal Wolsey, might last for
hours; and in them her accomplishments were dramatically
displayed.

While the evenings were given up to these performances,
Henry's days, which began at four or five in the morning, were

occupied with interviews, correspondence, hunting, jousting, tennis, archery, progresses from one palace to another, inspection of naval and other inventions and unremitting attendance at Mass. He seemed, as did the Cardinal—who often worked for nineteen hours at a stretch—to have time for everything, and was never tired or, really, out of patience; for his terrifying rages were as histrionic as they were effective; his famous good humour was sometimes equally conscious; and behind these alternating and impenetrable masks he was aware of much that he pretended to ignore. Indeed, his secretiveness—'If I thought that my cap knew my counsel, I would throw it in the fire,' he said once—was eventually brought to a fine art.[3] In his spare time he composed music and poetry (his Mass is still sung and his verses appear in more than one anthology); he wrote and spoke five languages, and played the harp, the virginals, the organ and the lute; he was a competent engineer, a fair architect and an enthusiastic astronomer; he wrote three books, the first and best known being the anti-Lutheran *Assertio Septem Sacramentorum* of 1521; he was a skilled theologian, in permanent touch with the Deity, and thus divinely guided (as he often pointed out) in all his actions. His marriage to Katherine of Aragon was little affected by his transient affairs with Elizabeth Blount and Mary Boleyn; for he had long been dependent on his wife's companionship and understanding, and continued so until directed by the Almighty to discard her.

Yet another outstanding characteristic, shared by the majority of Henry's courtiers, was that of giving way to floods of tears, either privately or in public, a habit of frequent occurrence in that age of brutal harshness and cruelty. These outbursts were chiefly indulged in by men; the women were more resilient (or less sensitive?) and did not cry nearly so much. It was not unusual for Henry, when addressing his Parliaments, to break down and weep —while continuing his harangue—with the result that lords, bishops and commons followed suit, and an orgy of grief, led by that huge, glittering figure, ensued. Wolsey did the same; and it often happened that a nobleman addressing his troops before a battle, or one minister disagreeing with another, would 'fall all to weeping', as an eye-witness puts it, and was rather reverenced than pitied for what was then looked on as a sign of sensibility. (Again, women were not so highly evolved; their feelings were less attractively shown by screams, or hysterical abuse.) These crises

34 THE CHALLENGE OF ANNE BOLEYN

were sometimes set off by a show of self-deprecation; the weeping potentate might turn away, mop his eyes and murmur something about unmanliness; but this did not often happen, and was in any case a formality.

So it is that when Shakespeare makes Wolsey say to Cromwell, 'I had not thought to shed a tear in all my misery', and gently reproaches that faithful servant (also in tears), for causing him to 'play the woman', the writer was drawing upon factual evidence provided by one of the first and most remarkable of historical biographies – the life of the Cardinal by George Cavendish, his gentleman-usher, whose observation of Anne Boleyn's influence on the King and his minister was intimate and unrivalled.

Cavendish, a man of gentle birth and good education, did not write his invaluable and fascinating memoir till some twenty years after the Cardinal's death; then, setting down his recollections in Queen Mary's reign, it would have been quite in order for him to censure the mother of the future Queen Elizabeth. He did not do so. Although Anne Boleyn is described as Wolsey's most dangerous enemy, she is not abused, or even criticized; her actions are allowed to speak for themselves.

This brilliant study, the work of one of the very few upright and kindly men in Henry VIII's entourage, was not printed till 1641; but the manuscript was in circulation throughout the sixteenth century, and used by Hall (thence by Shakespeare) and other chroniclers. Its unique quality cannot be overrated; for Cavendish was not only a 'natural' writer, but a man of keen and sympathetic intuition and undeviating loyalty. He adored his master, whose confidant he was proud to be; yet he did not minimize his faults, any more than he underrated the power and fascination of the woman who helped to bring about Wolsey's ruin.

Like others in that circle, Cavendish rejoiced in the luxury of Henry's Court; his descriptions of balls, feasts and masques create the background of Anne's early years there. Above all, it is to him that we owe the only full account of her relationship with Henry Percy, the eldest son of Lord Northumberland.

Cavendish says that Anne, 'for her excellent gesture and behaviour, did excel all other', and thus attracted Henry VIII, adding that she herself was not at first aware of her effect on him.[4] This seems unlikely; a king's favour, however casually given, is not usually unobserved; but it is possible that Anne, as she became increasingly drawn towards Henry Percy, discounted the King's casual gallantries. Also, the fact that her sister was now married to William Carey, and her brother George to Jane Parker, Lord Morley's daughter, may have turned her thoughts towards her own, long overdue establishment; for Percy, whose father had other plans for him, was a splendid match.

The delay in arranging her marriage might have been caused by talk of the mole on her neck and the malformation of her little finger; for many people believed the latter to be the sign of a witch, thus marked out by Satan as his instrument. Whatever the reason, Sir Thomas Boleyn had so far failed to find her a suitable husband, and now remained inactive; it was therefore inevitable that she should break all the rules by agreeing to marry the man she loved.

She and Percy had come to know one another in 1522-3, soon after she joined the Queen's entourage. For some time their growing fondness remained unnoticed, and was presently looked on as no more than a flirtation, one of many in a circle of lively young people whose duties threw them together at both public and private functions. Then, Cavendish reports, Lord Percy, who was one of Wolsey's attendants, and came with him to wait on Katherine, 'would resort for his pastime unto the Queen's chamber, and there would fall into dalliance among the Queen's maidens, being at the last more conversant with Mistress Anne Boleyn than with any other; so that there grew a secret love between them that, at length, they were ensured together, intending to marry'.[5]

This connection, seemingly of no great importance, began to shadow the Cardinal's radiance. Hitherto, Cavendish observes, his master had 'passed his life and time ... in such great wealth, joy and triumphant glory, having always on his side the King's especial favour'—and this over a period of thirteen years. But at last, he goes on, Fortune 'waxed something wroth with his pros-perous estate ... wherefore she procured Venus, the insatiate goddess, to be her instrument'.[6]

The goddess had an equally insatiate satellite. Anne Boleyn had been long aware of her own powers; now, having subjugated Percy, she contemplated marrying him, independently of their respective parents' approval; a characteristic defiance of conven-tion, which was to recur throughout her career. They exchanged vows, and sought one another out so openly that everyone came to know of their intentions. Talk of this rebellion reached the King, presumably through Katherine; he immediately desired Wolsey to put an end to it.

Cavendish concludes that Henry intended Anne to succeed her sister in his favour. Although the King did not make any definite advances to her until a year or two later, he may have wished her to remain available until he had made up his mind; and her marrying Percy would have removed her, intermittently, at least, from Court. Also, the Earl of Northumberland, one of his richest and most powerful nobles, not only had begun negotiations for his son's marriage to a Talbot heiress, Lord Shrewsbury's daughter, but had informed Percy of his intentions; and Henry's internal policy entailed his support of his principal servants in all family affairs.

So Wolsey, violently irritated by young Percy's putting him in the wrong, both with the King and with Northumberland, sent for him to the gallery of his palace of York Place, and in front of his gentlemen, of whom Cavendish was one, began, 'I marvel not a little of thy peevish folly, that thou wouldest entangle and ensure thyself with a foolish girl yonder in the Court, I mean Anne Boleyn.' He went on to describe Percy's prospects, scolded him for ignoring his father's wishes, emphasized the Earl's powers ('he would have matched you according to your estate and honour') and finally pointed out the young man's gross disloyalty to his sovereign. 'The King's Majesty himself', he said, 'will complain to thy father on thee.' He added that Henry had plans of his own for Anne—'though she knoweth it not'—and declared that she would be 'most glad and agreeable to the same'.[7]

Wolsey's rages could be even more alarming than his master's; for they were never lightened, as Henry's sometimes might be, by rays of unexpected (and calculated) good humour; and so, long before the end of this harangue, the unfortunate Percy was in tears. This did not prevent him defending himself eloquently and at length. Between sobs, he replied, 'Sir, I knew nothing of the King's displeasure therein, for whose displeasure I am very sorry. I considered that I was of good years, and thought myself sufficient to provide me of a convenient wife, whereas my fancy served me best, not doubting but that my lord my father would have been right well persuaded. And though she be but a simple maid, and having but a knight to her father, yet is she descended of right noble parentage.' He then reminded Wolsey of Anne's relationship with the Norfolks and the Ormondes, and went on, 'Why should I then, sir, be anything scrupulous to match with her, whose descent of estate is equivalent with mine, when I shall be in most dignity?' He concluded, rather too boldly, by asking the Cardinal to 'entreat the King's most royal majesty — most lowly on my behalf — for his princely benevolence in this matter, which I cannot deny nor forsake'.

This piece of impertinence so enraged the Cardinal that, turning from Percy to his awestruck followers, he exclaimed, 'Lo, sirs, ye may see what conformity or wisdom is in this wilful boy's head!' Rounding on him, he continued, 'I thought that when thou heardest me declare the King's intended pleasure and travail therein, thou wouldest have relented and wholly submitted thyself.'

Still 'all weeping', Percy protested, 'Sir, so I would — but in this matter I have gone so far, before so many worthy witnesses, that I know not how to avoid myself, nor to discharge my conscience.'

'Why,' Wolsey thundered, 'thinkest thou that the King and I know not what we have to do in so weighty a matter as this?' As Percy mumbled an assent, he added, 'I warrant thee! Howbeit, I can see in thee no submission to the purpose' — so fiercely that Percy's defences collapsed.

'Forsooth, my lord,' he begged, 'if it please Your Grace, I will submit myself wholly to the King's Majesty and Your Grace in this matter, my conscience being discharged of the weighty burden of my pre-contract' — i.e. to Anne.

Wolsey replied, 'Well, then — I will send for your father out of the north parts, and he and we shall take order for the avoiding of this hasty folly. And in the mean season, I charge thee — and in the King's name command thee — that thou presume not *once* to resort unto her company, as thou intendest to avoid the King's high indignation' — and with this fearful threat, swept from the gallery.[8]

Anne was unaware of the Cardinal's intervention when, with the King and Queen and their respective suites, she was bidden to a party at York Place. The splendour of this palace equalled, and in some respects surpassed, that of Westminster, as did the number of attendants, of which there were more than five hundred. Wolsey's household, says Cavendish, 'was furnished in all degrees and purposes most like a great prince ... his gentlemen ... clothed in livery coats of crimson velvet ... with chains of gold about their necks; and all his yeomen and other mean officers were in coats of fine scarlet guarded with black velvet'.

Suavely elegant, and 'all in red ... of fine taffety ... the best that he could get for money ... and also a tippet of fine sables about his neck', Wolsey was a brilliant host.[9] On these occasions the most hostile of Henry's nobles yielded to his wit and geniality; Henry always delighted in his company, and the Queen followed his example; for at this time she had no reason to distrust the Cardinal, who was useful to her in many ways.

For this, as for other parties, Wolsey's Master of Ceremonies had arranged a masque, which took place after dinner (a feast of some twenty dishes for each course) and had been carefully re-hearsed. In the great hall, a building described as the Château Vert had been set up; it was guarded by a group of young ladies, led by Anne Boleyn, and dressed in gold tissue with gold cauls. Henry, who had retired to change into his disguise, then laid siege to it with his gentlemen, all of whom wore different 'devices'; his was 'Ardent Desire'.[10] He and Anne headed the masque, which followed a form of courtship, and ended in a dance to 'all kinds of music and harmony ... with excellent voices, both of men and children', according to Cavendish. Supper ('viands of the finest sort') was then served, and the entertainment went on till the small hours.[11]

Meanwhile, Wolsey's messengers had been hurrying towards Wressil Castle, and a few days later the Earl of Northumberland came up the river and appeared at York Place. Before waiting on the King, he remained closeted with the Cardinal for some time. Wine was served; and then the Earl, escorted by Cavendish and his companions, joined his own suite in the gallery. There he sat down, and sent for Percy, who stood before him in silent apprehension.

'Son,' he began, 'thou hast always been a proud, presumptuous, disdainful, and a very unthankful waster—and even so hast thou now declared thyself.' He then accused the young man, who seems to have been too intimidated even to cry, much less to defend his actions, of 'misusing' his 'natural father' and his 'sovereign lord' by 'ensuring himself ... to *her*, for whom thou hast purchased thee the King's displeasure, intolerable for one subject to sustain!' After dwelling on the Cardinal's powers and his kindness to himself ('his displeasure and indignation were sufficient to cast me and all my posterity into utter subversion and desolation'), the Earl threatened to disinherit Percy, adding, 'I have more choice of boys who, I trust, will prove themselves much better.' Turning to both groups of gentlemen, he called upon them to witness his intentions; softening a little, he went on, 'Yet in the mean season, I desire you all to be his friends, and to tell him his fault when he doth amiss.' To the wretched and now broken youth, he said, 'Go your ways, and attend upon my lord's Grace, and see that you do your duty', and so departed to his barge.[12]

After prolonged negotiation, the terms of Percy's contract to the Lady Mary Talbot were agreed, and he was sent north in disgrace. Anne accompanied her father to Hever Castle.

Some time passed before she found out who was responsible for her banishment from Court and the ruin of her hopes. Then she said, 'If it ever lie in my power, I will work the Cardinal much displeasure' — 'as she did indeed hereafter,' says Cavendish, adding, 'whereat she smoked; for all this while she knew nothing of the King's intended purpose'.[13]

NOTES

1. *Ven. Cal. P.*, Vol. II, p. 918.
2. Ibid.
3. Cavendish, *Life and Death of Cardinal Wolsey*, p. 41.
4. Ibid., pp. 29–34.
5. Ibid.
6. Ibid.
7. Ibid.
8. Ibid.
9. Ibid.
10. *L. & P.*, Vol. III, pt. 2, p. 856.
11. Cavendish, op. cit., p. 29.
12. Ibid., p. 34.
13. Ibid.

IV

The King's Intentions

HENRY PERCY has been censured by some of Anne's biographers
for submitting to Wolsey and his father;[1] but this is to misunder-
stand the sixteenth-century attitude towards marriage. If he had
been disinherited, and therefore become outcast and penniless,
his separation from her must have followed; for Sir Thomas
Boleyn would have kept her under lock and key, while Percy was
confined in one of his father's castles, and years might have passed
before they met again.

This break in their lives had a lasting effect on both; for Percy,
never a strong character, sank into semi-invalidism, while Anne's
inate resilience hardened, changing her whole nature. She regained her gaiety and liveliness; her looks were unaffected, and
may indeed have improved; but all contemporary reports show
her as cold, calculating, and determined to a degree that eventually
changed the course of English history. So her intelligence took
charge, and she began to concentrate on the career her father had
failed to establish.

A rather suspect story describes Henry arriving at Hever Castle,
falling under her spell and speaking of her effect on him to
Wolsey;[2] but there is no evidence of his leaving London for Kent
at this time. In fact, the dynastic situation had become one of
such anxiety that it excluded all other considerations, even that of
the English reverses in France. It is unlikely that Henry thought
about acquiring another mistress at this point; for his concern now
centred on the succession – and on his wife.

The tragic history of Katherine of Aragon begins with her
marriage to Arthur, Prince of Wales, in 1501, at the age of fifteen.
Five months later he died, and Henry VII began negotiations
with King Ferdinand for her betrothal to the future Henry
VIII, whom she married after his accession in 1509. (The marriage
to Arthur had not been consummated; but a dispensation on the
grounds of consanguinity had to be obtained from the Curia.)
Between 1510 and 1518 Katherine had seven pregnancies, all of

which ended either in miscarriages or in dead children, with one exception, that of the birth of the Princess Mary in 1516; and after the Queen's final miscarriage in 1518 she did not again conceive. Apart from the fact that her daughter was not robust, the rule of a female sovereign could not be considered; for the Empress Matilda's attempts on the throne in the twelfth century had resulted in nineteen years of civil war. The situation was therefore very serious. If Henry were to die leaving no son, the claims of his Plantagenet cousins would produce anarchy (possibly invasion from France or Spain) and a recurrence of the York and Lancaster wars. Meanwhile, rumours of his divorcing Katherine—for which there were several precedents, including that of his brother-in-law Suffolk, thrice divorced before marrying Mary Tudor, and that of Louis XII from his first wife—rose and died away. Henry made no move, and was praised by Erasmus as 'the best of husbands'—not unreasonably;[3] for his mistresses, unlike those of Francis I, had had no political status, and had been accepted, however sadly, by Katherine, who was a devoted wife, an admirable consort and very popular with all classes. Now, in her thirty-ninth year, and, according to contemporary standards, past middle age, she could not hope to produce an heir. Yet between 1523 and 1525 Henry's affection for her prevailed, and they appeared to be on excellent terms. She had lost her looks, together with such elegance as she had ever possessed; but his long established dependence on her seemed unaffected—until they quarrelled, and her hold on him began to loosen.

In 1525 Henry's son by Elizabeth Blount was created Earl of Nottingham, Duke of Richmond and Somerset, Lord High Admiral of England and Knight of the Garter. Katherine saw this as a threat to her daughter's position as Princess of Wales, and protested. Henry replied by sending the nine-year-old girl, with her Court, to Ludlow. His resentment of his wife's criticisms increased with his perturbation about the war in France, the Emperor's breaking off his betrothal to the Princess Mary, and the danger of revolution at home, which was caused by the people's refusal to pay higher taxes. It was now, so he afterwards declared, that he remembered his confessor, Bishop Longland, speaking of a divorce some years earlier; but still he did nothing, and Katherine's fears of his legitimizing the six-year-old Richmond died down. She had no suspicion of plans for a divorce (which might now be described as a nullity suit) but others had; and it was impossible to find out whether the bestowal of Richmond's titles indicated his preceding his half-sister, or whether his father was contemplating another marriage. (This deviousness was characteristic of Henry, whose practice of deliberately confusing the issues was followed by his younger daughter, and exercised with bewildering success throughout her reign.) Further surmise as to Henry's intentions about the Boleyns arose when he made Sir Thomas Treasurer of the Household, and gave him lands in Tonbridge, Bramstead and Penshurst. Again, these rewards might be connected with the King's arrangements for Mary Boleyn, whose husband was made Gentleman of the Bedchamber and given his knighthood; or they could be associated with his ordering Wolsey to break off Anne's engagement to Henry Percy.

When Anne returned to Court, 'she flourished', according to Cavendish, 'in great estimation and favour with the King'. Her rage against Wolsey was based on the belief that he alone was responsible for terminating her understanding with Percy, and she was not yet privy, Cavendish says, 'to the King's secret mind, although that he had a great affection unto her'.[4]

Henry's feeling for Anne was known only to Wolsey; at this time, he had of course no intention of marrying her; and he seems to have approached her in rather an ambiguous fashion. Meanwhile, she was being courted by another married man, Sir Thomas Wyatt, whom she had not seen since their childhood. She encouraged him, presumably because his subtly poetic flatteries amused her. While refusing him the ultimate favours, she now began to assess the value set on chastity; for if she had become his mistress, she would have been dismissed from Katherine's service and sent back to the country; and as her father had done nothing for her, she appears to have decided to make her own arrangements. The sort of marriage achieved by her sister had no appeal for a young woman whose attractions were outstanding, and whose ambition had become limitless.

She was now one of the most noticeable figures in a reorganized Court; for the expenses of the war in France and Wolsey's failure to obtain money for his master through the added taxation of the euphemistically entitled Amicable Loan had brought on a financial crisis, and increased the Cardinal's unpopularity. Wolsey set about restoring his prestige with the King by dismissing a number of attendants and drawing up rules against waste in the household; as complaints of his own extravagance continued, he gave Henry his palace of Hampton Court, while retaining for himself the comparatively small mansion of The More in Hertfordshire. Henry was mollified, and immediately began to enlarge and modernize his new possession; but the resentment, amounting to hatred, of both nobles and people for the Cardinal remained. Wolsey was still an international power, and his influence with the King seemed to increase, although he was not responsible for Henry's approach to Charles V after the rout of Pavia, during which Francis I and his two sons were captured by the imperial troops. Henry's suggestion that the greater part of France should be divided between himself and the Emperor was disregarded; and this second failure to regain what he and many of his subjects thought of as his rightful inheritance threw a shadow between him and Wolsey, whom he blamed for all mishaps, and who, although still indispensable, began to feel a faint insecurity. So he turned towards those most favoured by the King, among whom were the Boleyns.

Anne continued to conceal her dislike of the Cardinal, who, seeing her as Henry's next mistress, treated her accordingly and thus became distrusted by Katherine; but at this time Anne seemed, or chose to seem, more interested in Sir Thomas Wyatt than in Henry. She, George Boleyn and Wyatt formed a coterie, in which the men exchanged ideas on poetry and music. In the next generation many of George's verses were confused with those of his friend; they also had in common an increasing dislike of their respective wives, for both were unhappily married. George Boleyn, who had already had a child by an unknown mistress, wrote on an anonymous manuscript entitled *Tourmens de Mariage*, 'this book is mine', as if to record his disgust with the situation.[5] He and Anne were devoted to one another, and neither seems to have had much use for their sister Mary, or her husband.

Wyatt's gifts as poet and musician drew him into the King's intimate circle, which consisted of Sir Francis Bryan, who was a cousin of the Boleyns, the Duke of Suffolk, and Anne's uncle, now third Duke of Norfolk, together with one or two younger men. With them, Henry jousted, hunted, exchanged verses and tried out his compositions; so sometimes he saw Anne privately and informally; yet such advances as he made to her were tentative, perhaps even hesitant.

For Henry's attitude towards women was a curious combination of crudity and fastidiousness. (The long-accepted picture of him as a ravening lecher is totally false, and has now been discarded.) He expected, and had hitherto received, instant subservience from those upon whom he had, in the contemporary phrase, cast his fantasy: wearying of these easy conquests, he seems to have paused before embarking on another, partly because his standards were higher and his tastes more capricious. At the same time brutal and sensitive, acute and egoistic, he watched the women who attracted him as a hunter observes his prey, concealing his deeper instincts under a mask of high-spirited gallantry. These instincts had been partially expressed in one of his earliest and best-known poems, beginning, 'Pastime with good company, I love and shall until I die', and reads like the apologia of a man who sees himself as a *preux chevalier*, specifically in the line 'Virtue to use, Vice to refuse'. His unsleeping consciousness of a regality which bordered on the divine complicated his approach to the other sex, as was shown by his passion for disguising himself as a shepherd or a Moor or a Turk, and then suddenly unmasking in all-conquering majesty. (So Jupiter appeared to Semele, with fatal consequences for that princess.) Proud of his magnificent physique, towering strength and overwhelming impact, he yet had to enhance them by dressing in the extreme of a fashion with which he will always be associated, and which Holbein has for ever impaled on the pages of Tudor history. His vast padded shoulders, glittering rings and chains, protuberant codpiece, slashed sleeves, brilliantly gartered hose and openwork shoes had to be more fantastic, more elaborate than anyone else's. He went to all lengths in everything— while exercising a rather sinister control—as if to be certain of a domination which charmed or terrified, according to his mood. The result was that no one, neither the wife who shared his bed for nearly twenty years, nor her five successors, nor his ministers, nor the companions of his pleasures, ever came to know him. He became, perhaps consciously, perhaps instinctively, deceptive, even to himself; and so, to this day, he appears as an enigma; at one moment a monster of cruelty, at another, 'more of a companion', according to Erasmus, 'than a king'. Tolerant, ruthless, hesitating, bold, intensely aware, and talented to the point of genius, he was always looking for the new and the original—and he found both in Anne Boleyn.

NOTES

1. Strickland, *Queens of England*, Vol. II, p. 191.
2. Ibid., p. 184.
3. Benger, *Anne Boleyn*, p. 177.
4. Cavendish, *Life*, p. 34.
5. Bapst, *Deux Gentilhommes-poètes de la Cour de Henry VIII*, p. 21.

V

Wyatt and the King

In the reign of Queen Elizabeth, George Wyatt, the poet's grandson, wrote a short memoir of the first Sir Thomas, in which frankness is combined with appropriate tributes to his sovereign's mother. That the Queen appears never to have mentioned Anne Boleyn — although she favoured her relatives — may have made his task more difficult; for his approach had to be circumspect; he must neither overpraise nor criticize his grandfather's inamorata.

When George Wyatt, writing in the 1590s, set about his task, taste in women's looks had not much changed in the last sixty years. A pale skin and fair or red-gold hair were still preferred, and dark colouring was deprecated when not condemned. So the memoir begins with a description of Anne as 'a noble imp ... not so whitely clear', but of a 'noble presence of shape and fashion', of whom Sir Thomas said, 'I could gladly yield to be tied for ever with the knot of her love.'[1]

This hope was not to be realized. Yet Anne's rebuffs inspired Wyatt's Muse, and exactly fitted in with the literary conventions of the sixteenth century, which ordained the lady's coldness and the lover's suffering. Groans, sobs, death-wishes and general misery on a Petrarchan basis were the favourite, in fact almost the only, themes of the poets of King Henry's day. That the caprice of the loved one might cause her to change from cruelty to kindness was not to be thought of; the King himself had set the tone by a rather hasty appeal to an anonymous charmer ('Whereto should I express My inward heaviness?'), and Wyatt would have been ashamed to stoop to describing a successful approach in the verses he composed, or adapted from the Italian. So Anne Boleyn's rejection suited him, while it did not prevent his advances to many other ladies, who were of course equally disdainful. His complaints soared and throbbed in a variety of rhythms, a succession of ingenious analogies and the ceaseless celebration of despair. Certain poems, specifically one mentioning a 'Brunet' and another referring to Anne's device of a white falcon, can be associated with his courtship of her. The famous sonnet describing his hopeless pursuit ('fainting I follow') of a hind about whose neck, 'graven with diamonds', he finds the message '*Noli me tangere*, for Caesar's I am, And wild for to hold though I seem tame', is directly based on one of Petrarch's, whose chase ends in the discovery that the quarry belongs to a king. 'Caesar' could stand for Henry VIII, and 'wild for to hold' for Anne: but not necessarily. Certainly *Noli me tangere* might have been her motto at this time. She remained chaste, with an eye on the future.

So it is that Wyatt's only breakaway from custom — in some verses describing a lady 'in a loose gown, with naked foot, stalking in my chamber', flinging her arms round him and, with a kiss, whispering, 'Dear heart, how like you this?' — bears no reference to Anne. Yet Wyatt continued to frequent her; and she allowed, indeed encouraged, him to do so, thus making it clear to Henry that she had more than one admirer. But as she could marry neither Wyatt nor Percy (the latter became the husband of Mary Talbot in 1524), she was still available; and Henry had no reason to suppose that she would refuse to become his mistress. There is a story — unauthenticated — that she met his first advances with the usual speech about her honour;[2] but if so, that was merely an accepted movement in the *pas de deux* of a courtship, which, it was assumed, must end in possession.

Some time in 1526 Anne had come to know, according to Cavendish, 'the King's pleasure, and the great love that he bare her in the bottom of his stomach',[3] with the result that much attention was paid her; her father and her uncle Norfolk began to see her value, and to plan how best to use it to their own advantage. Her submission could only be a matter of time; meanwhile, Wyatt continued to court her, and Henry seems not to have known that he was doing so.

It occurred to no one that Anne's aloofness might have had something to do with her love for Percy; indeed, no conclusions can be drawn on that point. Then, as now, her behaviour was attributed to cunning and ambition; what she really felt — or schemed — will never be known.

Meanwhile Wyatt, now separated from his wife, and Clerk of the King's Jewel House, became so familiar with Anne as to snatch from her, 'in sporting wise', according to his grandson, a jewel hanging by a chain from her pocket, 'which he thrust into his bosom; neither with any earnest request could she obtain it from him again', and he kept it under his coat. She then ceased to ask for its return. At this point, the King observed Wyatt 'hovering about' Anne, and took a ring from her, which he put on his little finger.[4]

A few days later, Henry, Wyatt, Sir Francis Bryan and the Duke of Suffolk, playing bowls, fell into dispute about the cast. Smiling, Henry said, 'Wyatt, I tell thee it is *mine*,' and emphasized his claim by pointing to Anne's ring. His tone exacerbated the poet, who replied, 'If it may like Your Majesty to give me leave to measure it, I hope it will be mine,' drew out chain and locket and measured the cast. Henry, recognizing them, kicked away the jack, exclaimed, 'It may be so — but then I am deceived!' and broke up the game. When he taxed Anne with having given Wyatt the locket, she replied that he had stolen it, and no more was said on either side.[5]

This example of the freedom Henry gave his courtiers is one of many, and illustrates the most disconcerting side of his character. No other Tudor — neither his father, nor any of his children — permitted the liberties taken by those to whom this king allowed argument, flat contradiction and even public censure. The more perspicacious of his intimates were aware that this freakish tolerance might give way to sudden fury or freezing contempt; and Archbishop Warham warned those who took advantage of Henry's jocund, shoulder-clapping friendliness that they were dealing with a despot, and that 'the anger of a prince is death'.

In her early years at Court, Anne grasped this danger; her boldness was limited, and may have been as carefully thought out as Henry's rather crab-like advances. She seems to have been aware that his pleasure in outspoken response was deceptive; while overlooking horseplay, he detested hooliganism; law-breaking and what is now called permissive behaviour were severely punished by a king whose prerogative in matters of chastisement was capriciously exercised. A courtier or minister who had long taken his privileges for granted, would suddenly be fined, imprisoned or, in extreme cases, condemned to death for offences against the King's lieges; or an equally unexpected reprieve might be enough to teach him a lesson. In such circumstances, no one quite knew how to proceed; and therein lay part of the power which enabled Henry, ceaselessly watching, constantly alert, to rule the most turbulent people — and the most treacherous nobles — in Europe. It would have been easy for the latter to have combined against him; for his private army consisted of two hundred yeomen of the guard. There were times when they wanted to do so; but they had not the courage; and the common people's trust in his abilities created a loyalty that finally became devotion.

Anne Boleyn, evolving her own spells, yet submitted to his. Their relationship was surprisingly equal, in spite of the fact that Henry pursued while she evaded and tantalized. Neither, in this time of what Cavendish describes as their 'secret love', mastered the other; so they achieved a balance which eventually uprooted and destroyed a regime. The preliminaries to their alliance were slow, and apparently indeterminate, deceiving those who over-simplified what they thought of as her tactics. She was as much in the King's power as he in hers. The result rather resembled a duel between two well-matched opponents than the hooking of an unwieldy and recalcitrant fish by a skilled angler.

In this, the first stage of his relationship with Anne, Henry said nothing to Katherine of the divorce which had been intermittently considered for some years. He visited the Queen every day, bringing with him any newly accredited foreign ambassador; on one of these occasions, Coresano, the Venetian envoy, was struck by Anne's looks, and described her as very beautiful.[6] This was not the general view; but the disadvantages of an olive complexion and a full mouth seem to have been outweighed by grace of bearing and eyes of extraordinary brilliance. The contrast between her appearance and that of her companions was therefore unforgettable. (So another Dark Lady, whose name has not come down to us, became celebrated, some sixty years later, for her 'mourning eyes' and the 'black wires' of her hair.)

In May 1526 the King's elder sister, Queen Margaret of Scotland, had applied to the Vatican for a divorce from her second husband, the Earl of Angus, on the grounds of his pre-contract to another lady. Henry, hearing this, wrote to her with the utmost severity, pointing out that the marriage vow was sacred and indissoluble.[7] His definition of his own status was based on the premise that he had been living in sin for eighteen years, as shown by two texts from Leviticus: 'If a man shall take his brother's wife, it is an unclean thing; he hath uncovered his brother's nakedness; they shall be childless'; and, 'Though he wist it not, yet is he guilty, and shall bear his iniquity.' Wolsey, who was planning a continental alliance for his master, agreed that the loss of six children, three of whom were males, proved that he had sinned, adding that this must be remedied by a dispensation for an annulment, as in the cases of Queen Margaret, the Duke of Suffolk and Louis XII. So Henry, convinced that he was a bachelor, felt it his duty to reprove his sister. By the time she received his letter, she had obtained the dispensation and was married to her third husband. In April 1527 the King, still having said nothing of his conclusions to Katherine, arranged to appear before an ecclesiastical court, headed by Wolsey, to answer to a charge of fornication. He went through the process of defending himself, accepted judgment and prepared his application for a divorce —as the word was then understood—to Clement VII, in which he queried, or rather denied, the validity of the brief issued by Julius II for his marriage to Katherine in his father's reign, while continuing to court her lady-in-waiting and allowing Wolsey to assume that his next marriage (in his view, his first) would be to a French princess. What his real plans were, whether he now visualized Anne as mistress or wife, remained a secret. He had ceased to cohabit with Katherine in 1526; but they appeared everywhere together as usual.

In his anti-Lutheran *Assertio Septem Sacramentorum* — the book for which the Pope gave him the title of *Fidei Defensor* in 1521 — Henry had cited many other passages from Leviticus, and had long known the pronouncement he was to quote over and over again. He now saw it, not only as applicable to himself, but further emphasized by other misfortunes: plague, losses in war and a financial crisis.

Anne's refusal to become his mistress seems not to have disturbed him unduly, perhaps because the dissolution of his marriage overrode all other matters, including that of the suggested betrothal of the Princess Mary to her cousin, the eight-year-old James V of Scotland, whom Henry now decided not to accept as his heir, although at one time he had said he might do so. In fact, the union of the two kingdoms was not feasible; the majority of the English people and many of the Scots would have rebelled against it. A marriage between Mary and her half-brother Richmond was then considered, with a view to their succeeding as joint sovereigns; but this scheme was also rejected.

On May 6th, 1527, the Spanish troops, advancing on Rome,

mutinied and sacked the city. Clement VII escaped the general holocaust by taking refuge in the Castle of St Angelo, where he remained as the Emperor's prisoner. This did not then affect Henry's and Wolsey's belief that Clement would grant the dispensation for a divorce, and it does not seem to have occurred to them that Charles, intervening on his aunt's behalf, would prevent the Pope's co-operation.

Henry therefore prepared to tell Katherine that they had never been married. (He did not know that she had already been warned of his approach to Clement VII by Mendoza, the Spanish Ambassador.) On June 22nd he told her that his wisest and most learned advisers had agreed that they were not, and never had been, husband and wife, that they must separate, and that she must decide where she would like to live. She was speechless; then she burst into tears. Henry attempted to comfort her. Finally, he rushed from the room.[8]

NOTES

1. Wyatt, *Anne Boleyn*, pp. 1–7.
2. Strickland, *Queens of England*, Vol. II, p. 192.
3. Cavendish, *Life*, p. 35.
4. Wyatt, op. cit., p. 19.
5. Ibid.

6. *Ven. Cal. P.*, Vol. IV, p. 121.
7. Chapman, *The Sisters of Henry VIII*, p. 141.
8. *Calendar of Spanish State Papers* (hereafter cited as *Span. Cal. P.*), Vol. III, pt. 2, pp. 193–4.

VI

The King's Great Matter

HENRY VIII was a deeply religious man, and a strict Catholic. His subtle and widely ranging intellectual powers operated outside the rock-like quality of his faith, beating against those inner convictions as the waves of a stormy sea assault the base of a lighthouse, leaving it unaffected. In this respect, he neither changed nor developed in the eighteen years between his accession and his first movement towards a divorce; nor did he alter during the next two decades.

In the spring of 1527 he received a shock with the realization that Anne Boleyn's refusal to become his mistress was not to be shaken — at least, not immediately; and as he had always been accustomed to his wishes being carried out with the minimum of delay, he may have begun to consider their relationship in a different light. In his thirty-ninth year he was utterly committed to the greatest passion of his life; the mercilessness, the savage loathing that sent Anne to the block nine years later sprang from the death of that love, and all it had cost him, his people and his ministers.

The processes of her mind are harder to assess; to describe them as tactical, or as the result of her father's and her uncle Norfolk's advice, is to underrate the effect of a complicated situation on a young woman of strong character and violent temperament placed in a situation she disliked. Quite apart from the breaking off of her agreement with Percy, and the fact that she was now almost past the marrying age, her years at the French Court had shown her that a woman of intelligence and determination could rise above her circumstances, as had the mistresses of Francis I; also, that the neglect and humiliation of Queen Claude — who resembled Katherine of Aragon in many ways — had been taken for granted by those in her service. So it was that when the rumours of Henry denying one marriage and seeking dispensation for another were confirmed, she saw the chance (not the certainty) of the greatest match of all.

Whether that stage in her attitude coincided with or caused his

THE KING'S GREAT MATTER

resolve to marry her, will never be known. Neither of them could
have guessed that six years were to pass before they became
husband and wife. Margaret of Scotland's dispensation to marry
Lord Methven had arrived after eighteen months; and Suffolk's
and Louis XII's divorces had been even more speedily obtained.
Also, Henry's support of and devotion to the Holy See convinced
him, as it did Wolsey, that his demand would be as easily granted —
why not? Neither of his brothers-in-law nor his sister had the
claim that he, England's *Fidei Defensor*, had upon Clement VII,
whom he thought of as an ally and a friend. In 1521, when he
desired Sir Thomas More to go through his anti-Lutheran book,
Sir Thomas had warned him of overstating the papal supremacy,
adding, 'I think it best therefore, that the part be amended, and
his [the Pope's] authority more lightly touched.' Henry replied,
'Nay, that it shall not! We are so much bounden to the See of
Rome that we cannot do too much honour to it.'[1]

Now, six years later, he was of the same mind; and his sin
required absolution. He has been accused — and will continue to
be so — of a conveniently elastic conscience which, after eighteen
years of marriage and the conception of seven children, brought
before him that highly apropos Levitical condemnation just as he
became infatuated with another woman.

This criticism is not unjust; but it is superficial. All religious
belief, not only of Henry's literal and static persuasion, is founded
on hypotheses with which reason has nothing to do. In many
cases — perhaps they are almost as numerous today as in the
sixteenth century — the divine will is often directly expressed.
When the believer, seeking a remedy for his desperate need, has
received news of it, he instinctively manufactures a pattern of
thought which is generally described as one of obedience and
faith. Such a procedure sometimes results in agreeably efficacious
fantasies: communication with the dead, hallucinations, visions,
and mystical experiences for which there seems to be no obvious
explanation. Thus, shrinking humanity is armed to face and overcome bewilderment, disaster and despair.

In this sense, Henry VIII was no exception. God, speaking
through the voice of the Jewish law-giver, had shown him the
way, and he must follow it. Then, the Almighty having been
appeased, his dynasty would be founded and his kingdom peace-
fully established through his marriage with Anne; and his

determination to ensure that dynasty's legitimacy was linked with her resolve to reach for the crown. At this point in his development – it came rather late – he could not enjoy a woman unless he was in love with her. (Some years afterwards, he explained this to his Council, in the frankest possible terms; and it is perfectly illustrated by his behaviour to his fourth wife, Anne of Cleves.[2]) His dark lady must therefore be the mother of his children; and until his marriage with her was accomplished, and acknowledged by Catholic Europe, their physical union must wait.

Meanwhile, she was given the status and nearly all the honours and privileges of a king's mistress and a reigning favourite. By some, notably the French Ambassador, she and Henry were thought to be lovers;[3] in 1532, when they became so, she immediately conceived; but, by then, the nervous strain caused by the apparently interminable delays of the divorce had taxed her resistance to breaking-point. Henry was not so affected; the certainty that he was carrying out, although against fearful odds, the commands of the Deity sustained him, until the wretched Clement's inability to co-operate forced him to take the law into his own hands.

Between 1527 and 1528 Queen Katherine's behaviour combined caution with optimism. She was Henry's lawful wife; their marriage had been based on the brief of 1503, and no one whose judgment she respected questioned its validity. She had seen Henry pursue, enjoy and then discard two mistresses; his disposal of Anne was therefore inevitable; and she prepared herself to endure, without complaint, any slight he might put upon her. To fall in with his views would be to imperil both their souls, and (so she declared) those of the English people. She partially exculpated Henry by deciding that Wolsey had put this hideous notion into his head, ended by blaming the Cardinal for everything, and thus refused to admit that her husband's impatience was turning into resentment; and this was natural, because he continued to visit and talk with her, leaving the question of the divorce to intermediaries; so she was doubly deceived.

And now Anne, according to Cavendish, 'began to look very hault and stout, having all manner of jewels, or rich apparel, that might be gotten with money. It was therefore judged by and by, throughout the Court, of every man, that she, being in such favour, might work masteries with the King, and obtain any suit of him for

her friends.'[4] She was still in Katherine's service, and they met —
sometimes over a game of primero, Pope July or chess — almost
every day. At this time, the Queen's attitude was one of contemptuous indifference. She had seen such creatures come and go
before. Pride — that terrifying, Spanish pride which yields to
nothing and embraces martyrdom — enhanced her natural dignity,
and enabled her to speak and act, both publicly and in private,
with smiling grace and unruffled calm.

At first, Henry did not object to this situation; for he disliked
all scenes but those made by himself. Then, seeing Katherine as
obstinate, undutiful and disobedient — for she was still his subject,
though not his wife — his irritation grew into anger, and, finally, to
hatred. But at this stage he seems to have felt an unwilling admira-
tion for the woman who could thus withstand both him and the
advisers he sent to reason with her.

Of these, Wolsey, the most powerful and ingenious, now perceived that Henry's demands were likely to be frustrated, not only
by the Queen's refusal even to consider the invalidity of her
marriage, but also by Charles V, whose imprisonment of the Pope
in 1527 would enable him to direct Clement's actions. Henry's
anger with Wolsey for not hurrying on matters convinced the
Cardinal that he had better proceed at once with the French
alliance; for Francis I, now released and eager for revenge on
Charles, must be recruited into Henry's service with the promise
that his sister-in-law, Madame Renée, should be Henry's wife and
the Princess Mary married to his eldest son. So Wolsey set off,
with a great retinue, for France.

His departure enabled Anne to turn the King's mind still further
against him, with criticisms of his dilatoriness and inefficiency; for
the legatine Court the Cardinal had set up to debate on the
annulment had not been unanimously in Henry's favour; he and
Anne blamed Wolsey for this, and for his inability to prevent
Katherine carrying out her threat of an appeal to the Curia, and to
her nephew, to support her cause.

At this point, Wolsey took the first step towards his own ruin,
in that he completely underrated Anne's intelligence and ability.
He should have remained at Court, and either soothed or submitted
to his master's anger. Shrinking from it, he yet trusted to his own
supremacy, even in absence. It did not occur to him how powerful
the young woman he had once described as a foolish girl had

become; nor was he aware, till too late, that she was and always had been his most dangerous enemy, and that she now headed the group of nobles who were plotting to bring him down.

Wolsey, that administrator of genius, had been indispensable for so long that he could not abandon the habit of relying on himself. Combining masterfulness and servility in his attitude towards the King, he discounted, and indeed despised, the other ministers of the Council. Furthermore, Henry deceived him as he deceived everyone, gentle or simple, cunning or naive, with whom he had to do. For eighteen years, Wolsey had been in the position of a man leading a tiger by a silken thread; and now, he did not feel the thread beginning to ravel in his grasp; nor that the beast was preparing, stealthily, to spring upon him. He knew that if he could arrange the divorce he would regain any influence he had lost. Speed was essential; but his and Henry's notions of speed were at odds. Wolsey thought in terms of years; his master desired settlement within a period of months.

Arriving at the English colony of Calais, Wolsey summoned all his gentlemen in order to tell them 'somewhat of the nature of the Frenchmen', according to Cavendish, whose description of the scene shows the Cardinal's endearingly insular side. 'Ye shall understand', he began, 'that their disposition is such that they will be at the first meeting as familiar with you as they had been acquainted with you long before, and commune with you in the French tongue as though you understood every word they spoke. Therefore ... speak you to them in the English tongue; for if you understand not them, they shall no more understand you.' Turning to one of his Welsh gentlemen, he went on, 'Rice – speak thou Welsh to him, and I am well assured that thy Welsh shall be more diffuse to him than his French shall be to thee.' When the laughter at this mild joke had died away, Wolsey gave his suite advice on 'gentleness and humanity' of behaviour to foreigners, and they departed to their lodgings more than ever devoted to their master.[5]

His meeting with Francis took place at Amiens on August 1st, 1527, and there the treaty of alliance was signed. The Cardinal then proceeded to Compiègne, where he received a fearful shock. Dr Knight, Henry's principal secretary, passing through on his way to Rome, assured Wolsey he had been sent in his support; but the Cardinal discovered that this was not the case. The King had not trusted him. Knight was empowered to treat separately with the Pope, and his orders cancelled Wolsey's. They embodied the request for a bull, or permit, for Henry to acquire another wife by marrying Anne out of hand, before the annulment of his marriage with Katherine, in other words, to commit bigamy. (Later on, Clement agreed to this arrangement, which Henry rejected.) So the French alliance was undermined.

The full extent of the King's duplicity was not revealed to Wolsey till he returned to England. Then he realized that Henry's letters praising his diligence were meant to deceive. A little later, he became aware that Knight had been instructed, not only to ask for the annulment of Henry's marriage, but also for a dispensation to marry whom he pleased, including anyone related to himself in the first degree of affinity through illicit intercourse. For since Mary Boleyn had been Henry's mistress, he was related to Anne (under canon law) just as he was related to Katherine through her marriage with Arthur. But Henry was on sure ground —through Leviticus. Anne was the sister of a mistress; Katherine had been a brother's wife; and so the Levitical embargo did not apply to Henry's marriage with Anne. He staked everything— including his conscience—on this point, and had worked out his new scheme during Wolsey's absence in consultation with those of his Council who, Cavendish says, were determined 'to bring their malice to effect against the Cardinal'.[6]

Wolsey therefore had to accept the King's resolve to marry Anne; he must work for her—or perish. She was not so foolish as to underrate Henry's affection for him—although she knew it to be shadowed by mistrust—and decided to treat him as a friend, to whom she was beholden, indeed humbly grateful, in view of the fact that he was now being forced to support her against Katherine.

Wolsey's reception at Hampton Court on the afternoon of his return was a portent of the disintegration of his relationship with the King. It illustrates an aspect of Tudor etiquette which, suddenly and sensationally flouted, showed the Cardinal that his present to Henry of that palace—the greatest gift ever bestowed on a sovereign by a subject—had availed him little or nothing.

At that time, it was the custom for an envoy returning from an important mission to announce his arrival through one of his gentlemen, who, kneeling before Henry, waited for orders as to where his master would be received. The King would then command the minister to attend him in his cabinet; or he might appoint a meeting for the following day.

On this occasion, Wolsey's gentleman found Henry surrounded by his courtiers. Anne Boleyn was at his side, and Mendoza, the Imperial Ambassador, who sent an account of the scene to Charles V, stood in the background. The messenger had barely finished his announcement, when Anne exclaimed, 'Where else is the Cardinal to come but where the King is? Tell him to come here.' Struck into silence, Henry's entourage—this included Norfolk, the Suffolks and most of the anti-Wolsey, Boleyn faction —waited, fearing that the Lady, as Mendoza called her, had at last gone too far and would be harshly put down.

Nothing happened. Henry consented with a nod; and a few minutes later Wolsey, travel-stained and weary, entered, knowing himself disregarded.[7] He behaved as if unaware of what amounted to an insult, and in due course talked apart with the King; but he realized, in that moment of humiliation, that he stood alone. He had not a single ally (for Francis I was notoriously unreliable) and so could count only on the frail hope of support from the Pope— whom he planned, as a last resource, to supplant, in the event of the Emperor keeping Clement in prison. He had long set his sights on the Chair of St Peter, with a view to ruling all, or nearly all, the kingdoms of the civilized world in his master's interests; thus the divorce would be easily obtained. Now, he must make one of a quartet who were to play out the long, the infuriatingly indecisive drama of Henry's second marriage. As he, the King, Katherine and Anne moved into their places, he endeavoured, as in his days of power, to prevail, and partially succeeded for two more years— an anxious, ailing wreck of a great man. For it was at this point that his magnificent physique began to break under the strain.

Anne Boleyn's attitude towards Wolsey now became one of subservient flattery, doubtless at Henry's suggestion; for the Cardinal's influence at the Vatican still exceeded that of any other English envoy. She set about showing herself to the King as gracious and charming, a fit companion, not only in his pleasures, but at all public and official ceremonies. These were invariably attended by Katherine, whom Henry treated with bland courtesy, often supping or walking with her, as if there were no dispute between them. Wolsey, with superimposed dignity and serenity, attended on all three, as well aware of the women's hatred as of the

King's increasing indifference to his advice. Valuing the past, Henry remained attached to the Cardinal, whom he addressed as his 'best beloved servant and friend',[8] and to whom he could talk as to no other. This exacerbated Anne and worried Katherine. Meanwhile, the subordinate participants in this *danse macabre* — the two Dukes and their wives, Councillors, bishops, secretaries, Gentlemen of the Bedchamber, foreign Ambassadors and Wolsey's newly appointed, clever young secretary, Thomas Cromwell — circled about their principals, recording their impressions in succinct and vivid phraseology. It was observed, in the contemporary idiom, that the Lady's gifts of a filed tongue and sugared words held and entranced the King; that he spent much time in the apartments set aside for her and adjoining those of the Queen; that Katherine, described by Cavendish as the perfect Griselda,[9] showed no sign of depression or alarm; that the Cardinal was working night and day for the divorce; and that Henry went about his usual activities, cheerful, energetic, protean, never alone — on his green-and-gold velvet close-stool, he was gay and relaxed, chatting and joking with his intimates — [10] shut up for hours in his cabinet dictating and composing, or singing, in his high tenor, to the organ in his chapel, or serving the priest at Mass.

Henry's background, whether that of Greenwich (his favourite palace), Westminster, Hampton Court or Bridewell, varied only in ingenuity of richness and elaboration. Hampton Court, newly decorated and enlarged by the King, who was his own architect, may have been the most convenient for himself and Anne. Still officially in the Queen's service, she had begun to form her own Court, and could provide Henry with a gayer and more talented circle than that presided over by Katherine. There were many among the older ministers, her uncle Norfolk being one, who disliked her boldness and disregard of convention; but young people of both sexes were attracted by her vitality, and copied her elegance. Her gowns of velvet, taffeta, and Lucca or Genoa damask at six shillings and eightpence a yard, edged with fur and lined with black satin, showed her preference for strong colours — orange-tawny, russet, carnation.[11] Her head-dresses, formerly set with semi-precious stones — cat's-eyes, tourmalines, Roman pearls — now glittered with Henry's presents of diamonds, rubies and emeralds. These enhanced the depth and brilliance of her eyes, and drew attention to her hair which, when released, fell almost to her knees. She seems to have moved well and, to judge by her portraits, avoided a superfluity of necklaces and rings. Cavendish describes her as 'gorgeous', and this adjective completes the picture of a young woman who appeared original and striking while following, when not leading, current fashion.[12] It is evident that she possessed taste, discrimination and sometimes, rather unexpectedly, a tranquil grace. (George Wyatt's grandfather handed down a memory of her 'mildness and majesty' of demeanour, before she became Queen.[13]) So the contrast between her and the stout, ever-smiling, sickly Katherine must have been painful to those who could feel compassion for that implacably patient lady.

Anne Boleyn did not move in beauty; she was one of those who can afford to dispense with it. Something of her power over Henry is illustrated by the little packet of letters he wrote to her between 1527 and 1529. They provide glimpses of a curious intimacy, in that it was sustained almost without change and thus without climax, over an extremely taxing six years. A study of these brief, scribbled missives shows that Anne achieved domination through means not often successfully practised by persons in an anomalous position.

NOTES

1. Roper, *Life of Sir Thomas More*, p. 255.
2. Froude, *History of England*, Vol. III, pp. 279, 319.
3. *L. & P.*, Vol. IV, pt. 3, p. 2409.
4. Cavendish, *Life*, p. 36.
5. Ibid., p. 48.
6. Ibid., p. 35.
7. *Span. Cal. P.*, Vol. III, pt. 2, p. 432.
8. Froude, *The Divorce of Catherine of Aragon*, p. 73.
9. Cavendish, op. cit., p. 35.
10. Baldwin Smith, *Henry VIII*, p. 20.
11. Loke, *An Account of Materials furnished for the Use of Queen Anne Boleyn* (hereafter cited as *Materials*), p. 22.
12. Cavendish, op. cit., p. 36.
13. Wyatt, *Anne Boleyn*, p. 2.

VII

The Love-Letters

SOME years before his approach to the Vatican for the annulment of his marriage, Henry VIII had two escapes from death. While hunting, he was thrown, fell head first into a ditch, was pulled out by his attendants and remained unconscious for several hours. Shortly afterwards, jousting with Suffolk, he forgot to lower his visor; the Duke's newly designed helmet prevented his seeing this or hearing the cries of 'Hold! Hold!' from the spectators; having couched his lance, he missed his brother-in-law's head by inches and, dismounting, burst into tears. Henry blamed himself for the mishap, and ran three more courses.[1]

These were portents that, followed by the Levitical warning about marriage with a brother's widow, could not be ignored. More than ever convinced that he must make his peace with the Deity, Henry ordered Dr Knight to press on with his request for the dispensation. In December 1527 the secretary obtained a promise of consent from Clement VII, who escaped from the Castle of St Angelo and took refuge in Orvieto. There, surrounded by Imperial troops and warned by the Emperor not to tamper with Queen Katherine's rights, he began to prevaricate, and Wolsey was empowered to take over the negotiations. Henry, assuming that this delay was temporary, instructed Sir Gregory Casale, one of his permanent agents at the Papal Court, to urge the Pope to 'consider the relief of the King's conscience, the preservation of his life, the continuation of the succession ... and the welfare of his subjects'.[2]

At this time, Anne Boleyn occasionally absented herself from Court, alternating between Hever Castle and London. Henry, who was in the habit of dictating all his correspondence, including that to relatives and friends, sent her a series of letters in his own hand. Seventeen of these have come down to us, nine in French and eight in English. At some point in the discussions over the divorce, they were stolen from Anne (presumably by a papalist or Spanish agent) and deposited in the Vatican archives, where they are still to be seen.

In his crabbed but even script, Henry adjures 'my mistress and friend' not to stay away any longer, 'that your affection may not by absence be dismissed', and compares his love for her to the heat of the sun. In this letter he sends her a bracelet enclosing his portrait, describes her departure as 'almost intolerable', and signs himself her loyal servant, in the *amour courtois* style of an earlier day.[3]

As contemporary etiquette required an exchange of gifts, Anne replied with a locket indicating her uncertain position; it was set with a diamond, on which a ship bearing a 'solitary damsel' was being tossed to and fro. Henry took this present as a proof of her affection, and declared himself his lady's 'secretary and most loyal and ensured servant', adding her initials within the drawing of a heart, inscribed 'H. autre ne cherche R.'[4]

Praying every day that God would vouchsafe them a complete union through Wolsey's negotiations, Henry still hoped for an early settlement. He was then plunged into gloom by Anne's postponement of her return. Surely this was not his fault — what had he done? The bearer of his letter would assure her of his devotion. Her next letters further distressed him, as being in some passages 'to my disadvantage'. A whole year had passed, as she very well knew, since he had been 'struck with the dart of love' — and yet, even now, he could not be sure that his love was returned. He begged her to 'make answer absolute to this my rude letter', and suggested a meeting. It may have been that he and his retinue then visited Hever, ostensibly to hunt, for later on he sent her a buck, 'killed by my own hand late yesternight, trusting that as you eat of it you will have in mind the hunter'.[5]

While they hunted together — she was as tireless and hard-riding as he — Dr Knight was recalled. He returned with a form of dispensation that enabled Henry to marry Anne, but did not touch on the invalidity of his union with Katherine. Wolsey, having convinced the King of its uselessness, sent Edward Foxe and Stephen Gardiner — one of his secretaries and later Bishop of Winchester — to ask that the cause, as it was now called, should be judged in England under his auspices. If the Pope demurred, they were to threaten him with England's secession from the Holy See. On their way to the coast they visited Hever with a letter from Henry in English. 'Darling,' it began, 'These shall be only to advertise you that this bearer and his fellow be dispatched with as many things to compass our matter and bring it to pass, as our wits could compass or devise', urged Anne not to keep the envoys too long, and concluded, 'written with the hand of him which desireth as much to be yours as you to have him'.[6]

Foxe and Gardiner found Clement at Orvieto with the remnant of his Curia in miserable circumstances, shabby, tearful and distraught. The Popes of the Renaissance were not spiritually minded, nor expected to be so. But two of Clement's predecessors, Alexander VI, a Borgia, and Julius II, a della Rovere, had been men of intelligence and political ability. Clement, a Medici, and thus chiefly concerned with the promotion of his own family, had neither quality. He made up for this with slipperiness and cunning; his skill in evading any inconvenient demand eventually defeated all envoys, Spanish, English and French. Tearing his handkerchief and weeping, he reiterated his loyalty to Henry, deplored his own helplessness and begged for time. His distress left the envoys unmoved; more frightened of their master's wrath than of poor Clement's hostility, they persisted — and got no further. Finally, His Holiness promised to grant them the kind of dispensation they required, on condition that it was not immediately acted upon; but he refused to allow the divorce to be judged in England. After further argument, he said that he would do his very best for Henry, in the face of the Emperor's wrath.[7]

These discussions, which took place during January and February 1528, reached a crisis when Gardiner and Foxe were told that the Pope now knew of Henry's intention to marry Anne Boleyn; also, that he had heard she was pregnant and 'unworthy'. Wolsey, categorically denying both charges, instructed the envoys to inform Clement of the lady's 'excellent virtuous qualities, the purity of her life, constant virginity, maidenly and womanly pudicity, soberness, meekness and humility, wisdom'. He described her aristocratic connections, her good education and manners, 'apparent aptness to procreation of children, and other infinite good qualities'.[8] Meanwhile, the Venetian Ambassador in London was reporting the Pope's consent to the marriage of Henry and Anne.[9]

By this time, Wolsey knew that Anne's supporters were influencing Henry as never before, 'fantasying in their heads', says Cavendish, 'that she should be for them a sufficient and apt instrument to bring their malicious purpose to pass ... And she,

having both a very good wit and also an inward desire to be revenged of the Cardinal, was agreeable to their requests ... They
would fain have attempted the matter with the King, but they
durst not ... and also, they feared the wonder wit of the Cardinal.'[10]

There was only one way for Wolsey to defeat the Boleyn cabal;
he must, somehow, obtain from Clement a guarantee of the invalidity of Henry's marriage to Katherine. For this, what was then
known as a decretal commission was required, and he ordered
Gardiner and Foxe to ask for it. This commission would empower
the judge of the case (Wolsey himself) to nullify Julius II's dispensation of 1503 for that marriage, thus leaving the King free and
depriving Katherine of the right to appeal. With this weapon the
Cardinal would be able to reinstate himself and conquer his
enemies.

Clement's reply to Gardiner's demand almost amounted to a
firm refusal; he suggested a consultation with his Cardinals, who
advised him not to grant the decretal commission. Gardiner then
announced, 'The King's Highness will do it without you,' adding
that when His Holiness's only friend, the King of England, was
taken away, the Holy See would fall to pieces. Clement, crying
bitterly 'and casting his arms abroad', the envoy reported, 'walked
up and down the chamber, we standing in a great silence'.[11] This
scene resulted in the grant of a general, as opposed to a decretal,
commission, and produced violent protests from Wolsey, who
therein perceived his own ruin, while assuring Henry and Anne
that all was going well.

As it now seemed to Anne that the Cardinal must be cajoled and
encouraged, she sent Heneage, one of his secretaries, a beguiling
little note. She was afraid that His Grace had forgotten her, as she
had received no token from him for a long time. She hoped he
might send her 'a morsel of tunny' or any 'good meat, such as
carps, shrimps or other'. She then asked for Wolsey's support on
behalf of the Archdeacon of Oxford, whose goods had been seized
'by that lewd person' (unnamed) of whom she had already complained to the King, and concluded, 'I beseech Your Grace to
pardon me that I am so bold to write unto Your Grace thereof; it
is the conceit and mind of a woman'. In a second letter she pleaded
for another friend, Sir Thomas Cheyney, gently adding, 'I am
sorry he is in Your Grace's displeasure'.[12]

Wolsey, well aware of the worth of such tributes, and how they must be paid for, managed to extort a third and more effective commission from Clement VII, with which Foxe returned to England, while Gardiner was ordered to engage Cardinal Campeggio to appear from Rome, with Wolsey, to judge the case in London. Foxe, received by Anne at Greenwich, was delighted with her praise of his efforts. She thanked him again and again, adding, 'I promise you large recompense'. Henry then came in, and she left them together. Foxe described his progress at the Vatican, concluding, 'His Holiness is willing to satisfy Your Majesty to the best of his power,' upon which Henry summoned Anne to hear the good news. But Wolsey, after considering the new commission, was neither pleased nor hopeful, and desired Gardiner to insist on the decretal; and so, in April 1528, the whole process began again.[13] It seemed to Henry and Anne that Clement's consent to the case being tried in England ensured their success; they were not then aware that a body of opponents—headed by Katherine, the Emperor and the pro-Spanish London wool merchants—were about to combine against them and the Cardinal.

While both sides prepared for the struggle, Henry and Anne were together at Greenwich; they passed the first weeks of May 1528 in the belief that judgment was almost certain to be in their favour, and that within a year they would be married. She was now in the penultimate stage of her attendance on the Queen. They were at cards, when Katherine suddenly said, 'My lady Anne, you have good hap to stop at a king, but you are not like others, you will have all or nothing.' Anne repeated this remark to Wyatt, whose grandson recorded it in his memoir.[14]

In June all arrangements for the case were halted by the sweating sickness, of which the death-rate rose at terrible speed. Henry sent Anne to Hever, and himself left London, moving from one country palace to another with a skeleton Court. His letters to her—'I implore you, my entirely beloved, to have no fear at all … for wheresoever I may be, I am yours' — reiterated his prayers for her safety.[15] When her father and brother both caught the disease, Henry came to the conclusion that women were not so susceptible to it as men. Then, hearing that Anne also was infected, he wrote in an agony, sending her his own doctor ('by which doing I trust soon to see you again, which to me will be more sovereign remedy than all the precious stones in the world') and lamenting the absence of 'mine own darling' and 'good sweetheart'.[16]

All the Boleyns recovered; when Mary's husband, Sir William Carey, died on June 22nd, Anne tried to comfort her by offering to promote Mary's sister-in-law, Eleanor Carey, an old friend and a professed religious, to the post of Abbess of Wilton Priory. Henry agreed, on condition that the lady's credentials satisfied Wolsey, who discovered that Dame Eleanor had had two children by different priests, and had later become the mistress of a layman. The Cardinal then put forward his own candidate, Dame Isabella Jordan, whom Henry also rejected, as being too old and of doubtful reputation. 'I could not,' he wrote to Anne about Eleanor Carey, 'for all the gold in the world, clog your conscience nor mine, to make her ruler ... [who] is of so ungodly a demeanour, nor I trust you would [that] ... I should so distain mine honour.'[17] To Wolsey, he wrote at length and severely, about his disregard of Isabella Jordan's ill fame, and received a cringing reply.[18]

All that month the death-toll rose. The King's interest in illness comes out in his letters at this time; he felt himself, perhaps rightly, something of an expert on cures, preventive and other, for all kinds of diseases, and kept a record of medicines, ointments and boluses; he was always ready to advise on such questions. If he had not been as anxious for Anne as for himself—he confessed daily and made a new will—he might have found a certain satisfaction in prescribing the remedies he continued to collect from a variety of sources.[19]

In July Anne, restored and reunited with Henry, wrote again to Wolsey, not so much in her former agreeable vein, as in one of exaggerated flattery which, in view of her real feelings, reads rather unpleasantly. 'Pardon me,' she began, 'that I am so bold to trouble you with my simple and rude writing ... I am desirous to know if Your Grace does well ... The great pains you take for me, both day and night, are never like to be recompensed.' She concluded by saying that she was 'alonely in loving you, next the King's Grace, above all creatures living'. At her desire, Henry added a postscript to this letter, which betrayed his and Anne's impatience about the case. 'Both of us desire to see you,' he wrote. ' ... The not having heard of the Legate's [Campeggio] arriving in France causeth us somewhat to muse, but we trust by your diligence shortly to be eased of that trouble.' Wolsey replied with a gift to Anne, which she acknowledged 'in most humble wise that my poor heart can think; I thank Your Grace for your kind letter and rich present ... I am most bound of all creatures, next the King's Grace, to love and serve Your Grace. I beseech you, never doubt that I shall never vary from this thought while breath is in my body.'[20] But what of Campeggio? Neither Anne nor Henry guessed that his delay had been ordered by Clement VII, with a view of placating the Emperor by an indefinite postponement of the case.

Anne then returned to Hever, where Henry was to join her. His next letter, written in English, gives a fairly clear picture of their increasingly intimate relations, and of the extent, short of possession, to which he now allowed himself to go. 'Mine own sweetheart,' he begins, 'this shall be to advertise you of the great loneliness I find here since your departing. I think your kindness and my fervency causeth it; for otherwise I would not have thought it possible that for so little a while it should have grieved me.' He then describes his work on his second anti-Lutheran book, and on his treatise about the invalidity of his marriage (four hours' intensive writing had given him a headache, hence this short note), and wished himself, 'specially of an evening, in my sweetheart's arms, whose pretty dukkys I hope shortly to kiss. Written by the hand of him that was, is and shall be yours by his will.'[21]

'Dukkys', a Tudor colloquialism for breasts, had thus become part of Henry's and Anne's little language. Its use in this context indicates the halfway-house – yet curiously static – aspect of their relationship.

In the 1520s and 1530s upper-class Englishwomen were encased in corsets of wood or iron, usually the latter; these covered the torso, pinched in the waist and enclosed the breasts, which were never displayed, or even thrust forward, as in the seventeenth and eighteenth centuries. It therefore becomes obvious that the embraces to which Henry refers involved partial undressing; and so his and Anne Boleyn's excursions into the *pays du tendre*, while failing to reach a climax and thus avoiding the risk of pregnancy, seem to have become their practice up to the last months of 1532. She then conceived, and continued to do so until he discarded her.

At intervals during those years it was thought by many that they must be lovers; and those who desired her downfall were sadly disappointed when it became clear that Henry was determined, not only on marriage, but on a legitimate succession. His decision gave Anne a qualified status and enhanced her power; but contemporary reports show her increasing inability to support the strain of being neither wife nor mistress.

This rationing of pleasure, ordained by Henry, did not, it seems, seriously disturb him; he was, as ever, strenuously occupied every hour of the day. Anne's position, providing no duties and constant appearances, was both taxing and invidious. Her resolve to become Queen of England supported her, but not all the time; and it was impossible for her to ignore the dislike, which grew into hatred, of the common people, or the mutterings of 'goggle-eyed whore' and 'night crow' from a number of sources. Ambition apart, she was sufficiently subjugated by Henry willingly to co-operate in a relationship which baffled the onlookers, and led some to believe that she was holding him off in order to lead him on, a process that would in fact have caused him to tire of her within a very short time. He knew how to charm her, as he charmed almost everyone he met, including those who detested all he stood for and all he did; and they were united in a pursuit which promised, in spite of setbacks, a happy ending.

So, as Cardinal Campeggio moved, with intolerable slowness, from Rome to Provence, from Provence to Lyons and thence to Calais, Henry and Anne saw themselves approaching the realization of their hopes and the last stage of the struggle. Wolsey knew better. He trusted no one at the Vatican, not even his own envoys; he had neither Henry's self-confidence nor his certainty of divine approval. He therefore braced himself for the opening of a conflict in which he must risk his whole career.

NOTES

1. Chapman, *The Sisters of Henry VIII*, p. 200.
2. Froude, *Divorce*, p. 53.
3. Byrne, *Letters of Henry VIII*, p. 54.
4. Ibid., p. 55.
5. Ibid, pp. 51, 58.
6. Ibid., p. 61.
7. Froude, op. cit., p. 62.
8. *L. & P.*, Vol. IV, pt. 2, p. 1741.
9. *Ven. Cal. P.*, Vol. IV, p. 121.
10. Cavendish, *Life*, p. 36.
11. *L. & P.*, Vol. IV, pt. 2, p. 1841.
12. Ibid., p. 1779.
13. Ibid., 1871.
14. Wyatt, *Anne Boleyn*, p. 6.
15. Byrne, op. cit., p. 69.
16. Ibid., p. 70.
17. Ibid., p. 71.
18. Ibid., p. 77.
19. Ibid., p. 73.
20. *L. & P.*, Vol. IV, pt. 2, pp. 1913, 1960.
21. Byrne, op. cit., p. 82.

VIII

The First Reverses

BEFORE Cardinal Campeggio left Rome for London, England and France declared war on Spain. By the time he set out, the English troops had been withdrawn; Admiral Andrea Doria had deserted Francis I for Charles V; Lautrec, Francis's best general, was dead and the French forces had been routed in Italy. Clement VII therefore ordered Campeggio to reunite Henry and Katherine, while placating the King and Wolsey with the decretal commission, which Campeggio was to bring with him, on condition that he was to show it to no one but Henry and Wolsey. The Emperor then desired his Ambassador, Muxetula, to threaten Clement with a return of his troops and further devastation, adding that His Holiness must forbid all proceedings for the divorce; if Henry persisted, then Clement must revoke the cause to Rome, and withdraw the decretal commission.

A few weeks later, Sir Gregory Casale's brother persuaded Clement to promise, in writing, not to withdraw either the general or the decretal commission. Clement consented; but he told the Emperor that the case would in fact be heard in Rome. Meanwhile, he instructed Campeggio to delay the hearing in London for as long as possible. Burdened with these conflicting orders, Campeggio, desperately ill with gout, arrived in London on October 8th, 1528, and retired to bed, giving out that he could see no one; the rumour went round that he was dying.

Henry then decided that Anne must leave Greenwich, where she had been established in semi-royal state, and stay at Hever while the case was being heard. 'Then I trust', he wrote to her, 'within a while after to enjoy that which I have so longed for ... No more to you at this present, mine own darling, for lack of time, but that I would you were in mine arms or I in yours, for I think it long since I kissed you.'[1]

After interviewing Wolsey, who warned him that the King was determined on the divorce, Campeggio was publicly received by Henry. A few days later, they talked alone for four hours, after which Campeggio informed Clement that 'His Majesty hath studied this matter with such diligence that I believe ... he knows more about it than a great theologian or jurist; and he told me ... in the plainest terms that he wanted nothing but a declaration that the marriage was valid or not, he himself presupposing always its invalidity; and I believe that if an angel descended from heaven, he would not be able to persuade him to the contrary.'[2] Campeggio, an ingenious and highly qualified lawyer, who knew England well (he was absentee Bishop of Salisbury, and had spent a year in London), then put forward a solution warmly supported by Henry; it was that Katherine should enter a nunnery, a step which would automatically dissolve the marriage.

This step would not only solve the dynastic problem, but would rather benefit Katherine than otherwise; for her life in such an establishment as then existed would provide her with her own servants and luxurious apartments in which she could receive relatives and friends; she would be able to follow any pursuits she liked, and be free to travel. Above all, her retirement would ensure the legitimacy of her daughter; for Henry promised that if she— nominally rather than literally—took the veil, the Princess Mary would succeed to the throne after any male heirs he had by another wife. If she refused, the Princess would be declared illegitimate. Also, it was obvious that neither the Pope nor the Emperor could possibly object to the Queen's honourable withdrawal from the rather degrading conflict of the case. All she stood to lose was Henry's frequentation of her bed; and that had ceased more than two years ago, and would never, he told Campeggio, be renewed. So, in high hopes, both Cardinals, assuming that Katherine would agree to their proposal, asked her to receive them.

Her refusal was definite and uncompromising. She said that she had no vocation for the religious life: that she was England's Queen and Henry's lawful wife. But she betrayed all the violence of injured pride by offering—in spite of having no vocation—to become a nun if the King became a monk. The absurdity, not untinged with malice, of this suggestion is understandable in view of the fact that Katherine hoped thereby to make Henry return to her; for she still loved him, and was determined to rout Anne Boleyn and quash the divorce by any means that came to hand. She repeated that she was principally concerned for her and

Henry's immortal souls. This concern was as deeply rooted and sincere as Henry's conviction that they had been living in sin for eighteen years; the difference lay in her obedience to the ordinances of her faith, and in her certainty that Julius II's dispensation of 1503 was flawless and incontrovertible, while his case was based on the Levitical pronouncement and the deaths of six children. The impasse was therefore complete and insoluble. Campeggio gave way to despair; Wolsey reiterated his warnings about England's secession from the Holy See. And then, unexpectedly, the English people entered the arena.

Rumours of Anne Boleyn's replacing the Queen had now reached the Londoners, with the result that Katherine was cheered whenever she left the palace, while Wolsey and Campeggio were stoned and cursed. The popular view was that Henry had tired of his old wife and wanted a new one. A more practical section of the public foresaw a breach between England and Spain, to the detriment of the wool trade, and so encouraged these demonstrations. Henry therefore convened a meeting of the City Fathers and other notables to the palace of Bridewell, in order to explain the situation, which he did in a speech of remarkable dignity and percipience. Instinctively aware that his subjects' principal grievance centred on Campeggio, he began by saying that he had had to summon a legate from Rome to decide whether or not he was living in adultery, and had done so 'for this only cause, before God and on the word of a prince'. 'I have reigned', he then reminded them, 'for twenty years, with victory, wealth and honour,' thereby claiming their support. 'But when we remember our mortality,' he went on, ' ... then we think that all our doings in our lifetime are clearly defaced.' Recalling the 'mischiefs and manslaughters' of the civil wars, he warned his listeners that 'if our heir be not known at the time of our death, see what shall succeed to you and your children'. Diverse great clerks, he continued, had assured him that the Lady Mary was not his lawful daughter, nor her mother his lawful wife. 'Think you, my lords,' he exclaimed, 'that these words touch not my body and soul?' When this appeal had sunk in, he described Katherine as a lady 'of high lineage and most gentleness and buxsomeness', from whom he had no wish to part. If it turned out that there was no fault in their marriage, he declared, then – 'There is nothing more pleasant nor more acceptable to me in my life,' adding, 'If the marriage might be good, I would surely choose her above all other women ... These be the sores', he concluded, 'that vex my mind, these be the pangs that trouble my conscience —and for these griefs I seek a remedy.'[3]

Not unnaturally, this piece of oratory has been described by most historians as one of unblushing insincerity and brazen disingenuousness. With great respect, it is suggested that there are certain persons, Henry being one, who can entertain diametrically opposite opinions at one and the same time, and with equal conviction. It is possible that, in thus describing his feelings for the Queen, Henry was neither lying, nor even deceiving himself. At that moment—in that climax of rhetoric and of concern for the sympathy of a bewildered and resentful audience—*he meant what he said*. Black became white, if only for half an hour; and this is shown by the effect on his hearers, whom he asked to circulate his defence. Some, says Hall, who records his address, 'sighed and said nothing', some grieved for the King, others for Queen Katherine: but all were at one in blaming Anne Boleyn, Wolsey and Campeggio, while pitying Henry, and going home to discuss his dilemma.

So, once more, Henry VIII scored a personal triumph. It was not his fault that he had no male heir; and his dialectic, touching the hearts of his hearers, may also have roused their fears. For the French Ambassador, who also was present, thought he heard a threat of punishment for those who persisted in making difficulties, and 'speaking wrongly' of His Majesty's motives. ('Il usa de ces termes qu'il n'y aura si belle tête qu'il n'en fit voler.') Cardinal du Bellay's English was by no means perfect; but he may have caught the note of terrorism omitted by the patriotic chronicler.[4]

Meanwhile, Katherine made it her business to appear more frequently than usual, smiling and waving in response to the applause of the citizens, who had no intention of concealing their loyalty. Of Anne Boleyn, they believed simply that she was, as we say now, no better than she should be, and, worse still, of low origin—had not her great-grandfather's grandfather started life as a mercer's apprentice? And was not their good Queen the daughter of a king and the aunt of an emperor? Snobbery and prudery (then, as now, among the outstanding characteristics of our island race) combined to place Anne in the dock and keep Katherine on the throne. As for His Majesty—he was unfortunate; but no doubt he would find a way out of the difficulty, if not interfered with by the hated Wolsey, and his foreign satellite who had no right to meddle in English affairs.

Embarrassed and annoyed by his people's demands, yet determined to appease them, Henry forbade Katherine to draw attention to her wrongs by any public appearances, and she obeyed without protest. (She does not seem to have realized that a patient Griselda is not the ideal companion for an increasingly worried man.) Then Henry, further put about by complaints of delay and neglect from the lady of Hever Castle, summoned Anne to a party at Greenwich, given by himself and Wolsey for the French Ambassador, on November 10th, 1528. Here the Queen presided, splendidly dressed. It would never have occurred to Henry to eliminate her on such an occasion. His care for the conventions nearly always prevailed over anger and frustration.

Du Bellay and his suite were escorted by Henry and Wolsey into the great chamber of the palace, where a fountain had been set up; on one side of it was a hawthorn tree, from which gold ornaments were hanging. As the audience took their places, masked dancers surrounded the tree, followed by a group of players, one of whom described, in Latin, the 'tragedy' of the captured Pope, explaining that the Holy See had been thrown underfoot by the tyranny of the Emperor. St Peter then appeared in chains, and kneeling before Wolsey, asked to be set free, upon which the Cardinal appealed to the powers of France and England to combine in liberating the saint. This scene was followed by the entry of two boys representing the sons of Francis I, who complained that they were still held as hostages in Spain. Their release concluded the play – and then the dancers, led by a dark-haired lady, 'in strange attire', according to Hall, 'richly apparelled in cloth of gold', took the floor.

It now became obvious that both play and ballet had been planned round this glittering and bejewelled figure who, dancing like the daughter of Herodias, was joined by three groups of gentlemen, masked and in fancy dress. Circling round the fountain to the sound of lutes and viols, they all danced together till the music ceased. Then the ladies, still led by their principal, unmasked, approached du Bellay's entourage and claimed them as partners in the next round.[5]

Cavendish, well accustomed to such displays, presently followed them in to supper; but even he was overcome by the magnificence of the feast. 'I do both lack wit in my gross old head and cunning in my bowels', he recalls, 'to declare the wonderful, curious imaginations invented and devised.' He then described the 'beauty, gesture and goodly proportion' of the ladies, 'who seemed to all men more angelic than earthly', adding that they conversed with their guests in fluent French.[6]

Whether earthly or angelic, Anne Boleyn's performance was designed to show her status to Henry's French allies, whom Wolsey was now trying to convince that his master intended to marry Madame Renée. Du Bellay did not believe this. On December 9th, 1528, he reported that Henry had given Anne 'a very fine lodging' at Hampton Court. Far greater attention was paid her, he went on, than to the Queen. He concluded that the King 'meant the people by degrees to endure her, so that when the great blow comes, it may not be thought strange', and noted that the demonstrations against Anne had been sternly put down.[7]

In Christmas week the Ambassador wrote from Greenwich that open house was being kept by Henry and Katherine, adding that Anne Boleyn 'is there also ... having her establishment apart, as I imagine she does not like to meet with the Queen.'[8] While supporting the divorce, du Bellay was doubtful about Anne's relationship with Henry; he feared that they would become lovers, and then the King would tire of her; but his spies discovered no advance in the intimacy of this strange pair; and as Henry, despite Wolsey's pleading, had refused to consider marrying Madame Renée, his support of Francis against the Emperor might be abandoned. All depended, du Bellay concluded, on Anne's chastity and Henry's restraint. He trusted in neither.

Meanwhile, Campeggio had succeeded in postponing the hearing. He must wait, he said, for Clement's written assurance (described as the 'pollicitation') that he would not revoke the decretal commission. He and Wolsey pleaded again with the Queen, reminding her that Jeanne de Valois, taking the veil so that Louis XII might marry Anne of Brittany, had been much admired for her co-operation. She made no reply, and ignored Henry's threatening messages. She could afford to do so; for she had received from her nephew a copy of a document which seemed almost certain to destroy Henry's case. This was a supplementary brief to Julius II's dispensation of 1503, eliminating all the flaws in the first one, through which Wolsey had planned to prove the invalidity of her marriage to the King. While writing to Charles for support and advice, she said nothing of this second brief to Henry, who continued to visit her, sometimes arguing and enraged, sometimes amiably chatting, as if they had never disagreed. She submitted to both approaches with a calm that must have been extremely trying. Anne's power over him was partially founded on her explosions of impatience. He could deal with these, and seems to have enjoyed doing so; with Katherine he could do nothing. When Anne, from Hever, accused Campeggio of pretending to be ill and refusing to meet her, while blaming Henry for the resultant delay, he wrote to her gently about 'suppressing of your inutile and vain thoughts and fantasies with the bridle of reason ... The unfeigned sickness of this well-willing legate', he went on, 'doth somewhat retard his access to your presence; but I trust verily, when God shall send him health, he will ... recompense his demur.'[9]

Then, in a stormy interview with Katherine early in 1529, Henry was told of the second, and hitherto concealed, brief of dispensation. It was a crippling blow. Some time passed before he and Wolsey decided how to meet it. While they debated, Campeggio, instructed by Clement VII, burnt the decretal commission.

NOTES

1. Byrne, *Letters of Henry VIII*, p. 84.
2. Ibid., p. 86.
3. Hall, *Henry VIII*, from *The Union of Two Noble and Illustre Famelies of Lancastre & Yorke* (hereafter cited as *Chronicle*), pp. 754–6.
4. *L. & P.*, Vol. IV, pt. 1, p. 2020.
5. Hall, op. cit., p. 735.
6. Cavendish, *Life*, p. 72.
7. *L. & P.*, Vol. IV, pt. 3, p. 2177.
8. Ibid., p. 2207.
9. Byrne, op. cit., p. 85.

IX

Campeggio's Decision

ANNE BOLEYN was now twenty-five. For nearly twelve years she had had little or no contact with her family, except for her step-mother, who sometimes accompanied her when she left Hever Castle for Greenwich or Hampton Court. Then, having dispensed with a chaperone, she had her own establishment in these palaces and was entirely independent.

In January 1529 her father returned from his embassies abroad, to be later created Earl of Wiltshire, while George Boleyn became Viscount Rochford. They then joined the group headed by Anne and her uncle Norfolk, with support from the Duke of Suffolk, who, as the King's brother-in-law and favourite companion, appeared more influential than was really the case. The widowed Mary Carey had no place in this clique, and no attempt was made to find her a second husband. She may have resented Anne's re-taining her hold over Henry, but this was not apparent. Lady Rochford's jealousy was, however. She and her husband were on increasingly bad terms, not only because he was unfaithful to her, but on account of his and Anne's affection for one another. Jane Rochford, a spiteful and unhappy woman, was ignored by the Boleyn faction, all of whom were optimistic about the divorce, although set on destroying Wolsey. While counting on the Cardinal's failure to obtain it, Norfolk and Suffolk planned to force the Pope into granting the kind of dispensation Henry needed. On this point, Suffolk and his wife were at odds; for she and Katherine had been devoted to one another for many years. The Queen-Duchess, as Mary Tudor was called, urged her husband to remonstrate with the King, which he eventually did; this merely resulted in an estrangement between her and Henry, and she retired from Court.[1]

A deeper split in the Boleyn group was caused by Norfolk's dislike of his niece, her resentment of his managing ways and her father's indifference to her difficulties. Wiltshire was interested only in his own promotion and more than ever absorbed in adding to his income; using Anne, he too disliked her, and rebelled against the power by which he continued to profit. So it was that George Rochford alone supported her; a gay, handsome, moderately gifted young man, he was not suited to the diplomatic career for which he had been trained, and could neither intrigue against nor win over her enemies; such efforts as he did make were undermined by his wife.

As the central figure in a faction divided against itself, Anne had no one to turn to but Henry; and he was now occupied in trying to solve the fearful problem of the second brief. He and Wolsey came to the conclusion that the hearing must be postponed until their agents at the Curia had persuaded Clement to pronounce it a forgery. The holograph remained in the Spanish archives, and as Charles V refused to part with it, copies only were available Francis I had one, Queen Katherine another. While Henry's envoys at the Vatican persisted in their attack, those in Madrid inspected the original and reported it to be forged; but Clement would not commit himself. Then, just as he seemed to be giving way, he fell seriously ill and was thought to be dying. This was the worst of Henry's setbacks, so far; for Clement might be replaced by one of the Emperor's Spanish Cardinals, which would ensure Katherine's triumph.

These delays further exacerbated Anne Boleyn; she refused to admit that they were inevitable. The discussions and arguments about the disputed brief, and the unsuccessful attempts to prove its falsity, seemed to her irrelevant. She knew only that she had been promised marriage, that it had not materialized and that with every month her position became more taxing. When her cousin, Sir Francis Bryan — who was known in Court circles as 'the Vicar of Hell' — was sent to promote Henry's cause in Rome, and met with the usual meaningless assurances from Clement VII, his reports were kept from her at Bryan's request; by this time, he and most of his associates feared her scorn of their efforts, and its effect on the King. 'I would have written to my mistress that shall be,' Bryan told Henry, 'but I will not write unto her until I may write that shall please her most in this world.'[2] Du Bellay, who admired Anne and much enjoyed her company[3] — they hunted together at Windsor and elsewhere — overheard her abusing Wolsey, and came to the conclusion that, whatever the result of the case, the Cardinal's power was on the wane. According to

Cavendish, Wolsey maintained his influence over Henry, which he reinforced by arranging 'banquets and solemn feasts' for the King and Anne.[4]

From February till April 1529 Clement's illness prevented his conferring with the English envoys. Then, forced to do so, and at the same time warned by the Emperor, he wrote to Henry apologizing for his inability to pronounce on the validity of the second brief, and adding that he must hear both sides before making a decision. Once more, he was attacked by Casale, who denounced the document as a forgery; the Englishman was followed by Charles V's Ambassador, Miguel Mai, threatening to execute any Cardinal who spoke against his master. Poor Clement, sobbing out that he was 'between the hammer and the anvil', promised Charles, for the third or fourth time, that he would revoke the hearing to Rome, while telling Henry that he would give him a dispensation to take another wife. When Henry insisted that the nullity of his marriage to Katherine must be established first, he received no answer; so, once more, he had to soothe Anne's impatience, which he did by sending Gardiner, the most forceful and competent of his envoys, to the Vatican. Anne followed up this advance by giving Gardiner, whom she addressed as 'Master Stephen', a present of cramp-rings, with an encouraging and cheerful letter. 'I hope for good news,' she concluded.[5]

But one defeat followed another. On May 5th, 1529, Bryan wrote to Henry from Rome, 'I can do you here no service. I dare not write to my cousin Anne the truth of this matter ... If she be angry with me, I most humbly desire Your Grace to make mine excuses.'[6] This failure, and Clement's final refusal to declare the disputed brief a forgery, caused Henry and Wolsey to change their ground, and press on with the hearing, which was to open at Blackfriars under Wolsey's and Campeggio's auspices. Then the Italian Cardinal fell ill. He was pursued by Henry's advisers, bearing huge tomes of theological and patristic literature, from which they lectured him as he lay in bed. 'God help me!' he wrote to Clement.[7] He was sent instructions so to conduct the case as to leave it unsolved, while establishing neutrality between Henry and the Curia.

Three days before the hearing, du Bellay became very anxious; he believed that Henry had 'come too near' Anne Boleyn. ('Si le ventre croît, tout sera gâté,' he wrote, but was presently reassured.[8])

As he waited for the result from Blackfriars, and the Cardinals prepared for what they knew would be a pompous farce, Cavendish recorded his disapproval of the whole procedure; his remarks epitomize the reaction of the English public to the case. He describes it as 'the strangest and newest sight and devise that ever was heard or read ... that a king and queen to be convened and constrained ... to appear in any court as common persons ... to abide the judgement and decrees of their own subjects,' going on to deprecate the 'inordinate carnal love' which had engendered such a step.[9] Ultimately, Henry profited by what appeared to be his total defeat at Blackfriars; it precipitated — but did not cause — a revolution in government which was long overdue.

Just before the hearing Queen Katherine made her confession to Campeggio, and swore, on the sacrament, that her marriage to Arthur had not been consummated. Meanwhile, Anne was advised to retire again to Hever, where news of the case reached her by degrees, the oratory of the protagonists being spread over several weeks. The final and most dramatic moment came when Campeggio rose to announce his decision. He did not touch on the fact that the Queen's famous protest and her refusal to acknowledge the authority of the court had made her contumacious, but stated simply that the whole case, having been conducted under the aegis of the Curia — which forbade any action being taken during the summer vacation — was now revoked to Rome, and would be adjourned until October. Suffolk, realizing that such a postponement was likely to be indefinite, 'gave a great clap upon the table', according to Cavendish, and 'with a very hault and stout countenance', exclaimed,' "By the Mass! It was never merry in England since we had Cardinals amongst us!" ' and was reproved by Wolsey, who now faced total ruin.[10]

When Anne heard the result of the hearing, she refused to come back to London; she gave out that she intended to remain in the country until she was forced to return. At last Henry came himself to fetch her, and stayed at Hever till he had reconciled her to the situation.[11] She blamed Wolsey for this new impasse; and Henry then perceived that all the Cardinal's foreign policies had been destroyed by one peace being signed between Clement VII and the Emperor at Barcelona, and another arranged between the latter and Francis I at Cambrai in 1529. The English were left out of both agreements.

Seemingly unperturbed, Henry took Anne on progress into Northamptonshire. It was his practice to hunt during all this, the 'grease', season, i.e. from August till October, when the harts were fat and best for killing. At his hunting-lodge of Grafton, he was approached by Wolsey, whom he received, says Cavendish, 'with as amiable a cheer as ever he did', talking alone with him before going in to dinner. One of Cavendish's friends, who was waiting on Henry and Anne, told him that she 'kept there an estate more like a queen than a simple maid' — and was behaving accordingly.[12]

During dinner, she made no secret of the fact that Henry's reception of Wolsey had annoyed her, and began, 'Sir — is it not a marvellous thing to consider what debt and danger the Cardinal hath brought you in with all your subjects?' 'How so, sweetheart?' Henry asked. 'Forsooth,' she told him, 'there is not a man within your realm worth five pounds but he has indebted you unto him by means' — referring to the Amicable Loan. Henry dismissed this. 'Well, well,' he said, 'as for that, there is in him no blame — for I know that matter better than you, or any other.' 'Nay, Sir,' Anne insisted. 'Besides all that, what things hath he wrought within your realm to your great slander and dishonour! There is never a nobleman,' she went on more heatedly, 'within this realm, that if he had done but half so much as *he* hath done, but he were well worthy to lose his head.' As Henry said nothing, she added, 'If my lord of Norfolk, my lord of Suffolk, my lord my father, or any other noble person within your realm had done much less than he, but they should have lost their heads for this.' 'Why, then I perceive', said Henry dryly, 'ye are not the Cardinal's friend?' Anne seems to have felt herself warned. She said, 'Forsooth, Sir — I have no cause, nor any other that loveth Your Grace, no more have Your Grace, if ye consider well his doings.' At this point the meal came to an end, and they withdrew to another room.[13]

Henry then summoned Wolsey for a second talk alone, appearing, as before, in the best of humours. Next day, the Cardinal came to wait on him, as arranged, to find that he and the Lady Anne Rochford, as she had now become, had gone out hunting. All that morning and afternoon, he stayed on, hoping to see his master. But Anne had arranged a picnic meal; she and Henry did not return until dusk — and then Wolsey, denied an audience, was told to go back to Hertfordshire. A week or so later, du Bellay reported that 'Mademoiselle de Boulen' had made her 'Friend' promise that he would not receive the Cardinal, 'for she thinks that he could not help having pity on him'. He added that the two Dukes, having brought down Wolsey, meant to grasp at the wealth of the Church, by an attack on the clergy. King and Cardinal never met again.[14]

Henry returned to London in the autumn of 1529 in order to authorize Wolsey's indictment under the Statute of Praemunire. (In the reigns of Edward III and Richard II this offence was defined as that of introducing a foreign power into the country, obeying an alien process and thus denying the prerogative of the sovereign.) This deprived him of the Chancellorship, the Great Seal and other benefices; while refusing to sign the act of attainder which would have sent the Cardinal to the Tower, and doubtless to execution on charges of embezzlement and high treason, Henry took for himself the palace of York Place, and ordered Wolsey to retire to the Bishop of Winchester's residence at Esher, where the Cardinal remained, temporarily unmolested. It was at this point that Wolsey's ablest but hitherto obscure under-secretary, Thomas Cromwell, took the step which involved him in the fortunes of Anne Boleyn. He had accompanied his master to Esher, and there, in the Great Chamber of the palace, Cavendish came upon him leaning against the window-sill, a missal in his hand. He was following the office, but 'prayed', says Cavendish, 'not more earnestly than the tears distilled from his eyes'. 'Why, Master Cromwell, what meaneth all this your sorrow?' Cavendish exclaimed. 'Is my lord in danger, for whom you lament thus? Or is it for any loss that you have sustained by any misadventure?'

Wiping away the tears, Cromwell described his situation as 'an unhappy adventure', in which he had lost all he had worked for. When Cavendish advised him not to do anything precipitate, he replied that he had been dismissed from the Cardinal's service. 'I intend, God willing,' he added, 'this afternoon, when my lord hath dined, to ride to London, and to the Court—where I will either make or mar, or I come again.' Cavendish approved this plan, and so they parted.[15] In the event, Cromwell, an administrative genius, both made and marred—to her destruction and, eventually, to his own—the young woman whom the King delighted to honour. He could not then have visualized the results of his services to Henry VIII, one of which was to make Anne Queen of England.

While Wolsey waited for orders to move on, Henry and Anne inspected the treasures of York Place, which had been laid out on tables. There they found masses of gold and silver plate set with jewels, also tapestries, silks, velvets, gold tissue and a thousand lengths of fine holland cloth.[16] What most pleased Anne was the rearrangement of the rooms. Henry planned to enlarge and modernize the whole structure, in which he allotted no apartments to the Queen, while the palace, renamed Whitehall, would be his principal dwelling-place in the city. Within the next few months he had himself redesigned the interior decorations, adding galleries, of which the ceilings, the Venetian Ambassador reported, were 'marvellously wrought in stone'. Each gallery was lined 'with a gold wainscot of carved wood, representing a thousand beautiful figures'.[17]

Anne Boleyn's installation in this riverside palace gave her the status of a consort; that her relationship with Henry remained as before, one of intimacy yet not of possession, seemed incredible to those who watched every move made by the King. Yet pages, waiting-women, Ladies and Gentlemen of the Bedchamber, bribed to reveal their mistress's state, reported as formerly. The situation was static; and foreign envoys contemplated, amazed, the spectacle of a monarch in absolute control, not only of his kingdom, but also of his desire for the woman he so loved that he would not let her out of his sight, and who went with him everywhere, receiving his guests as if they were husband and wife.

Queen Katherine remained at Westminster, accompanying Henry to Windsor, Greenwich or Hampton Court, where he visited her, generally in the evenings, as usual. Desperately anxious and miserable, she behaved as if her rival did not exist. Described by some as 'the sainted Queen', she added to the role of patient Griselda that of the thrifty housewife, sending to the Keeper of the Wardrobe for Henry's linen—and mending his shirts herself.[18] So the ruler of the richest Court in Europe, whose expenditure on dress and jewels ran into the modern equivalent of some £20,000 a year, would find his stout, ceaselessly smiling wife bent over patches, buttons and draw-strings, ready to talk or to listen—or to endure. Katherine was much admired for this gesture. Whether it exacerbated Henry or not, he remained in-scrutable and impervious. When it came to correct attitudes, he could compete with the best, as he showed by his first private talk with Eustace Chapuys, who had replaced Mendoza as Imperial Ambassador in August 1529.

Yet perhaps long-established habit and the memory of those beautifully darned shirts were in the King's mind, when he began by praising Katherine, and saying how much he regretted parting with her; but alas! God's will must be obeyed. He then turned to the corruption of the Roman clergy and the need for reform in the Church, while Chapuys, who had been instructed to use 'douceur et amitié' in his mission of reuniting Henry and Katherine, listened rather coolly to the King's account of Clement VII's broken promises.[19]

Chapuys, a middle-aged Savoyard, was a highly qualified legal expert, with few illusions. His detailed, bi-weekly reports to his master provide the fullest contemporary evidence of the struggle over the divorce; yet they must be cautiously received: for though he was fluent in French, Spanish and Latin, his English was not such as to enable him to understand everything said when Henry's courtiers were talking to one another. Also, the Emperor's orders that he should prevent Henry setting aside the Queen, so prejudiced the Ambassador against 'the Boleyn faction, that he collected all the derogatory gossip about the Concubine', as he called her, without troubling to find out whether it was true or false. To him, she was the personification of evil, the Woman on the Beast, the Great Whore of Babylon; and her satellites—Norfolk, Suffolk, Cromwell and Wiltshire—seemed to him, not only a degraded but an inefficient gang of rogues and predators. So he underrated Norfolk's cunning, Cromwell's ingenuity, Anne's intelligence and the influence of the group they led. Nor did he understand the English people (those barbaric islanders) or grasp the nature of their relationship with the King.

Finally, Chapuys discounted a new element in Henry's policy—his extremely subtle use of the Lutheranism he had attacked in his *Assertio*, and the Boleyn party's patronage of that heretical sect; this was the principal weapon in their sudden—and highly popular—move against the clergy. Henry's careful assessment of Anglo-Lutheran feeling had begun several years before he decided to marry Anne Boleyn. It was later enhanced by his interest in Tyndale's *Obedience of a Christian Man*, which she put into his hands shortly after the hearing at Blackfriars, together with Simon Fish's *A Supplication for the Beggars*. Both works were revolutionary, combining virulent attacks on clerical privilege, and the abuses arising out of what they described as an intolerable situation. There are three accounts of Anne's share in the propagation of the *Obedience*, two written some sixty years later by Foxe the martyrologist and George Wyatt respectively, and a third by an anonymous contemporary, whose version is that preferred by modern scholars.

This letter describes how one of Anne's ladies, Mrs Gainsford, betrothed to a Mr Zouch, was reading Tyndale's pamphlet, when he, 'among other love-tricks, plucked it from her'. Knowing that such works were forbidden, Zouch concealed the *Obedience*, but was 'so ravished ... that he was never well but when he was reading of that book', even in the royal chapel. This alarmed Mrs Gainsford, who begged him to return it, but—'he was as ready to weep as to deliver the book'. One of Wolsey's gentlemen then discovered and reported the matter to his master, who prepared to tell the King of Zouch's illicit reading; but, by this time, Mrs Gainsford had confided in Anne, who herself obtained and read the *Obedience*, marked certain passages with her fingernail and brought it to Henry. One of its opening phrases—'The King is in this world without Law, and may at his lust do right and wrong, and shall give accounts but to God only'—so struck him that, after he had read the whole book, he is reported to have said, 'If a man should pull down an old stone wall, and should begin at the lower part, the upper part might chance to fall upon his head,' adding, 'This is a book which all kings should read.'[20] In fact, Henry later perceived that to undermine clerical power in England must precede national independence of the Vatican. On Fish's *Supplication*, which contained very severe strictures on the English clergy and the monastic institutions, he made no comment, but sent for the author and his wife and promised them his protection.[21]

In her daughter's reign Anne Boleyn's patronage of Tyndale and Fish was affectionately recorded. Her motive in putting their works before Henry may be connected with her awareness of his politico-theological views. She knew more than one method of attracting and keeping his interest, and was well able to discuss such matters when he chose to raise them. His belief in the semidivinity of monarchy was perceived by all his intimates; and Anne naturally subscribed to it, thus strengthening his dependence on her. Both the *Obedience* and the *Supplication* implied support of

what is now known as Caesaropapism; and in that sense, both
suggested a solution to the problem of the King's great matter.

NOTES

1. Chapman, *The Sisters of Henry VIII*, p. 208.
2. *L. & P.*, Vol. IV, pt. 3, p. 2264.
3. Ibid., p. 2296.
4. Cavendish, *Life*, p. 70.
5. *L. & P.*, Vol. IV, pt. 3, p. 2382.
6. Ibid., p. 2398.
7. Scarisbrick, *Henry VIII*, p. 224.
8. *L. & P.*, Vol. IV, pt. 3, p. 2509.
9. Cavendish, op. cit., p. 78.
10. Ibid., p. 90.
11. Herbert of Cherbury, *The Life and Raigne of King Henry the Eighth*, p. 258.
12. Cavendish, op. cit., p. 94.
13. Ibid., p. 96.
14. *L. & P.*, Vol. IV, pt. 3, p. 2679.
15. Cavendish, op. cit., p. 105.
16. Ibid., p. 99.
17. *Ven. Cal. P.*, Vol. IV, pp. 286–7.
18. Mattingly, *Catherine of Aragon*, p. 221.
19. Scarisbrick, op. cit., p. 246.
20. Foxe, *Acts and Monuments*, Vol. IV, p. 658.
21. Pocock, *Records of the Reformation*, pp. 52–3; Scarisbrick, op. cit., p. 247.

X

Threats and Promises

AN eminent and learned English author has observed that 'It is difficult to find any medieval or Renaissance writer who does not take it for granted that, from highest prelate to humblest friar, the majority of clergymen are disreputable.'[1] This judgment was amplified in the Act of Accusation against the Clergy submitted to Henry VIII by the 'Reformation' Parliament of November 1529.

At great length and in meticulous detail, the corruptions resulting from the abuse of clerical privilege were set forth, and finally accepted as factual, not only by the King, but by his people, in whom resentment had risen to fury at the injustices caused by 'spiritual' courts, financial exactions, pluralism, nepotism and other grievances. Henry referred the Accusation to the bishops, who, having hitherto made and passed their own laws for the clergy, were now required to obtain his and Parliament's consent before their resolutions became statutory.

National feeling on these points had been intensified by the revocation to Rome of the hearing for the divorce. While still supporting Katherine against Anne—whom they continued to detest and abuse—most people saw Campeggio's decision and Wolsey's enforced agreement with it as another example of clerical arrogance and meddling; that an Italian bishop, whose revenues came from a diocese in which he had never set foot, should be empowered to dictate terms and give orders to an English king was intolerable. Henry was expected to stand up for his rights, the more especially because, fourteen years earlier, he had announced that 'We are, by the sufferance of God, King of England, and the Kings of England in time past have never had any superior but God.'[2]

The Commons' appeal, welcome though it was to Henry, did not at once have all the effect he hoped for, although the revocation had already been met by his answer, given through Wolsey, that when and if he did appear in Rome, he would do so at the head of an army, whose banners might well prove more terrible than the Emperor's landsknechts. His position was now that of negotiator between the bishops, the Commons and his newly elected Council, which was headed by Norfolk, Suffolk, Wiltshire, and Sir Thomas More as Chancellor.

At this time, Henry began to see his way to the divorce, and thus to marriage with Anne Boleyn, by threatening the Curia more fiercely than Wolsey had been able to do. Clement was told, not only that the English Church might secede—while remaining Catholic—but that further vacillations and refusals would cause Lutheranism, that poisonous heresy, to spread throughout the kingdom, as it had in Germany and Switzerland. As *Fidei Defensor*, Henry indicated that he was determined to avoid this disaster by continuing to burn heretics—on condition that the nullity of his marriage to Katherine was authorized by the Pope. He then began his new campaign against papal jurisdiction, which was partially supported within the kingdom. 'God', Hall records, 'illumined the eyes of the King.'[3] His attitude towards Anne Boleyn was thereby slightly shifted.

He was still deeply in love with her, and determined on marriage. But that objective was now subordinated to the achievement of the Caesaropapism which eventually resulted in the divorce of Katherine by Archbishop Cranmer, the Royal Supremacy and the rather unwilling acceptance of Anne as Queen of England. Yet Henry still believed—wrongly, as it turned out—that he would be able to force Clement to do what he wanted, and warn off Charles V by indicating the consequences of his power through a different type of envoy. One of these—and a more inept choice can hardly be imagined—was Anne's father, who was sent to interview the Emperor at Bologna, and whose mission completely failed.

The last months of 1529 saw the defeat of the bishops on several points and the amendment of a number of grievances. So the Boleyn faction, now headed by Norfolk, seemed ready to defy the Curia; but still the agile Clement managed to slip out of making any decision vetoed by the Emperor; still Henry insisted that the nullity suit must be granted by the Pope; and still Anne, who 'ruled all', according to du Bellay, continued to protest.[4]

Then it became necessary to decide what should be done with Wolsey. Commons, Lords and the general public were clamouring for his blood. He wrote imploring Anne to intercede for him with Henry, and received no answer.[5] While Cromwell, now a member of Parliament, pleaded for him in the Commons, he was reported to be very ill, too ill to leave Esher. Henry, apparently much concerned, sent him a kind message and his own physician, Dr Butts, from whom he required an account of the Cardinal's progress. With Anne, he received Butts at Whitehall, and began, 'How doth yonder man, have you seen him?' 'Yea, Sir,' the doctor replied. 'How do you like him?' Henry pursued. 'Forsooth, Sir,' said Butts, 'if you will have him dead, I warrant Your Grace he will be dead within these four days, if he receive no comfort from you shortly — and from Mistress Anne.'

'Marry,' Henry replied, 'God forbid that he should die! I pray you, good Master Butts, go again unto him and do your cure upon him, for I would not lose him for twenty thousand pounds.' 'Then', Butts explained, 'must Your Grace send him first some comfortable message, as shortly as is possible.' 'Even so will I,' Henry promised, 'by you. And therefore make speed to him again.' The King then gave Butts a ruby ring, as assurance of his favour to the Cardinal, adding, 'And tell him that I am not offended with him in my heart, and that shall he believe, and God send him life very shortly. Therefore, bid him be of good cheer, and pluck up his heart, and take no despair. And I charge you, come not from him until ye have brought him out of all danger of death.'

All this time, Anne had said nothing. Henry, determined on her co-operation — which might not have been forthcoming if they had been alone — turned to her and said, 'Good sweetheart — I pray you, at this my instance, as ye love us, to send the Cardinal a token, with comfortable words; and in so doing, ye shall do us a loving pleasure.'

Anne knew better than to hesitate. She at once removed a gold tablet from her girdle and gave it to Dr Butts, 'with very gentle and comfortable words in commendation to the Cardinal'.[6]

The effect of the doctor's mission was immediate; Wolsey's health improved — or seemed to do so — and through Cromwell he obtained Henry's permission to leave for The More. Walking in the park with Cavendish, the Cardinal quoted an ancient saying, which he took as a warning of his own fate. 'When the cow rideth the bull,' it ran, 'then, priest, beware thy skull.' As Cavendish could make nothing of the rhyme, his master explained that a dun cow was one of the Tudor emblems, and thus symbolized Henry VIII. 'The bull', he said, 'betokens Mistress Anne Boleyn, because her father hath the same beast in his cognisance.'[7]

Henry's interview with the Cardinal and his refusal to sign the act of attainder gave rise to the rumour that after a short absence Wolsey would be reinstated. Norfolk was then heard to say that if this happened, he would 'eat the Cardinal alive',[8] but he need not have concerned himself. Wolsey had been permanently discarded; and the King, still on progress, was taking a holiday from state affairs.

With Anne, and a Court that included Foxe and Gardiner, he moved into his hunting-lodge at Waltham, which was too small to accommodate all his entourage. The two ministers were billeted in a neighbouring house, where they met an old Cambridge acquaintance, Thomas Cranmer, who was tutoring the sons of a local magnate. Dining together, they talked of the divorce; and after some discussion Cranmer said, 'You go not the next way to work as to bring the matter unto a perfect conclusion and end.' He then put forward his own solution, which was that both universities should be consulted about the marriage with Katherine. Himself convinced of its invalidity, he later won over a number of the Cambridge fellows to his views. 'He has the sow by the right ear,' Henry exclaimed, when he heard of Cranmer's abilities, summoned him to Greenwich for further discussion and told him to study the problem 'with an indifferent eye'.[9]

So Cranmer's attachment to the Boleyn family, whose chaplain he presently became, was inaugurated; his affection for Anne endured until her death. A shy, retiring scholar, whose theological principles later moved towards Henrician Catholicism, he was neither a sycophant nor a climber; his sympathy with Anne's difficulties sprang from a disinterested and genuine devotion. She came to depend on him as on no one else.

Cranmer's idea of canvassing the English universities was at once put in hand by Henry's commissioners, whose efforts with the Cambridge dons were rewarded by their declaring that marriage with a brother's widow was unlawful; and a month later the Fellows of Oxford came to the same conclusion. Here, there were protests from some of the younger dons, who, supported by the townswomen, organized violent and noisy demonstrations against their seniors, stoning and mobbing them. Henry dismissed them as 'rebellious youths', and they subsided, unpunished. It was then arranged that the continental universities should be consulted, and this campaign was planned for the spring and summer of 1530.

Meanwhile, Henry gave orders that the rise of the Boleyn family should be celebrated by a banquet, which was to take place at Whitehall, before he left London to join the Queen at Greenwich for Christmas.

This occasion was marked by further honours being paid to Anne. She sat on the dais at Henry's right hand, thus taking precedence over all the other ladies, including the Duchess of Suffolk, who, as the King's sister, ranked second only to the Queen. Mary Tudor, a spirited and outspoken young woman, insisted that her husband should protest; when he did so, Henry, already irritated by Suffolk's unnecessary advice — which was that he should not marry Anne till he had disposed of Katherine — dismissed him from Court. Suffolk retaliated by telling his brother-in-law that Anne had once been Sir Thomas Wyatt's mistress. Henry, apparently unmoved, denied the charge, and the Suffolks retired to the country, where the Duchess remained, rather than submit to her former lady-in-waiting preceding her; she seems not to have objected to Suffolk's returning alone.[10]

The story that Wyatt and Anne had been lovers was a pointless slander. Her enemies were so eager to seize any weapon against her, that a scandal of this kind would have been publicized without hesitation, especially by the foreign ambassadors, who were instructed to report all such rumours. That Wyatt had pursued her, and that she had refused him her favours, was well known; in any case, he had been sent on a mission to Spain shortly after the incident of the stolen locket.[11] But the King's disregard of Suffolk's mischief-making complicated the imbroglio of which Anne was the central figure; for she had to appear to be on good terms with the Duke. Yet her resolution, and her certainty of Henry's support, enabled her to withstand other and cruder methods of attack.

One of these came to her in the form of a book, 'pretending old prophecies', which she found lying on a table. The first page was headed by the letter H, the second by A, the third by K, and all were illustrated. She then read warnings of her 'certain destruction' if she married the King. Unperturbed, she called to her maid, 'Come hither, Nan — see, here is a book of prophecies.' As the girl obeyed, she went on, 'This, he saith, is the King, this the Queen, mourning, weeping and wringing her hands — and this is myself, with my head off.' 'If I thought it true,' the maid exclaimed, 'though he were an emperor, I would not marry him with that

condition!' Her mistress said, 'Tush, Nan, I think the book a
bauble. Yet,' she added, after a pause, 'for the hope I have, that the
realm may be happy by my issue, I am resolved to have him—
whatever may become of me.'[12]

This incident, recorded by George Wyatt half a century later, is
perhaps somewhat *ben trovato*. But whether true or false, it may be
taken as an example of the stubborn resolve with which Anne Boleyn
faced her situation. Few of her contemporaries would have cared to
bet on her marriage with Henry, and no doubt she knew this, just
as she knew the nature of the impasse before herself and the King.

Now, for the first time in three years, Henry was at a loss; he
could not make up his mind whether to go on pressing his cause at
the Vatican, or to wait for the result of his appeal to the continental
universities. So there came a pause in the struggle; and it was then
that Eustace Chapuys noticed a change in the King's behaviour.
His outbursts of rage were more frequent, and not always histrionic; also, he did not attempt to conceal his anger with Clement
VII, who, in February 1530, told the English envoys that he was
desirous to do their master's pleasure, and promised to solicit
Charles V on Henry's behalf. Let him marry Mistress Boleyn, the
Pope added—and then, later, perhaps something might be arranged
about the invalidity of the marriage with Katherine. Henry refused
to commit bigamy; this nonchalant suggestion, once entertained,
now infuriated him; he said he would use it against Clement when
he denounced him as a heretic.[13]

When Chapuys reported this speech to Norfolk, the Duke refused to take sides. 'I would rather have lost one of my hands than
that such a question should have arisen,' he said, 'but it is entirely
a matter of law—and conscience,' he added blandly. He ended the
conversation by saying that if the Emperor continued to use the
second brief of Julius II as a weapon, King Henry would 'consider
himself the most abused prince in Christendom'.[14]

Returning to Greenwich, Chapuys described Henry's treatment
of Katherine as 'worse than ever', for he spent most of his time
with Anne, and when he did visit the Queen, it was in order to urge
her taking the veil. Chapuys then advised her how best to appeal to
the Emperor, whose response was kindly but not constructive. Her
agonized letters to the Pope resulted in his forbidding the English
Parliament even to discuss the divorce—which produced another
wave of anti-clerical feeling.[15]

This reassured Anne, who still feared Wolsey's return to power. When one of Henry's gentlemen spoke up for the Cardinal, she refused to speak to him for three days, according to Chapuys; but to please Henry, she sent to inquire for Wolsey's health. 'She is an accomplished mistress of intrigue,' the Ambassador told his master, adding that the French envoys at the Vatican were 'saturated' with English money, and so working for the divorce.[16]

In this time of frustration and anxiety Anne and Henry were more closely bound, and thus perhaps more at one, than if they had been husband and wife. Most people found it difficult to resist his personal magnetism; and she was no exception. He had lived all his life in public; and she now found herself in the same position. The reports show that she became more amenable when their prospects were bad; with improvement, her impatience recurred. During the greater part of 1530 she seems to have realized that she must be content with what she had already gained—including her own palace—while waiting for marriage. Quite apart from what Chapuys described as the King's 'miserable amour' for her, and her own ambitions, she and Henry were temperamentally suited, and so able to endure an extremely trying situation, over which the experts continued to disagree; for the continental universities, all heavily bribed, were by no means unanimous in Henry's favour; and even if they had been, Charles V, still in control of the Curia, was determined to stop the divorce; while the Pope, confiding in the French Ambassador, said that he would be glad if the marriage between Henry and Anne were effected, 'provided it is not by my authority'. And the Nuncio accredited to Henry's Court was 'heart and soul' for the King, according to Chapuys.[17] Yet matters had to remain at a standstill, as long as Katherine insisted on the second hearing taking place in Rome—where Henry, supported by Parliament, refused to go—and Clement took no action.

Then, as the King's visits to Katherine resulted in fiercer arguments and increasingly bitter recrimination, Anne's self-control began to give way, especially when he complained to her of his failure to move the Queen. Chapuys's spies told him that she berated Henry, not only for his inability to persuade Katherine, but for seeing her at all. The King seems to have felt that until the divorce was effected he must observe the conventions by appearing with Katherine on certain public occasions, and this enraged Anne; yet their relationship remained unchanged. This puzzled

Chapuys, whose interpretation of their disputes was, naturally, biased; for he was now almost sure of Katherine's triumph, while his hatred of Anne intensified. She was everything he most feared and detested—a bold, provocative, brilliant creature, whose behaviour seemed to him insolent, unfeminine and immodest. And he had no use at all for her circle of gay, gallant young people, with their gambling, their versifying and lute-playing, and their disregard of the formalities. Also, he was quite disgusted by the Nuncio's complacent acceptance of their and Henry's flatteries.

In the early summer of 1530 the King began work on a plan which he believed would force Clement into action by showing him that the whole country, as represented by its leading men, desired judgment for the divorce; if he refused it, England's secession would cease to be a threat and become a reality. While looking on this step as final (it was in fact the first of a series), Henry anticipated, and may have prevented, another outburst from Anne by giving her a quantity of furniture, jewels and horse-trappings of great splendour.[18] His eye for such details seldom failed; but his awareness of public feeling was not, at this time, quite so well developed. Once more, he had to accept defeat.

NOTES

1. Huxley, *The Devils of Loudon,* p. 14.
2. Scarisbrick, *Henry VIII,* p. 249.
3. Hall, *Chronicle,* p. 250.
4. *L. & P.,* Vol. IV, pt. 3, p. 2679.
5. Ibid., p. 2714.
6. Cavendish, *Life,* pp. 120–21.
7. Ibid., p. 128.
8. Froude, *Divorce,* p. 132.
9. Parmiter, *The King's Great Matter,* p. 124.
10. Chapman, *The Sisters of Henry VIII,* p. 121.
11. Thomson, *Sir Thomas Wyatt and His Background,* p. 24.
12. Wyatt, *Anne Boleyn,* p. 12.
13. Froude, op. cit., p. 133.
14. *L. & P.,* Vol. IV, pt. 3, pp. 2682–3.
15. Ibid, p. 2781.
16. Ibid.
17. Froude, op. cit., p. 135.
18. *L. & P.,* Vol. IV, pt. 3, Appendix.

XI

Taking the Offensive

THE large and formidable party supporting Queen Katherine was
headed by Bishop Fisher, who wrote a number of books and
pamphlets against the divorce, and was one of those who believed
that the Emperor would, if necessary, invade England on his aunt's
behalf. This group, which included Archbishop Warham and the
Duchess of Norfolk (she had parted from her husband, who was
living with a mistress), gravitated towards Chapuys; his view
seems to have been that there would be no need for his master to
declare war, because the majority of the English people, led by
certain nobles, would rise against the Council and depose Henry, if
he discarded his wife and married Anne Boleyn.

Such delusions were perfectly natural. It was not the first time
(nor would it be the last) that a foreign envoy had been misled
through ignorance of national feeling. Meanwhile, those who
feared and detested the Boleyn faction thought that Norfolk
would eventually desert his niece's cause for that of the Queen;
for his disapproval and jealousy of Anne were well known. In fact,
the Duke had no intention of working against Henry, although he
could not conceal his dislike of what he had to do. If only, he told
Chapuys, Katherine and Anne were both dead, then His Majesty
could marry suitably and for the good of his people. Now, if
Charles V ordered the Pope to do so, he would 'dance in a clown's
coat through the streets of Rome'. But, sooner or later, Clement
must yield to the King's requirements and pronounce against the
Queen.[1]

That unhappy lady was, and still is, regarded as a martyr;
indeed, at one point the question of her being canonized actually
arose. A great deal has been written about Henry's cruelty towards the wife who loved and served him for nearly twenty
years; the manner of her response to his demands is worth recon-
sideration.

Her principles, rightly and inevitably, eliminated all question
of the invalidity of their marriage; but during these last years of

94

crisis her behaviour towards Henry had neither dignity (except in public) nor common sense; nor did she show the faintest understanding of his character. Her six years' seniority, and the fact that in their youth he had depended on her judgment, resulted in her thinking of him — and treating him — as an easily led, well-disposed creature of impulse, who, properly influenced, was bound, at long last, to come to a better frame of mind. So he must on no account be indulged or placated, but scolded, threatened and, above all, reminded of his duty by her appearance at his side on every possible occasion. In her letters to the Pope and her nephew her point of view is shown as that of one absolutely sure of being in the right, and knowing exactly how to deal with a devious, incalculable, tirelessly resolute man, who knew far more than she could ever have begun to learn about his power, the use he might make of it, and in what it consisted. Unfortunately, Katherine's ignorance, stupidity and tactlessness were those of a bigot and a fanatic, whose thirty years' residence in England had taught her nothing of the varying currents of opinion outside her own constricted circle, and who was incapable of perceiving that since her marriage to his brother both the King and his people had changed, and were continuing to do so. Nor does she seem to have realized that her insistence on her rights, combined with her virulent abuse of Anne Boleyn, as a shameless woman Henry 'dragged about' with him,[2] were driving him into hatred and contempt for herself, and for everything she represented. Finally, she chose to ignore his belief that the God they both worshipped had told him what he ought to do. Her letters show that his talk of conscience, sin and the dictates of Leviticus sounded in her ears like the foolish babble of someone temporarily unbalanced; and what may have most exasperated him was her making excuses for his convictions, and laying the blame on others, as if he, who had been King of England for twenty-one years, had neither knowledge, nor intelligence — nor even authority.

Yet Henry did not now order her to leave him, possibly because, by continuing to visit and appear with her, he still hoped to bring about her capitulation. Also, his rather tenuous sense of justice may have prevented his sending her away, apart from the fact that she refused to go when he made it plain that that was what he wanted. Irritated beyond bearing, he yet was sorry for her; and he could not utterly reject the claims of the past, nor their shared affection for the Princess Mary, a pretty, delicate girl of fourteen, to whom he was devoted.

Katherine's tragic misconceptions eventually helped to solve Henry's dilemma; but between 1530 and 1532 they added to it, while enhancing his need of Anne. Putting up with or soothing her rages enabled him to forget the Queen's impregnable righteousness. Turning from the rock and the desert of Katherine's spiritual arrogance to the shimmering oases of Anne's moods, he emerged ready for further efforts; and he now put them into practice.

He had long been aware that his Council and a number of his nobles, while disliking Anne, had accepted his resolve to marry her, longed for an end to the dispute, and were increasingly enraged by the interference of Charles V and the shilly-shallying of Clement VII. They so detested the latter that, according to Chapuys, they could not bear to hear him mentioned.[3] The Ambassador, failing to perceive the significance of this hostility, was merely disgusted; it did not occur to him that Henry saw it as a secret weapon, to be used when all else failed.

Henry now prepared to proceed cautiously. He knew that if he did not, he would lose the support of Parliament, and of his people; and their approval was more vital to his purpose than that of Clement, or Charles V, or Francis I. These potentates would be difficult, if not impossible, to manœuvre; he knew more than one method of handling those he had ruled for two decades. His gift for subtle manipulation later amounted to genius; in the summer of 1530 he was feeling his way towards success.

With his Council, Henry composed a courteous, bold, not quite belligerent petition to Clement VII, asking him to acknowledge the invalidity of his marriage to Katherine, and pointing out that the majority of the continental universities had pronounced in his favour. Some seventy nobles, abbots and bishops were asked to sign this document, which, although it granted the authority of the Holy See, put forward the usual threats of secession, so phrased as to make it clear that further delay would not be tolerated. When these menaces were objected to, the petition was toned down. A few days later, Henry summoned this group of advisers again, and suggested that the divorce should be effected in England, without the Pope's permission.

This proposal was greeted with dismay; and one of those asked for his signature knelt and implored his master not to take such a desperate step.[4] Henry at once gave in, and confined himself to a personal letter to Clement, pointing out the injustice with which he had been treated. After considerable delay, Clement told the English envoys that he would allow Henry to take two wives, while ensuring the legitimacy of any children by both of them.

Henry ignored this suggestion, and once more refused to go to Rome — this time, on the grounds that no Englishman could legally be summoned to appear before a foreign court; he then announced that the case must be submitted to the Archbishop of Canterbury. A month later, he desired his envoys to defy the Pope's jurisdiction. They were to tell Clement that those who did not were 'Englishmen papisticate', as opposed to the 'entire Englishmen' representing national opinion and ancient custom.[5] So he inaugurated his withdrawal from papal authority. It was of course a slow process; and as Anne Boleyn had, ostensibly, no share in it, she began to despair. She therefore asserted herself; and a series of scenes ensued, which were reported by Chapuys.

The first of these took place when Henry and Anne were alone, and no record survives of what was said. A few days later, Chapuys and Norfolk were interrupted in a heated discussion about the divorce by her father, whose abuse of Clement VII was such that the Ambassador had to leave the room. 'If she and Lord Wiltshire remain in power, they will entirely alienate this kingdom from the Pope,' Chapuys told his master.[6]

A fortnight after this dispute, Henry summoned Chapuys for a talk in one of the galleries of Whitehall, and raised the prevailing question angrily and at length. At last the Ambassador said, 'I beg Your Majesty not to enter upon so delicate a subject until I have received orders from the Emperor.' Henry persisted, pointing out that Charles V had thwarted him in every possible way. Then Chapuys, looking up, saw a woman he believed to be Anne Boleyn, sitting by a window overlooking the gallery. Henry moved away, and went on to explain that he had spoken 'unceremoniously' of the Emperor, because the imperial envoys at the Vatican had slandered him to Clement VII. As the argument continued, Chapuys came to the conclusion that Henry had shifted his position for fear that Anne might overhear 'something that would offend her'.[7] This scene was followed by another, which took place in front of several people, and was reported to the Ambassador.

The King had recently left his Council in a rage. They were

useless, he told them, adding, 'The Cardinal is a better man than any of you.'[8] He then found Anne in tears; she sobbed out that she was wasting her life and sacrificing her good name – and for what? As Henry protested, she declared that she would leave the Court and never see him again. When he tried to reason with her, she repeated what Chapuys decided was an attempt at blackmail, but which may have been an outburst of genuine alarm; for Henry's remarks about Wolsey had been reported to her, and she knew that the Cardinal, planning to return, had approached the Queen. She may also have known (as her father did) that Wolsey had written to the Pope, offering his support against the divorce, and putting forward a plan for her dismissal.

The prospect was appalling. She could only threaten to with-draw from an untenable situation which was intensified by the fact that Wolsey had come to London, and was staying with Norfolk – was the Duke also betraying her?

Henry then burst into tears. 'Do not speak of leaving me!' he exclaimed. She implored him to arrest Wolsey, and he promised to send him to his diocese, but would not consent to his arrest. 'He could not appease her,' Chapuys concluded, 'and nothing but Wolsey's arrest would satisfy her,' adding that Anne was deter-mined to bring down the Cardinal.[9]

The Ambassador's interpretation of this scene did not allow for the fact that Anne was really terrified of what Wolsey might do; she knew that Henry was still fond of him, and had discounted all rumours of his approach to the Vatican and to Charles V. Her only hope was to present the King with a choice; yet to count on his need of her had an element of risk, for he was now so discouraged as to have reached a stage of indecision. This mood did not last; but she may well have feared that it might lead to some arrange-ment for the succession from which she would be excluded. She did not trust him – nor her father, nor her uncle; and so she gave way, regardless of what would be said of her. She was surrounded by enemies; and her reputation, according to the Venetian Ambassador, who had arrived a few weeks earlier, was that of a kept woman – which she was – and of a harlot: which she was not.

This envoy, Savorgnano, told the Signory that if Henry did succeed in marrying Anne Boleyn, the people would rebel, partly because they believed that the votes of the continental universities had been unfairly obtained; he did not realize that what most concerned them was the possibility of a cessation of the wool trade with Spain. Describing London as 'a very rich, populous, mercantile, but not beautiful city', he then reported on the Court, where he was received by the King and Queen. He was much impressed by Henry's 'handsome presence, singular beauty, many accomplishments and charm of manner', but disapproved of his rumoured 'repudiation' of Katherine, whom he found 'prudent, good, very popular, stout and always smiling'. He rather naively added, 'She is neither disheartened nor depressed.' This was the more remarkable, in that Henry was now 'living with a young woman of noble birth, though many say of bad character, whose will is law to him, and he is expected to marry her should the divorce take place, which it is supposed will not be effected, as the peers of the realm ... and the people are opposed to it.' Savorgnano concluded that no other queen was wanted. He was rather surprised that Henry, who was very religious, held the Pope 'in such small account'. He also noted his care for the Princess Mary who, with her mother, had her own apartments at Hampton Court.[10] Neither Savorgnano nor his successor, Falier, met Anne during the summer and autumn of 1530; nor did they understand why Cardinal Wolsey was in disgrace.

In September 1530 Wolsey set off for York with a train of six hundred attendants, including his Italian physician, Agostini, who had just informed on him to the Council. According to Agostini, the Cardinal had said that all his hopes rested on the Queen, and that he had advised the Pope to take stronger measures on her behalf by calling in 'the secular arm'. He followed up this hint at a Spanish invasion by telling Clement that he ought to excommunicate Henry and order him to dismiss Anne Boleyn.[11] The King accepted the evidence and commanded Wolsey's arrest; this duty fell to Henry Percy, who had recently succeeded his father as Earl of Northumberland.

So the cup of vengeance was placed before the young man whom the Cardinal had humiliated and abused; but the impact of Wolsey's personality was such that Northumberland, entering his palace of Cawood, while the doomed man was dining ('at his fruits', says Cavendish), paused, mumbled a greeting, and dared not proceed.[12]

Wolsey, who knew what he had come for, welcomed him suavely, and with a flow of words which further embarrassed the

Earl, led him into his bedchamber, where a great fire was burning. 'And they being there all alone,' Cavendish recalls, 'save only I, that kept the door according to my duty ... the Earl, trembling, said, with a very faint and soft voice unto my lord, laying his hand upon his arm, "My lord, I arrest you of high treason."'[13]

Wolsey was spared the ultimate horrors: for he had been mortally ill for some time. He reached Leicester Abbey on the night of November 29th; there, after a few days' suffering, he died (it seems of dysentery) and was buried next to Richard III in what Chapuys described as 'the tyrants' sepulchre'.[14]

'I wish that he had lived,' said Henry, when Cavendish, who found him shooting at the butts in the park of Hampton Court, told him of his master's last hours. After some talk of the money owed Henry by Wolsey, and Cavendish's unpaid wages—'Ten pounds, is it not so?'—the King took the gentleman-usher into his own service. Cavendish concludes his exquisite masterpiece as one speaking from a medieval past, with 'O madness! O foolish desire! O what inconstant trust and assurance in rolling fortune!'[15]

Shortly after the removal of her old enemy, Anne Boleyn was attacked again, this time by the newly accredited Nuncio, Del Borgho, who demanded her dismissal from Henry's Court—'an outrageous measure', Norfolk told Chapuys, and refused to pass on this piece of impertinence to the King.[16] Defiantly, Anne celebrated Christmas week by putting her servants into liveries embroidered with her device of a white falcon and the words 'Ainsi sera, grogne qui grogne'. Then, hearing that this was a Burgundian and therefore a Spanish motto, she ordered the new doublets to be laid aside, and her attendants appeared in their old habits.[17]

Meanwhile, at a consistory of the Cardinals, Clement VII was asked, not only to denounce Henry's divorce, but to forbid him to cohabit with any other woman, 'especially a certain Lady Anne'. If he married her, they added, His Holiness should declare their union null and void. 'The Pope says', Chapuys told Norfolk, 'that he has done enough for your King.'[18] Encouraged by what seemed to her Clement's firmer attitude, the Queen asked Henry to talk with her alone. The ensuing discussion, which she reported to Clement, would have utterly defeated any other woman.

NOTES

1. Froude, *Divorce*, p. 143.
2. *Span. Cal. P.*, Vol. IV, pt. 2, p. 254.
3. Froude, op. cit., p. 148.
4. Scarisbrick, *Henry VIII*, p. 259.
5. Ibid., p. 263.
6. *Span. Cal. P.*, Vol. IV, pt. 1, p. 790.
7. Ibid, p. 803.
8. Ibid., p. 3035.
9. *L. & P.*, Vol. IV, pt. 3, p. 3035.
10. *Ven. Cal. P.*, Vol. IV, pp. 252, 286–7, 293.
11. Froude, op. cit., p. 140.
12. Cavendish, *Life*, p. 152.
13. Ibid., p. 155.
14. *L. & P.*, Vol. IV, pt. 3, p. 3054.
15. Cavendish, op. cit., pp. 154, 188.
16. *Span. Cal. P.*, Vol. IV, pt. 1, p. 128.
17. Friedmann, *Anne Boleyn*, Vol. II, p. 128.
18. *L. & P.*, Vol. IV, pt. 3, p. 3060.

XII

Cromwell's Solution

ON this occasion the Queen did not confine herself to arguments about the validity of her marriage. Putting aside her own wrongs, she told Henry that his relationship with Anne Boleyn was scandalous and degrading; for she placed her in the same category as Elizabeth Blount and Mary Boleyn, whose status she had once more or less philosophically accepted. Henry replied that Anne was not his mistress; he was keeping her at his side because he intended to marry her, and no one, certainly not the Pope, he added, would change his decision. This announcement temporarily silenced Katherine. She reported it to Clement VII as being the truth.[1]

Henry was not in the habit of lying unless it was necessary to do so; and he had never attempted to conceal his relations with Mary Boleyn and Elizabeth Blount from Katherine, or from anybody else. Also, to tell the truth on this point helped to destroy her case; for he must have known that she would believe what he said. He therefore forced Katherine to face an obstacle which might change her attitude; that it did not—that she still counted on his return to her, and regarded his feeling for Anne as a transient aberration—strengthened his resolve to bring about the divorce, and increased his hostility towards herself. At this juncture Katherine does not seem to have dwelt on her rival's ambitions, or to have pointed out that it was the crown and not the man that Anne desired.

That Anne Boleyn was incapable of affection—that she remained a coldhearted, scheming adventuress throughout these last years of trial and frustration—has long been the accepted view of her character. In fact, the role of the calculating siren was beyond her. She clung to Henry, and was subjugated by him, as indeed were most of his intimates, however much they feared or disapproved of his actions. The streak of violence in Anne's temperament, intensified by her anomalous position, made it difficult, and eventually impossible, for her to plot and plan; while appearing to Chapuys, and others, as a mistress of intrigue, she was not even mistress of herself; and Henry's decision not to consummate their relationship until they were married finally drove her into attacks of hysteria which further undermined her resistance to his power.

For Henry VIII, although sentimental and sometimes romantic, was sexually cold, completely ruthless—and so dedicated to the cause of his Supremacy as to be able, at times, to relegate Anne, while arranging his next move, not only towards the divorce, but towards national independence of the papacy. By the beginning of 1531 this had become his goal, and his marriage to her a subsidiary consideration. His first, frenzied demands for a nullity suit were being replaced by a series of elaborate manœuvres for an absolutism which must be impregnable; and in this advance his principal adviser was Thomas Cromwell.

Cromwell, now in his middle forties, was the son of a blacksmith. He had spent some years in northern Italy and the Netherlands, where he studied banking and commerce, returning to London to train as a lawyer. He then entered Wolsey's service, where he remained until the autumn of 1529, when he became Member of Parliament for Taunton, a Councillor, and in the course of these duties privy to Henry's intentions and problems. He had a house and garden in Throgmorton Street, and kept a good table for his many friends, as also for the poor, two hundred of whom he fed every day. Witty, urbane and cultivated, he was popular in City circles, but disliked by the nobles, one of whom had to admit that, while he was 'a great taker and briber, he spent ... honourably and freely, like a gentleman (though he were none) and helped many honest men, and preferred his servants well.'[2] Chapuys, who disapproved of him in theory, enjoyed dining at his house, and was impressed by his powers of conversation, his collections of *objets d'art*—and, above all, his library.

Among the books Cromwell had brought back from Italy was one that might be compared to a high explosive: Marsiglio of Padua's *Defensor Pacis*, written in 1324 and still, after two hundred years, the most revolutionary theological work in contemporary literature. The author describes the clergy as physicians of the soul and without jurisdiction in state affairs. No pope, he goes on, can claim supremacy as the successor of St Peter, who did not precede the other apostles; and he finds no evidence of the saint ever being in Rome, nor that he became a bishop. The Bible, he concludes, is the only source of divine law.

Cromwell was not in a position to arrange for the translation of this highly controversial and heretical book till two years after he publicized Marsiglio's pronouncements by describing England as an empire (whose ruler acknowledged no superior power) governed by a Supreme Head, to whom both spiritual and temporal bodies were 'bound to bear, next to God, a natural and humble obedience',[3] thus supporting Tyndale's theory of kingship. Therefore, Cromwell concluded, Henry did not come under the Pope's authority, and his case could be settled only within the realm.

The King, having denounced Tyndale as a heretic and forbidden the common people to read his translation of the Bible (perhaps because he had declared against the divorce in his *Practice of Prelates*), welcomed the Marsiglian concept and announced himself as head of the clergy, whom he had already condemned and fined under the Statute of Praemunire. On January 24th, 1531, Henry modified his claim with the limiting but rather meaningless clause of 'so far as the Law of Christ allows'. According to Chapuys, this step towards independence so delighted Anne that 'it was as if she had gained Paradise'.[4] He then reported Henry as 'blinded' and 'indiscreet', adding that the Lady was 'braver than a lion ... so sure is she of her affair.'[5]

Any improvement in her prospects nearly always had a disturbing effect on Anne, who now made a scene with the King, on the grounds that one of his gentlemen had been rude to her; she was so angry that the quarrel lasted till her father intervened. 'Then,' says Chapuys sourly, 'they were more loving than ever.'[6] But Henry's visits to the Queen, although brief and infrequent, still enraged Anne. She said to one of Katherine's ladies, 'I wish all the Spaniards in the world were in the sea.' Reproved, she went on, 'I do not care anything for the Queen, I would rather see her hanged than acknowledge her as my mistress.'[7] She and Henry were then cast down—he complained of sleepless nights—by 'displeasing' letters from his agents at the Vatican, and there was talk of her retiring to Hever. Her father countered this gossip by giving a banquet for her, the King and the French Ambassador, which was followed by a farce about Wolsey in which the actor playing the Cardinal was shown descending into hell.[8] On February 21st Chapuys reported Anne as 'more openly acknowledged than ever', and the Queen told him that she had written to Clement VII asking him to insist on her rival's removal from Court. When there was no reply to this demand, she said, 'The King would not have declared his Supremacy if His Holiness had done as I asked,' concluding—and delusion could hardly have gone further—that Anne and her father were responsible for Henry's claim; he himself was not to blame.[9] Norfolk then told the Ambassador that the English people, while loyal to Katherine, would no longer tolerate the Pope's interference, adding that if Clement himself were to appear before them, they would set about him.[10] Chapuys's only hope lay in the Queen's determined attitude and the general detestation of the young woman he now described as the *Manceba*, or harlot; he failed to grasp that Anne's reputation had become symbolic, and was in no way connected with her actual character and behaviour.

Envy of any woman whose sexual magnetism has made her the subject of lurid gossip, and has given her privileges and luxuries denied to the majority, is apt to provoke furious abuse and, sometimes, attack, on the grounds that this favourite of fortune is in fact a criminal who, most unfairly, continues to reap, unpunished, the harvest of her misdeeds. Such a person seems to represent certain sins which her adversaries themselves would not hesitate to commit, if only they had the opportunity to do so. Neglected, unattractive or impoverished individuals of both sexes are often driven into a madness of hatred when faced with the spectacle of someone whose triumphs are the result of beauty or charm, or a combination of both. The downtrodden housewife, the overworked husband, the persecuted outcast—any of those whose lives have been soured through no fault of their own—are roused to a frenzy of loathing when this kind of success becomes a matter of public concern; and censure and slander may be accompanied by violent action.

This jealous and bitter resentment is as common today as it was in the sixteenth century. (As recently as 1963 a beautiful and alluring girl had to be protected by the police from screaming mobs, mostly of women, when she was subpoenaed in a case of national security.) Anne Boleyn, therefore, could not hope to escape the enraged detestation of those who made a heroine of her former mistress; for poor Katherine, plain, dull and dowdy, stood for all the disappointments and frustrations they had had to endure: while Anne was described by persons entirely ignorant of her circumstances as 'a common stewed whore' whose advent had brought disaster on the kingdom.[11] She was the personification not only of evil, but of an assault on religion, crops, cattle, fine weather—every aspect of daily life.

The effect on Anne of the general odium is hard to define. She seems to have ignored it: but it must have intensified the appalling strain under which she moved; for she was completely dependent on a man she could not trust. An inexperienced person would have relied on Henry VIII. Anne knew, none better, the depth and range of his moods and caprices. This fearful awareness produced, every now and then, quarrels and scenes made by her and dealt with, more or less patiently, by the King, who could afford to wait, as she could not, for his plans to mature. He was now sure of victory; she was on a knife-edge, and no longer able to consider escape. Yet her spirit remained high and unbroken, astonishing Chapuys, whose accounts of her actions were wildly prejudiced; for he reported everything he heard to her detriment, while ignoring any word said—by Cranmer, for instance—in her praise.

It now seems amazing that Henry and Anne should have been able to wait for the consummation of their relationship for six years; but as the reports from the Vatican gave them the impression that the divorce would be granted within a month, or less, they were effectively deceived. Meanwhile, Henry maintained his usual standard of piety, while defying Clement's threat of excommunication. 'Let the Pope do what he will,' he said to Del Borgho, loudly enough to be overheard by several courtiers, 'I shall never consent to his being judge in that matter. I care not a fig for all his excommunications, I shall do what I think best.'[12] This outburst was amplified by Sir Thomas More in his address to the Lords on March 30th, 1531. He said that His Grace was not pressing for the divorce because he had fallen in love with another lady; his only concern was to free himself from the sin of fornication.[13] Katherine was then informed of the opinion of certain bishops that her marriage to Henry was 'more than illegal',[14] with the result that her letters imploring Clement to take action became desperate as her position weakened. When Chapuys told her that His Holiness might yet drive the Lady from Court, her hopes rose—and sank, as no reply came from Rome, and Henry and Anne feasted the French Ambassador, and drank the health of Francis I.[15]

The King then added to Anne's difficulties by inaugurating tactics of delay with the Curia, so as to organize and ensure the acknowledgment of his Supremacy within the kingdom and on the Continent. While appearing to temporize, and sending friendly messages to Clement, he replied to the clergy's objections to his claim with subtle and ingenious dialectic. He was not, he explained, the Head of the Church in a mystical sense—that position was Christ's, and anyone denying that authority was guilty of blasphemy. He claimed to be Head of the Church *in England* merely, and thus of the English clergy, as their temporal sovereign. 'Their persons, acts and deeds', he added, 'are under the power of the Prince by God assigned.' He acknowledged the clergy's authority as preachers and ministers of the Sacrament—'but for the rest, they are subject to Princes'. A few days later, he told Del Borgho that he had no intention of setting up a 'nouvelle papalité' in England. Having refused to plead his cause in Rome, he agreed to Clement's proposal that it should be heard in Cambrai; but Katherine insisted on appearing at the Vatican, thus creating another impasse.[16]

A month later, a priest, preaching before Henry, pointed out that the Emperor Constantine had refused to judge between two bishops, in order to emphasize his submission to the clergy. 'That is a lie!' the King shouted, and walked out of the chapel.[17] He then had to deal with Anne's jealousy of the Princess Mary. No excuse can be made for her attacks on a girl whose only crime was her loyalty to both parents. Henry's affection for his daughter alarmed Anne, who behaved as if the fifteen-year-old Princess had power to work against her. When Henry praised and defended Mary, Anne lost all control of herself, and so berated him that he complained of her to Norfolk. 'She is not like the Queen, who never in her life used such ill words to me,' he said, choosing to forget Katherine's more calculated scoldings.[18] Beset by both women, he sank into temporary depression; then he appeased Anne by magnificent gifts of bracelets, brooches, diamonds, rubies, and a gold basin and ewer.[19] He would have done better to have discussed with her his new approach to Clement VII; but his inherent secretiveness made that impossible.

After a long conversation with the King, Francesco Bardi, a Florentine merchant, reported, 'Nothing else is thought of in that island every day, except of arranging affairs in such a way that they no longer need the Pope,' adding that Clement's unpopularity was partly caused by his failing to protect the Queen, whose relations with her husband were now nearing a climax.[20] On May 14th Henry dined with her for the last time; with what Chapuys described as 'supernatural courage', she again urged him to dismiss 'that shameless creature', and then asked his leave to visit the Princess Mary. Henry, unmasking his batteries, replied, 'Go, if you wish—and stop there.' She announced, 'I would not leave you for my daughter—or for anyone else in the world—' and he left the room.[21]

Katherine was then told to expect a deputation, led by Norfolk, from the Council, who urged her to appear for the hearing in Cambrai. The Duke began by saying that His Grace, as Supreme Head, could not submit to the jurisdiction of the Curia, or leave his kingdom for Rome. Calmly, Katherine replied that Henry's authority was temporal, adding that only the Pope had power to judge her cause. 'Your Grace's marriage is detestable and abominable before God,' Dr Lee broke in, and was supported by Bishop Longland, Henry's confessor. The argument continued on these lines until the Council, defeated, left to report their failure to Henry, who said, 'I feared it would be so, considering the courage and fantasy of the Queen.'[22] He then had to deal with Anne's complaints of Sir Henry Guilford, Controller of the Household, and also one of Katherine's supporters. 'When I am Queen,' she told him, 'you will be deprived of your office.' 'When that time comes, he replied, 'you will have no need to deprive me, for I myself shall give up my office.' He tried to return his white staff to Henry, who refused to accept it, and said soothingly, 'Do not trouble yourself about what women say.'[23]

Suffolk chose this moment to enter the arena. 'The Queen', he told Henry, 'must obey Your Highness in all but two matters— God and her conscience'—and was ordered not to meddle. Chapuys thought that both the Duke and his wife wanted openly to side with Katherine, but dared not go so far.[24]

Meanwhile Anne, irritated by what she considered Norfolk's lack of co-operation, criticized his methods. He replied by retiring from Court, after telling Chapuys that the Queen had been 'most unwise' in rejecting the Council's advice.[25] The Duke was right. Katherine's plan of remaining at her husband's side in order to defy—if not provoke—his rages was now defeated.

NOTES

1. Friedmann, *Anne Boleyn*, Vol. I, p. 130.
2. Dickens, *Thomas Cromwell and the English Reformation*, p. 38.
3. Ibid., p. 55.
4. *L. & P.*, Vol. V, p. 47.
5. Ibid., p. 10.
6. Ibid., p. 27.
7. Ibid., p. 10.
8. Ibid., p. 28.
9. *Span. Cal. P.*, Vol. IV, pt. 2, p. 3.
10. *L. & P.*, Vol. V, p. 45.
11. Ibid., p. 425.
12. Scarisbrick, *Henry VIII*, p. 290.
13. Parmiter, *The King's Great Matter*, p. 290.
14. *L. & P.*, Vol. V, p. 83.
15. Ibid., p. 59.
16. Scarisbrick, op. cit., p. 279.
17. *L. & P.*, Vol. V, p. 216.
18. Ibid., p. 101.
19. Ibid., p. 125.
20. Parmiter, op. cit., p. 148.
21. *L. & P.*, Vol. V, p. 110.
22. Ibid., p. 134.
23. Ibid.
24. Ibid., p. 128.
25. Froude, *Divorce*, p. 172.

XIII

The End in Sight

LIKE an underground river, the English people's disapproval of
Henry's and Cromwell's innovations now became turbulent, sometimes rising to the surface, as one bold spirit after another protested, from market-place, pulpit or tavern, against the new
decrees. Those who had no stake to place in the gambling-hells of
Court and Council were the most vociferous. Clinging to tradi-
tions and customs they had constantly grumbled about in the past,
some of them rejected, without recognizing it as such, a revolution
in the government, with abusive and, often, treasonable comments,
risking hideous punishment rather than forgo the free speech they
had always taken for granted. Their especial dislike — that of
Henry's matrimonial conflict — was aggravated by his rather unstable alliance with their ancient enemy. The more sophisticated
perceived the connection between his withdrawal from the papacy
and his need of French support; the majority, hating and despising
a nation they had fought twice within the last twenty years, looked
towards Spain and the Emperor to protect their sainted Queen
from the machinations of Anne Boleyn.

Among those who spoke most effectively was a young woman
called Elizabeth Barton; she had been noted for her gifts some two
years before Henry applied for a divorce, and now led a chorus of
censure and warning. First heard of as a servant in the household
of Thomas Cobb, bailiff to Archbishop Warham, she had there
fallen seriously ill, recovering to find herself afflicted with what
seems to have been epilepsy. This was then diagnosed as demon-
iacal possession, presently giving way to trances, and what is now
known as 'clairaudience', as Satan retreated and an angel took
charge. Her master, feeling himself unqualified to deal with
phenomena of this kind, consulted his parish priest, who, after
listening to some of Elizabeth's mumblings and shoutings, decided
that she was divinely inspired, partly because she 'spake very godly
... concerning the Seven Deadly Sins and the Ten Command-
ments.'[1] He reported the information produced by her Voices to

the Archbishop, who put her under the jurisdiction of a monk,
Father Bocking. This director assured her of what she was only too
willing to believe, that she had become the instrument of the
Deity, and compared her to St Bridget of Ireland and St Catherine
of Siena.[2]

Elizabeth, a girl of strong character and some ambition, flying
higher than the Maid of Orleans — who had been quite contented
to follow the highly practical commands of that same St Catherine,
together with those of St Michael and St Margaret — demanded an
interview with no less a person than the Mother of the Saviour, and
was conducted to her chapel. Our Lady duly appeared to her,
whereupon, 'her face was wonderfully disfigured, her tongue
hanging out, and her eyes in a manner being plucked out and laid
upon her cheeks ... There was then heard a voice speaking within
her belly ... her lips not greatly moving: she all that while continuing ... in a trance.'[3]

Elizabeth's miraculous powers having been thereby confirmed,
she became the mouthpiece of those who set out to put down
heresy. Her tongue was not now on (or in) her cheek, for she spoke
clearly of the joys of heaven and the pains of hell to a number of
experts. She then ordered Warham, who had promised the King
that when the divorce was granted he would marry him to Anne,[4]
not to perform that impious ceremony, was paid by Sir Thomas
More to pray for him, and finally announced her intention of
speaking to Henry himself, in order to tell him of his misdeeds.
This interview, presumably the result of the King's curiosity, took
place early in 1531.

Elizabeth, later known as the Nun of Kent (it had not been considered necessary for her to take the vows), told Henry that if he
divorced Katherine, he would 'die a villain's death' within six
months. She added that God was already much displeased with his
behaviour, described him as an 'infidel Prince', and threatened
him with divine vengeance if he married Anne Boleyn. 'After such
marriage,' she later announced to her coadjutors, 'he will no longer
be king of this realm ... one day, nor one hour ... I command him
to amend his life ... that he take none of the Pope's right ... [and]
that he destroy all ... new learning.'[5]

Henry's tolerance, perhaps enhanced by superstition, enabled
him to submit to these objurgations, and Elizabeth was allowed to
return to her nunnery, which now became the sixteenth-century

precursor of the Abbey of Lourdes. Here many cures were effected, and large sums amassed, in spite of Satanic attempts to defeat Elizabeth's efforts with 'stinking smokes' and unpleasant smells. (These were afterwards discovered to have been caused by Father Bocking's implantations of brimstone and assafoetida.[6]) Undeterred, the Blessed Virgin continued to direct her protégée as to how to eliminate heresy and schism, and Elizabeth's *Book of Oracles* (she was of course illiterate) soon ran into many hundreds of words. Her reputation — she was now established in the convent of St Sepulchre in Canterbury — spread throughout the kingdom, and beyond it, as did that of Father Bocking. After glancing through her book, Henry said to More, 'I esteem the matter as light as it is lewd,' to which the Chancellor replied that he found it 'a right poor production, such as any woman might speak of her own wit'.[7]

At first, Queen Katherine had enough sense to ignore the Nun's revelations, as did Anne, who, 'speaking with greater assurance than formerly', according to Chapuys,[8] saw the preliminary stage of her triumph approaching, when she, Katherine and Henry moved from Hampton Court to Windsor in the third week of June 1531. While the Queen remained in her own apartments, Henry and Anne went out hunting; and Chapuys informed the Emperor that they did so *unchaperoned*, riding alone together and followed at a distance by a single equerry and two grooms. Charles was disgusted; his Ambassador concluded that this indecency indicated a bigamous marriage within the next three or four months.[9]

In fact, Henry, as determined as ever on a legitimate union — how to bring it about he had not yet decided — was resolved finally to separate himself from the Queen. Very early in the morning of July 11th, he and Anne, with all their baggage, left Windsor for Greenwich. Katherine, who did not hear of their departure till the following day, wrote to him, expressing her regret that he had not come to say goodbye to her. Infuriated, Henry replied that he had not done so because she had 'brought shame and dishonour' on him, and forbade her to write again, or to send him any messages. Katherine at once wrote back, reiterating her loyalty, and pointing out that God (Henry's special ally) was more powerful than himself. This produced another angry letter from Henry. She had lied, he wrote, about the non-consummation of her marriage to Arthur; also, the Pope had no power to forbid the divorce, and so she must mind her own business and 'cease complaining to all the world'. He concluded, brutally enough, by telling her to prove the virginity on which her case had been based. When Katherine showed Chapuys the letter, he said that Anne must have dictated it; but the King had now reached the point, as his subsequent actions show, where exasperation needed no further stimulus.[10] He ordered Katherine to leave Windsor for The More, where she established herself with a train of four hundred servants, and where she was visited by two Venetian envoys, who reported her as 'always with a smile upon her countenance'.[11] Henry then commanded her to retire to a smaller house near Dunstable, while the Princess Mary, who up to now had been with her mother, was sent to Richmond. Henry and Katherine never met again.

For the next two weeks, he and Anne made use of the 'grease' season to hunt, chiefly from Windsor. This strenuous routine seems to have made life easier for her; violent exercise, with intervals for hearing Mass three times a day and five times on Sundays, suited her better than appearing in state with the King in order to receive a number of people of whose dislike she was well aware. Riding at a hand-gallop through the forest, followed by attendants in Tudor liveries of white and green, so as to 'shoot flying', she was agreeably distracted until dusk. Then, having supped, she had to wait for Henry to come to her after the hours spent in his closet with ministers and secretaries. He sometimes worked until after midnight, correcting, annotating, 'crossing and blotting out', according to Erasmus, who observed that his letters were often redrafted three or four times.[12] His erudition, passion for learning and extraordinary memory were those of a virtuoso who prided himself, says a contemporary, on being 'a perfect theologian, a good philosopher and a strong man at arms, a jeweller, a perfect builder'.[13] So there remained little leisure for 'dalliance' with Anne; this generally took the form of dancing or music. Then, on October 16th, 1531, he organized a final attack on Katherine, through a group of bishops and nobles.

She replied to their proposals as before. She also said that, far from being moved by his conscience, Henry had yielded to 'mere passion', and should reinstate her without delay. She then knelt, declaring herself his 'true and lawful wife', adding, 'I will go even to the fire, if the King commands me,' and went on to say that she was ready to leave for the Tower and the block, rather than forgo her rights. There could be no answer to this offer of public martyrdom, and once more the envoys were routed.[14]

In the following week Chapuys received a very disturbing letter from the Emperor's proctor at the Vatican, Dr Ortiz, who had been urging Clement to excommunicate Henry, 'in consequence of this public sin and scandal to all the world'. The trouble was, Ortiz continued, that no evidence of Henry's cohabitation with Anne had yet been produced.[15] If the Concubine was not his mistress, then what was she? Meanwhile, Ortiz had again 'remonstrated' with His Holiness, but to no effect.[16] This letter was followed by one from Chapuys to the Emperor, gloomily reporting that Anne, who, with Henry, had been supping with the Speaker of the House of Commons, 'governs all'.[17]

Dr Foxe was now Anne's almoner, and an encouraging adviser; but she was afraid that Fisher's dauntless attacks on the divorce might influence public opinion, and so renewed her own on the Princess Mary, whom Henry met, seemingly by accident, in Richmond Park. When Anne heard that he had greeted the girl affectionately, regretting that he saw so little of her, she exclaimed, 'I will not have it, nor hear of her.'[18] She now knew Mary to be far from negligible, in that the people acclaimed her as heiress-apparent, thus placing her before any children Anne herself might have.

When she returned to Whitehall, her days were less fully occupied. With her ladies, she might play chess or gamble — Henry paid her debts — practise her music, play with her dogs, try on new gowns and head-dresses, or take up her embroidery. (A specimen of her work is preserved at Hever Castle.) But these pursuits did not prevent tension mounting, as the dispatches from Bennet and Carne, Henry's envoys at the Vatican, brought further news of Clement's indecision and the Emperor's threats. The King became very depressed, to the point of curtailing the Christmas revels. He had no heart for them, it seemed.[19]

On New Year's Day he received a gold cup from Katherine, which he did not acknowledge, and from Anne a set of ornamental daggers. He then redecorated Anne's rooms with hangings of cloth of gold and crimson satin.[20] A few days later, he complained to Del Borgho of Katherine's 'high words', and deplored her obstinacy and the Pope's vacillations.[21] While Clement told the Consistory that he did not intend to be hard on Henry, he continued to placate the Emperor. 'That devil of a Pope', said the French Ambassador to Chapuys, 'has embroiled and sown dissension throughout Christendom.'[22]

So again, the King's great matter seemed to be at a standstill — until, with the opening of Parliament on January 13th, 1532, it became clear that Thomas Cromwell had been working for his master through the Commons' Supplication against the Ordinaries. This was the penultimate movement towards the Royal Supremacy. Implementing and enforcing the Accusation against the Clergy of 1529, it deprived them of nearly all their privileges, reducing their status, Chapuys considered, to that of shoe-makers.[23] A Convocation of Bishops fought stubbornly and at length against this attack, yielding at last to the combined pressure of Parliament and Henry. On May 11th the King made it the subject of one of his best-known speeches to a delegation from both Houses. 'Well beloved subjects,' he began, 'We thought that the clergy of our realm had been our subjects wholly — but now we have well perceived that they be but half our subjects, yea, and scarce our subjects' — and handed them a copy of the oath of loyalty to himself taken by the bishops on his accession, together with that taken to the Holy See. He then sent the prelates away, so that they should 'invent some order, that we be not thus deluded of our spiritual subjects'. Other remarks hinted at a charge of high treason — and a few days later the bishops surrendered.[24]

In the course of this four months' struggle the divorce had not once been mentioned; ostensibly, Henry's purpose was that of reforming the Church through his decision to rule it, independently of the papacy; and on that point, both Parliament and the common people, long and furiously resentful of clerical privilege and injustice, supported him. So he triumphed, not as a tyrant, but as a constitutional monarch; having thus established himself, he was in a position eventually to divorce Katherine and marry Anne.

Anne's grasp of these altered circumstances was shown by gentler and more dignified behaviour, and she was reported as looking 'very beautiful'.[25] She ceased to make scenes, and to complain of slights, real or imaginary, from Henry's courtiers; also, she could afford to ignore the insults of the Nun of Kent, the attempted assaults on her person by mobs of women (from one of which she only just escaped by crossing the river in a covered barge[26]) and the censure of her status made in Henry's presence.

On one of these occasions, a certain Father Peto, preaching in the royal chapel on the story of King Ahab and the murder of Naboth, had taken for his text, 'Where the dogs licked the blood of Naboth, even there shall they lick thy blood, O King.' His peroration was directly addressed to Henry. 'And now, O King,' he began, 'hear what I say to thee ... I must tell thee truly that this marriage is unlawful, and I know that ... I must speak it. There are other preachers ... which ... persuade thee otherwise, feeding thy folly and frail affections upon hopes of their own worldly promotion ... These, I say ... seek to deceive thee. Take heed, lest thou, being seduced, find Ahab's punishment, who had his blood licked up by the dogs.'[27]

Henry and Anne, with their courtiers, sat out the rest of the service; the King took no action. But Peto found it prudent to leave for Canterbury, where he continued to preach in the same vein. On the following Sunday, Henry commissioned Dr Kirwan to take Peto's place, which he did to some effect, describing him as 'dog, slanderer, base, beggarly friar, rebel and traitor. No subject', he went on, 'should speak so audaciously to his Prince.' After approving Henry's intended marriage to Anne, he apostrophized his rival with—'I speak to thee, Peto, which makest thyself Micaiah, that thou mayest speak evil of kings: but now, art not to be found, being fled for fear and shame, as unable to answer my argument.'

At this point, another friar, Elstowe, was heard from the roodloft, defending Peto. 'I am here as another Micaiah,' he shouted, 'and will lay down my life to prove those things true which he hath taught.' He then challenged Kirwan, accusing him of trying 'by adultery to establish the succession, betraying thy King for thine own vainglory into endless perdition'.

Other members of the congregation now sprang up, and began to argue on both sides. At last, Henry, rising, called out 'Silence!' and left the chapel. Next day, Peto and Elstowe, summoned before the Privy Council, were told that they ought to be sewn up in sacks and thrown into the Thames. 'Threaten such things to dainty folk, which have their hope in this world,' Elstowe replied. 'We fear them not.' Both men may have been prepared for imprisonment, or even death; they were merely ordered to leave the kingdom, and departed to Antwerp, where they continued their propaganda, corresponding with Fisher, More, Queen Katherine and a number of Spanish priests.[28]

Anne then tried to win over the monks of Greenwich, whose warden, Father Forest, had been Katherine's confessor; she succeeded with one or two, who were punished by Forest. He then preached at Paul's Cross on the same lines as Peto, inveighing against Cromwell and the Supplication, but without referring to the King. Henry sent for him, spoke tolerantly of his sermon, and won him over by a gift of 'a great piece of beef from his own table'. He was then congratulated by the Duke of Norfolk, presumably for his criticisms of Cromwell, who had just been made Master of the King's Jewels.[29] Forest, delighted, did not realize that falling back in order to spring was an exercise Henry had brought to a fine art. He was allowed to persevere in his attacks for some time, before he was seized, to perish more horribly than most.

NOTES

1. Froude, *History*, Vol. I, p. 193.
2. Ibid., p. 195.
3. Ibid., p. 196.
4. Ellis, *Original Letters*, Third Series, Vol. II, p. 137.
5. Froude, op. cit., p. 199.
6. Ibid., p. 198.
7. Ibid., p. 197.
8. *Span. Cal. P.*, Vol. IV, pt. 2, p. 198.
9. Ibid.
10. *L. & P.*, Vol. V, p. 167.
11. Mattingly, *Catherine of Aragon*, p. 243.
12. Baldwin Smith, *Henry VIII*, p. 43.
13. Ibid.
14. *L. & P.*, Vol. V, p. 226.
15. Ibid., p. 231.
16. Ibid.
17. Ibid.
18. Froude, *Divorce*, p. 174.
19. Ibid.
20. Mattingly, op. cit., p. 243.
21. Ibid.
22. Froude, op. cit., p. 181.
23. Scarisbrick, *Henry VIII*, p. 299.
24. Ibid.
25. *L. & P.*, Vol. V, p. 501.
26. *Ven. Cal. P.*, Vol. IV, p. 304.
27. Froude, *History*, Vol. I, p. 228.
28. Ibid., pp. 228–30.
29. Ibid., p. 227.

XIV

Triumph

THE conferences between Henry VIII and his Parliament during the negotiations that arose out of the Commons' Supplication against the Ordinaries were frequent and prolonged. Meanwhile, his agents continued their pressure on Clement VII, whose attitude towards the divorce fluctuated as before. The Emperor's assiduous bribery of the Consistory was outdone by the more lavish expenditure of the English; this enabled the Cardinals to take fees from both sources and to remain inactive.[1] When Dr Ortiz implored the Pope to denounce Henry for openly consorting with a mistress, Clement smoothly replied that he had received no evidence of mortal sin. 'It is the custom in England', he explained, 'for Princes to converse intimately with ladies. You cannot prove that, in this case, there is anything worse,' adding that he had already forbidden the King to 'frequent' (cohabit with) Anne Boleyn.[2] He then wrote to Henry, describing himself as his 'loving father'. 'I cannot believe', he went on, 'that you have put away the Queen for this Ana. It is a scandal to the Church, and you must take her back.'[3] When Henry's agents told Miguel Mai that their master had in fact never been legally married to Katherine, he replied, 'If that is so, then he ought to marry her now.'[4] 'He will marry the Concubine,' a Spanish Cardinal then told Charles V, 'in order to maintain his alliance with Francis I.'[5]

In England, Katherine's supporters began to despair. 'What news?' a monk asked the Abbot of Whitby after a meeting in York. 'Evil news,' was the answer. 'The King's Grace is ruled by one common stewed whore, Anne Boleyn, who makes all the spirituality to be beggared, and the temporality also.' The Abbot then accused Anne's father and her uncle Norfolk of 'setting down' the clergy.[6] At this point, Henry, reasoning with Del Borgho, said mildly, 'I am surprised that the Pope should persist in this fantasy of wishing me to recall the Queen. It is my affair,'[7] while Anne observed that 'too many priests' were supporting Katherine,[8] in spite of the fact that a sermon advocating the divorce had been heard at Paul's Cross. On this occasion, a woman, standing up to denounce the priest as a liar, shrieked out that the King had 'destroyed the law', and was arrested.[9]

As soon as Henry's sessions with Parliament were over, he made arrangements to meet Francis I at Boulogne in the autumn of 1532. As he intended to take Anne with him, she set about renewing her wardrobe; one of her dresses was of black satin with a black velvet cloak. This rather unusual outfit cost £49. 4s. 4d.[10] and may have given rise to the rumours of her having bewitched the King by 'potions'.[11] Surely Satan had thus robed her for this purpose? Three men were imprisoned in the Marshalsea for abusing her on these grounds;[12] but nothing could stop the women's demonstrations when she and Henry rode out hunting. One day, they were so pursued and shouted at that he decided to retire. (It was on this expedition that one of her greyhounds killed a cow.) On his return Henry sent for Chapuys, and announced, 'I am resolved to celebrate this marriage in the most solemn manner,' adding that preparations for the ceremony were already being made.[13] Chapuys concluded that it would take place in France. But Henry intended that Francis should first receive Anne as the future Queen of England, preferably in Calais. On September 1st he therefore created her Marquess (not Marchioness) of Pembroke—a Tudor title—in a ceremony of great splendour.

Anne was now in her twenty-ninth year and, according to contemporary standards, middle-aged; but she had nothing to fear, as far as her looks were concerned. In a gown of crimson velvet furred with ermine, she was attended by a train of courtiers and their wives in the presence-chamber of Windsor Castle. Supported by the Countesses of Rutland and Sussex, and Norfolk's daughter Mary (this girl was betrothed to Henry's bastard son, the Duke of Richmond), Anne, uncoifed, slowly approached the King, who sat under his canopy of state. As she knelt before him, her hair touched the floor. He then announced that, with the consent of his nobles, 'We do make, create and ennoble ... the Lady Anne Rochford to be Marquess of Pembroke, and also, by putting on of a mantle, and the setting of a coronet of gold upon her head, do truly invest unto her this name and title—and to her heirs male.' The charter granting Anne a pension of £1,000 a year having been read out by Bishop Gardiner, she said, 'I humbly thank Your Grace,' and after three obeisances retired to the sound of trumpets to change her dress for the banquet. Next day, Henry presented her with a quantity of jewels and gold plate; these last were engraved with the royal arms and true lovers' knots.[14]

Anne now spent much time hunting with Guillaume du Bellay, brother of her old friend Jean, who came over to arrange the details of the meeting with Francis, and whom she feasted at the end of September. 'Madame Anne', he told his master, 'has presented me with a hunting cap, bow and arrows and a greyhound. I do not tell you this as a boast ... but to show how much King Henry prizes me ... for whatever that lady does is ordered by him.' Du Bellay went on to say that Anne ought to receive a personal invitation from Francis, and then discussed what French ladies should be asked to meet her; they might be headed by Francis's sister Marguérite, now Queen of Navarre. 'As to the Queen of France,' (Eleanor of Austria, Francis's second wife and the sister of Charles V) 'not for the world would this King meet her, for he says he would as soon see the Devil as a lady in Spanish dress.'[15]

Yet although Anne's triumph seemed to be nearing completion, she was still vulnerable. Henry of Northumberland and his wife had disliked one another ever since their marriage; that dislike soon turned to loathing, and they were living apart. The Countess, desiring absolute freedom—she may have wanted to marry some one else—brought what would now be called an action against her husband, on the grounds that he had been pre-contracted to Anne, and appealed for a divorce. He denied the charge, which was at once publicized by Katherine's supporters, in the hope of preventing Henry's second marriage. The King was inclined to suppress the case; but Anne insisted on bringing it before the authorities, and was thus able to prove that, while Henry Percy had once mentioned a pre-contract to Cardinal Wolsey, none had been made.[16] The Earl took no action in the matter, and presently sank again into an invalidism which may have been hypochondriacal, or, possibly, the result of his enforced parting from Anne and his unhappy marriage. Dragging out a miserable life, he was to reappear twice more in hers before he died in 1537, a crushed and degraded figure.

This successful defence, and the death of Archbishop Warham, further consolidated Anne's position. The vigorous and fearless aspect of her character shown by her rebuttal of Lady Northumberland's attempts to discredit her, delighted Henry; at this time he had no use for meek or subservient women. He flew into a rage which was not, for once, histrionic, when Chapuys spoke of the Pope's 'order' to him to abandon Anne; the Ambassador, resigned to her state visit to France, told Charles V that the King 'cannot leave the Concubine for an hour'.[17]

They were to set sail on October 9th. On the 1st, Henry desired Katherine to relinquish certain jewels, as being crown property, to Anne. Advised by Chapuys, the Queen replied, 'I will not give them up to a person who is the scandal of Christendom and a disgrace to you.' This dispute continued till the eve of the King's departure, when the jewels arrived. Chapuys was not able to discover what threats Henry had used, but noted that he had been avoiding the Princess Mary, who was still at Richmond.[18]

On arrival in France Henry was informed that Queen Marguérite of Navarre would not allow Anne to be presented to her (the fact that they had seen a certain amount of one another during the latter's service to the late Queen Claude was ignored) and so, leaving her with her suite of twenty ladies and their attendants at Calais, he proceeded to Boulogne, where he remained for a fortnight. During this visit he set himself to win over, not only Francis and his sister, but also their entourage, with whom he played cards and dice, taking care to lose large sums. He gave pensions to a selected number of courtiers, gold chains to lesser dignitaries, and was particularly gracious to the French King's sons. He then proposed returning Francis's hospitality at Calais; his host's acceptance was preceded by the gift of a jewel to Anne: but as he had not promised to receive her, Henry arranged for her to appear in disguise.

With seven ladies, all dressed in cloth of gold and crimson satin, she entered Henry's tent after supper, and danced before the two Kings; as she approached Francis, Henry leant forward and twitched off her mask. She and Francis then talked together for a few minutes.[19] After three days of festivities, Francis returned to Boulogne, and Henry and Anne prepared to leave; but storms in the Channel enforced their remaining in the English colony till November 13th, when they crossed at some risk, reaching Dover to find that services of prayer for Henry's safety were being held in London and Canterbury. Here, the King was visited by Elizabeth Barton, who reiterated her warnings and threats.[20] Henry received them without comment. He was now relying on Francis I's promise of support at the Vatican; though Jean du Bellay, his good brother and cousin, had advised him to marry Anne at once.

Meanwhile, the newly appointed Venetian Ambassador coldly reported her as 'not one of the handsomest women in the world. She is of middling stature,' he went on, 'with a swarthy complexion, long neck, wide mouth, bosom not much raised, and in fact has nothing but the King's great appetite, and her eyes, which are black and beautiful — and take great effect on those who served the Queen when she was on the throne.' The envoy ends this rather denigrating account with 'She lives like a queen, and the King accompanies her to Mass — and everywhere.'[21]

It was not only to Mass that Henry now accompanied the woman he had sworn to marry six years ago. He was no longer young — and the time had come to put an end to further dallying. At some point between the middle of November and the beginning of December 1532, he consummated the relationship which had nearly caused a revolution in England, convulsed the Courts of Europe, and brought the Emperor to the verge of an invasion. News of this momentous step was duly reported to Clement VII, who immediately wrote to Henry, describing himself as 'grieved' by that monarch's immoral act, and yet again desiring him to reinstate Katherine and abandon Anne. On December 19th he wrote declaring that if Henry did not obey him within a month, he would annul 'any marriage' he might choose to make.[22] When Miguel Mai described Henry's 'madness' for the Concubine to the Emperor, his master exclaimed, 'I cannot believe that the King will be so blind as to marry her!'[23]

During Christmas week Henry and Anne visited the Tower, where the royal apartments had been newly decorated in her honour.[24] A little later, she began to suspect that she was pregnant. In the second half of January 1533 this hope was confirmed. On the 25th of that month she and Henry were married, very early in the morning, in an attic in the west turret of Whitehall, by the Bishop of Lichfield.[25] The King was attended by Henry Norris (one of his Grooms of the Bedchamber) and George Rochford. Anne was accompanied by her train-bearer, Lady Berkeley.

Three years and four months later, Anne, her brother and Norris were arraigned, found guilty of, and executed for, high treason.

NOTES

1. Froude, *Divorce*, p. 191.
2. *Span. Cal. P.*, Vol. IV, pt. 1, p. 486.
3. *L. & P.*, Vol. V, p. 358.
4. Ibid., p. 393.
5. Ibid., p. 262.
6. Ibid., p. 425.
7. Ibid., p. 475.
8. Ibid., p. 514.
9. *Ven. Cal. P.*, Vol. IV, p. 335.
10. Strickland, *Queens of England*, Vol. II, p. 216.
11. *L. & P.*, Vol. V, p. 501.
12. Ibid., p. 288.
13. Ibid., p. 526.
14. Strickland, op. cit., p. 217.
15. *L. & P.*, Vol. V, p. 521.
16. Friedmann, *Anne Boleyn*, Vol. I, p. 159.
17. *L. & P.*, Vol. V, p. 571.
18. Ibid., p. 591.
19. Hall, *Chronicle*, p. 794.
20. Froude, *History*, Vol. I, p. 245.
21. *Ven. Cal. P.*, Vol. IV, p. 365.
22. *L. & P.*, Vol. V, p. 649.
23. Ibid., p. 642.
24. Ibid., p. 679.
25. Strickland, op. cit., p. 224.

PART II

Queen of England

Semele ... was tenderly loved by Jupiter ... and was at last persuaded to entreat her lover to come to her arms with the same majesty as he approached Juno ... As he had sworn by the Styx to grant Semele whatever she required, he came to her bed attended by the clouds, the lightning and the thunderbolts. The mortal nature of Semele could not endure so much majesty, and she was instantly consumed ...

J. LEMPRIÈRE

I

The Act of Appeals

IN his forty-second year Henry VIII reached his apotheosis, although he was already thinking of himself as having passed middle age—and even, sometimes, as an old man. While the slender but solid outlines of the athlete had sunk beneath the formidable bulk by which he will always be remembered, the impression he made on critical newcomers was that of a magnificently proportioned being, whose height, breadth and ease of movement were so combined as to emphasize a consciously exercised domination. Position and power naturally ensured the alarming impact of his presence; also, he had his own, his special, brand of majesty. Whether he sat, walked or stood—frowning, amused, or coldly observant—he was unique: and, above all, strange.

He was thought to resemble his maternal grandfather, Edward IV. That likeness can be accepted—with this difference; the Plantagenet King's soft, sensuous expression was replaced, in Henry Tudor's case, by one of stern withdrawal and icy disapproval. That he was not only prudish, but puritanical to the verge of fanaticism, seems to have become clear to Holbein as he noted and reproduced, in a number of portraits and drawings, that small, pursed mouth, the arched, raised eyebrows, and a frigid glance which still appears to condemn, while it appraises, the spectator. Henry's distaste for bawdry has been recorded by several contemporaries, some of whom expected to find in England's King Hal—the games-player, the huntsman, the gross eater, the tireless dancer—a genial response to coarse jests and obscene allusions. The King's angry rejection of this kind of approach contrasted, startlingly, with his informality, his warmth of manner, his capacity for remembering some personal detail in the lives of unimportant people; these sudden changes first astounded and then endeared him to the majority of his humbler subjects—or bedesmen, as they called themselves. Adversaries became loyalists, as he flattered and cajoled, while towering above them—the semi-divinity of legend, the hero of a hundred anecdotes and reminiscences. Those whom he talked with or consulted daily —but never intimately—learned to cater for his moods, yet were not always quite prepared for them, while they sometimes grew to love him. Seeming to reciprocate, he never really did so; his unsleeping awareness of the difference between himself and the rest of the world set him apart, an idol to be placated rather than relied on; for no one knew—perhaps Henry did not always know— what he actually believed, when, in ringing appeal or harsh admonition, he spoke to his people as the privileged representative of a merciless Deity.

Such a man must find a secret refuge from his weaknesses; and Henry found his when he fell in love with Anne Boleyn. She stood up to him, as we say now; moreover, she knew when not to do so. Until this treatment became, through exhaustion and strain, repetitive and therefore wearisome, her intuition bound them to one another for nearly nine years—a long time, in that age of hurry and rush and revolution. The pace of life, as Henry and Anne lived it, was, sometimes literally, murderous: hardly to be imagined by those who know only the leisured sequences of the twentieth century, and see her, not as dangerous or sinister, but as a victim, the doomed creature of a king's caprice. In her own day, Anne's foreign elegance and unfashionable swarthiness showed her as a sort of monster to many of her contemporaries. Those huge, 'black and beautiful' eyes, admired by the Venetian connoisseur, were deprecated by the English, as were her slenderness and her long hair; surely these were the attributes of a sorceress, a malignant spirit—and then, her manners! Uncertain, tempestuous to the point of hysteria (she laughed when she should have cried, and burst into mocking or defiant speech when silence would have been more suitable), she became odious to all except those she allured and entranced.

For Anne, also, stood apart: but not on a height. In that tumultuous, crowded pageant of kings and nobles, self-seeking administrators, stealthy traitors and hostile envoys, she was not so much an original as an anomaly, the enemy of convention and custom: intolerable, enviable, flouting, shocking. It was foretold that she would one day have to pay for her success. And in January 1533 her destruction was already shaping itself, looming nearer with every week of the pregnancy which had been so long postponed, and was about to give her the crown of Edward the Confessor.

She had been counting on a public and ceremonious wedding, especially now that Cranmer, her only faithful friend, was Archbishop of Canterbury. It could not be: not only because the divorce was still in debate, but because one of the most important laws ever passed in England—the Act in Restraint of Appeals, which was finally to stabilize her position—did not become statutory until a year later. Cromwell was putting the finishing touches to decrees which would then form the basis of modern government and cast into limbo the principles of medieval Catholicism. Yet his genius succeeded in presenting this, his peculiar creation, as scrupulously constitutional, while bestowing on Henry a quasi-Byzantine autocracy.

This Act, amplifying Richard II's Statute of Praemunire of 1398, and thus achieving a traditional quality, forbade any appeal to Rome in testamentary or matrimonial causes. All ecclesiastical jurisdiction came under the control of the monarch, whose Supremacy was thus irrevocably established, and England for ever freed from foreign authority. Anyone disobeying this law was guilty of high treason.

Inconsistency of public feeling was shown by the people's acceptance and modified approval of the Act, which contradicted their loyalty to Queen Katherine, and their dislike, not only of Anne, but of all her family. The merchant classes supported Henry's independence of the Papacy as soon as they realized that trade with Spain and the Low Countries would remain unaffected. The majority of the nobles followed their lead; and as the jealous enmity towards the clergy of the poorer sections of the community had not been entirely assuaged by the Supplication against the Ordinaries, they too, although continuing to abuse Anne Boleyn, were behind their King, whose marriage was still a secret; indeed, most of them hoped and believed that he and Katherine would be reunited, and that the beloved Princess Mary would eventually succeed her father.

The time had not yet come for Henry to destroy these comforting beliefs; nor did the foreign envoys know that he and Anne were, although bigamously, husband and wife. Two days after their wedding, Chapuys and Norfolk were discussing a plan for an Anglo-Spanish alliance; but the Ambassador warned his master that Cranmer would probably authorize 'a new marriage'. This information resulted in the Pope again ordering Henry to 'remove' Anne from his Court.[1]

What chiefly annoyed Chapuys was the attitude of Del Borgho, whom Henry bribed and flattered, taking him in his barge to the opening of Parliament, and praising him for his co-operation. When Chapuys remonstrated with the Nuncio, he coolly replied, 'I am a poor gentleman, living by my service, and it is right for me to act thus.' But later, he told Henry that he ought to recall Katherine, and treat her better. 'I shall do nothing of the kind,' said the King, 'and for good reasons—her disobedience and her severity towards me.'[2]

In the same week, that of February 9th, Chapuys told the Emperor that if he would only force Clement to excommunicate Henry, the people, supported by the nobles, would depose him and welcome a Spanish invasion—and then, Anne, 'hated by all the world ... will not escape with her life and jewels.'[3] Urged by Del Borgho to pronounce 'speedy sentence' on the King, Clement remained inactive, merely advising him to take two wives, while Henry and Anne now spoke openly, in Chapuys's presence, of their forthcoming marriage.[4] To a priest, asking for employment, she was heard to say, 'If you wish to enter my service, you must wait a little, till I am married to the King.' And a few days later, she told her ladies, 'I am as sure as death [an unfortunate analogy] that the King will marry me shortly,' adding that she and Henry were planning to betroth the Princess Mary to one of Francis's sons.[5]

Queen Katherine had no share in this arrangement; she was beginning to realize that Charles V, now embroiled in a war against the Turks, could do little or nothing for her, and that Clement's inaction had destroyed her cause. When Chapuys urged her to persist, she replied that the Pope had kept her waiting for three and a half years, and that his orders to Henry to dismiss Anne Boleyn had been consistently disregarded; she added that even if the King did send that wicked woman away, he would eventually recall her, and then, 'He would cause me more suffering than before.'[6] She went on to speak of her marriage to Prince Arthur, which, thirty-two years ago, was reported to her father as having been consummated—and to deny that affirmation.[7]

A deadlier blow was now dealt her by the Pope's consent to the consecration of Cranmer—the Archbishop had once taken a wife, but Clement may not have known this—with the approval of the Consistory. As Chapuys thought that Cranmer would eventually marry Henry and Anne, the Pope's action seemed to him to support the King, in spite of his promise to Charles V that if the marriage did take place, he would excommunicate Henry.[8] For the next two months the wedding still remained a secret. Anne, aware that her pregnancy could not be concealed much longer, then decided, in what appears to have been an outbreak of hysteria, to force the issue.

Her old admirer, Sir Thomas Wyatt, had now returned from his mission abroad, and was accustomed to wait in her ante-chamber, together with other members of her Court. On this occasion Chapuys, also there, and on the watch, drew back as she suddenly appeared, unattended, and said to Wyatt ('Whom she loves well,' the Ambassador reported), 'Will you send me some apples?' and, without waiting for an answer, went on, 'For the last three days I have had a savage desire for apples! The King tells me that this means I am with child—but I told him, No! No!'

Silence fell on the embarrassed gathering as she gazed from one to another. Then, bursting into peals of laughter, she rushed from the room.[9]

According to Chapuys, Wyatt appeared 'ashamed', No doubt he was sorry for Anne; in common with the rest of her circle, he suspected that she and Henry were married, but had to subscribe to the official view that the wedding had not yet taken place—as did her father, who persuaded the Earl of Rutland to promise that he would approve it in the House of Lords when the announcement was made.[10]

Anne then tried to recoup her indiscretion by telling Norfolk that, if she were not soon pregnant, she would make a pilgrimage directly after Easter.[11] Yet still Henry refused to acknowledge either her condition or their marriage, while arranging, with the Council, that Cranmer—who had already declared that His Majesty was free to take a wife—should pronounce sentence of divorce.

In March the King sent George Rochford to Paris, to inform Francis I of his marriage and of Anne's pregnancy, under a vow of secrecy, and to remind him of his sworn support at the Vatican, in the event of an excommunication.[12] This mission was not a success, partly because Francis took against Rochford, and also because he was arranging an alliance between his second son and the Pope's niece, Catherine de' Medici.

Rochford was still in Paris when Anne celebrated Shrove Tuesday by giving a great banquet for Henry, Chapuys, her step-grandmother the Dowager-Duchess of Norfolk, the Duke of Suffolk and Audley (he had succeeded Sir Thomas More as Lord Chancellor) in a room hung with tapestries. The principal feature, a favourite form of decoration in that day, was a cupboard, some six feet high, with open shelves supporting rows of cups, bowls and ewers, all of beaten gold.[13]

The King, who had refused to accept Clement's latest brief ordering him to dismiss Anne, was in high spirits, chatting and laughing with the guests. Presently he turned from her to the old Duchess, who was sitting on his left, and said, 'Hath not the Marquess a grand *dot*—and a rich marriage, in all that we see?' He pointed to the cupboard and added emphatically, 'It belongs to her.'[14]

Chapuys, reporting this incident, was now more than ever concerned for Queen Katherine, who had been ordered to leave for a manor some forty miles from London. He resolved to expostulate with Henry; still he did not believe that the marriage to Anne had taken place, partly because it was referred to as imminent in a sermon preached before her and Henry a few days later. After describing the marriage to Katherine as invalid, the priest went on, 'All His Majesty's good subjects ought to pray God to pardon his offence [of fornication] and enlighten him to take another lady. He might take a lady', this obliging supporter explained, 'of humbler condition, in consideration of her personal merits.'[15]

Next day, Chapuys approached Henry as he was walking in the garden of Greenwich Palace. Before he could begin to speak, the King described his efforts to please Charles V, adding that Clement's embargo would be destroyed by Francis I. With a laugh, he exclaimed, 'His Holiness will get ugly bastinadoing, should he defy the French King.' Then, suddenly serious, he declared that Charles had done him wrong—'much wrong', he repeated, ignoring the Ambassador's protests. At last Chapuys decided to speak out. 'The Queen,' he said, taking care to use a gentle tone, 'and Your Majesty's people, and all the world, blame you—very much.' Unmoved, Henry replied, 'Neither you nor the Queen has any

Anne Boleyn as a young woman. Though contemporary sources always emphasize the fact that Anne was dark-haired, here she is portrayed with the
currently fashionable auburn hair—an indication that the artist was anxious

A letter from Anne Boleyn to her father, written when she was eleven years old
From a manuscript at Corpus Christi College, Cambridge, England

Anne's father, Sir Thomas Boleyn, Earl of Wiltshire and Ormonde (1477–1539) and Lord Privy Seal
Holbein

Henry Percy, Sixth Earl of Northumberland
Artist unknown

Sir Thomas Wyatt
Holbein

Thomas Cromwell
After Holbein

Cardinal Wolsey
Artist unknown

Katherine of Aragon
Artist unknown

One of Henry VIII's love letters to Anne Boleyn, written in September, 1528, in which he tells her of the expected visit of Cardinal Campeggio which they both hoped would result in the annulment of Henry's first marriage. He writes, 'I would you were in mine arms, or I in yours, for I think it long since I kissed you.'
From the Vatican Library

A portrait of Henry VIII
Holbein

Anne Boleyn in later life
Holbein

Henry VIII and the Pope, who has been depicted upside down as a visual acknowledgment of Henry's antagonism towards the Papacy
Artist unknown

Pope Clement VII,
Giulio de Medici
Artist unknown

Francis I, King of France,
1515–47
Jean Clouet

Archbishop Cranmer
G. Flicke

The falcon emblem granted to Anne by Henry VIII when
she was created Marquess of Pembroke in 1532

The Armorial Achievement of Henry VIII and Anne Boleyn

The Duke of Norfolk
Holbein

Mary Tudor, daughter of Katherine of Aragon
H. Ewarth

Jane Seymour
After Holbein

Hever Castle as it is today

right to complain,' adding, 'The Queen must be condemned' —
implying a charge of fornication. 'If Your Majesty makes this
marriage,' Chapuys persisted, 'I fear the Queen will leave for
Spain. Here, she is much adored.'[16]

Brushing aside this remark, Henry began to speak of the
Consistory. 'I blame them', he said, 'for trying to force me to
Rome.' Again, Chapuys attempted to convince the King of his
errors, but to no effect. 'I know very well what I have to do,' he
said, pointing out that, with his French ally, he could afford to
defy the Emperor. He then began to abuse Clement VII. Arrogant
and vain, the Pope should not, Henry declared, let people kiss his
foot, nor assume power over the kingdoms of Christendom. 'I
have seen a book', he told the Ambassador, 'in which it was maintained that all Christian Princes are but feudatories of the Pope!
I intend to put an end to such ambitions, and to repair the errors
of King John and Henry II — and I am determined to reunite
Church goods to the Crown.' As Chapuys stood aghast, the King
explained, 'I am bound to do so by my coronation oath.'[17]

From this conversation Chapuys concluded that Katherine's
cause was now 'desperate', but not quite lost. After a talk with Del
Borgho, who told him that Henry was resolved to preserve his
Supremacy, he decided that the marriage to Anne would take
place at Easter, and wrote to the Emperor, asking to be relieved
of his post.[18]

In April, the invalidity of Henry's marriage to Katherine and
the celebration of that to Anne were announced to both Houses of
Parliament. On the 10th of that month, Norfolk and Suffolk told
Katherine that Henry was now Anne's husband, and that henceforth her status would be that of Princess-Dowager. She was
offered a large income, a palace and the company of her daughter
for her consent to this arrangement. She replied that she was
Queen of England, adding that she would rather 'beg her bread
from door to door' than accept either the allowance or the title.[19]

Chapuys then wrote to the Emperor, imploring him to invade,
and again promising the support of the nobles, who would (of
course) lead the English against their King. 'Your Majesty must
root out the Lady and her adherents,' he urged. 'This accursed
Anne has her foot in the stirrup, and will do the Queen and the
Princess all the harm she can. She has boasted that she will make
the Princess her lady-in-waiting, or marry her to some varlet.'

Chapuys felt bound to add that Francis I would not allow that last degradation;[20] nor was this piece of gossip borne out by Anne's having to accept, however unwillingly, Henry's plan of a French marriage for his daughter. The Ambassador complained of the King's refusal to let anyone, meaning himself, speak for Queen Katherine. Finally, he accused Clement VII of secretly giving Henry permission to marry Anne. On April 15th, he resolved to attack the King once more. Henry received him pleasantly. No doubt he appreciated the envoy's courage.

'I cannot believe', Chapuys began, 'that a Prince of Your Majesty's great wisdom and virtue will consent to the putting away of the Queen.' As Henry said nothing, he went on, more severely, 'Since Your Majesty has no regard for men — all of whom you despise — you should have some respect for God.' Henry blandly replied, 'God and my conscience are on good terms.' Chapuys then pointed out the iniquity of dismissing Katherine after twenty-five years of marriage. Henry, adopting what seems to have been a casual tone, said, 'It is not so long a time. If the world', he added, 'thinks this divorce so extraordinary — then, still more, the world finds it strange that the Pope should have dispensed it [his marriage to Katherine] without having the power to do so.'

Chapuys refused to discuss this reference to the supposed consummation of Katherine's first marriage, and produced letters of protest from Charles V, which Henry put aside, saying, 'I wish to have a successor to my kingdom.' Chapuys replied, 'Your Majesty has a daughter endowed with all imaginable goodness and virtue — and of an age to bear children. Nature obliges Your Majesty to restore the throne to the Princess Mary.' Henry declared that he knew better, and went on, 'I wish to have children,' apparently so phrasing his reply as to show that he meant the birth of a son. Chapuys, emboldened by this seemingly easy reception of his criticisms, said, 'Your Majesty is not sure of having them.'

This insolence produced an explosion. Henry shouted, 'Am I not a man like other men?' The Ambassador dared not answer. The high, harsh voice repeated, 'Am I not a man like others?' Silence. Then, once more — 'Am I not a man like other men?'[21]

Still Chapuys said nothing. At last, Henry went on in a more ordinary tone, 'You are not privy to all my secrets.' From this, the Ambassador concluded that the rumours of Anne's pregnancy were true; yet he could not bring himself to believe that she and Henry were married. When the King told him that Katherine's marriage to his brother had been consummated, Chapuys reminded him, 'Your Majesty often confessed that the Queen was a virgin.'

Not in the least put out, Henry coolly replied, 'I admit it. It was spoken in jest. A man —' he explained, 'jesting and feasting, often says things that are not true.' Seeing the Ambassador once more stunned into silence, he exclaimed triumphantly, 'Now — have I paid you off? What more would you have?'

As Chapuys repeated his pleas for the Queen, Henry's mood changed again. Frowning, and more than usually formidable, he interrupted with, 'All such remonstrances are useless. The Emperor has no right to interfere. I shall pass such laws in my kingdom [i.e. the Restraint of Appeals] as I like.'

'Your Majesty's subjects are too frightened to interfere on the Queen's behalf,' Chapuys replied. Henry said, 'The marriage to Prince Arthur *was* consummated. I blame the Emperor. The Princess-Dowager is no more my wife than she is yours —and I shall treat her as I wish, in despite of anyone who may growl at it. If the Emperor troubles me — I can defend myself.'

Chapuys then fell back on the King's disregard of Clement's briefs. 'You sting me!' Henry angrily exclaimed — and the Ambassador apologized.[22]

So ended a remarkable conversation, in which Henry's thrice repeated assertion of his virility seems to have been one of triumph, rather than — as has sometimes been said — that of uneasy defiance. For Anne's pregnancy ensured, so he believed, the first of several sons. As ever, the Almighty was on his side.

It was characteristic of Henry that, while shocking and horrifying Chapuys, he continued to exercise his personal magnetism. The Ambassador reported him as 'naturally kind and generous'. But, he continued sadly, 'the Lady has so perverted him that he does not seem to be the same man.' Once more, Chapuys begged his master to invade; if he did not, Anne would destroy the Queen as she had destroyed Wolsey. In fact, she was to blame for everything. Henry, misled and bewitched, remained guiltless.[23]

NOTES

1. *L. & P.*, Vol. VI, p. 33.
2. Ibid., p. 62.
3. Ibid.
4. Ibid.
5. Ibid.
6. Ibid.
7. Ibid.
8. Ibid.
9. Ibid., p. 82.
10. Friedmann, *Anne Boleyn*, Vol. I, p. 187.
11. Ibid., p. 193.
12. Ibid., p. 194.
13. *L. & P.*, Vol. VI, p. 95.
14. Ibid.
15. Ibid., p. 107.
16. Ibid., p. 163.
17. Ibid.
18. Ibid., p. 128.
19. Ibid., p. 150.
20. Ibid.
21. Ibid., p. 163.
22. Ibid., pp. 163–5.
23. Froude, *Divorce*, p. 216.

II

The Crown of St Edward

IT was inevitable that those combating the Restraint of Appeals should remind Henry that he had acknowledged and supported the papal supremacy in his *Assertio* of 1521. The King calmly replied, 'If we, being deceived by false pretence of evil-alleged Scripture, gave to you [the clergy] that which ought to have been refused, why may we not, our error now perceived ... take it [back] again? We Princes wrote ourselves inferiors to popes ... now, we write not as we did.' To another critic he explained that, having read and studied more, he had discovered the truth.[1] It did not occur to him to give up the title of *Fidei Defensor* bestowed by the Holy See, which remains on the coins of his Church of England successors.

To the victors the spoils ... The tactics that silenced both Chapuys and the dissentient English were reinforced by Henry's arrangements for Anne's attendance at Mass on April 14th, 1533. She entered the chapel 'in royal state', according to the Ambassador, loaded with jewels, dressed in cloth of gold and attended by sixty ladies; Mary of Richmond carried her train, and she was prayed for as Queen. 'It looks like a dream,' Chapuys wrote despairingly, 'and even those who take her part know not whether to laugh or to cry.' After the service Anne was instructed by Henry to hold Court. He stood aside, so as to note any reluctance on the part of his nobles, some of whom, Chapuys thought, appeared rather gloomy, while the King had to order one or two to kneel and kiss his wife's hand.[2] But there could be no holding back as that hard, piercing glance observed every sulky look, every unwilling movement; and so Anne received the homage of the whole assembly, the majority of whom were eager to show their adherence to the risen star.

Meanwhile, Clement VII, having made some further gestures of disapproval, philosophically received the news of what was thought to be Henry's coming marriage. Confronted by Cifuentes, the Emperor's newly accredited envoy, he was told that it would be the result of 'la Ana's' pregnancy, and 'a public sin'. He said, 'If the marriage does take place, we must seek a remedy.' His cool tone enraged the Spaniard, who exclaimed, 'You should do justice at once!' 'What will the Emperor do?' Clement inquired. 'His Majesty will act like a good—and powerful—Prince,' Cifuentes angrily replied.[3] Clement promised that he also would do justice, thus implying an annulment of the marriage, followed by excommunication.

In the last week of April Henry gave orders that Anne should be prayed for at all services. This caused disturbances, and in a London church the congregation, 'with great murmuring and ill looks', left the building. Henry sent for the Lord Mayor and gave him a scolding. 'Take order', he said, 'that nothing of the kind happens again. No one should be so bold as to murmur against my marriage.' When the unfortunate man tried to lay the blame on the merchants and their apprentices, he was told to imprison and fine them if they repeated these demonstrations.[4] In the same week the King sent two nobles to tell the Princess Mary of his marriage; they added that when she wrote to her mother, she must not address her as Queen. The Princess received these instructions without comment; she then left the envoys to go into dinner, a meal to which they were not invited.[5]

On April 28th Henry sent out his first batch of instructions for Anne's coronation, which was to take place on Whit Sunday, June 1st. He saw to every detail himself, beginning with the procession of barges from Greenwich to the Tower, where he would be waiting to receive her. She was to wear a skirt and tasselled mantle of cloth of gold furred with ermine, and a gold coronet set with jewels. He then issued orders for flags for the barges, for the decorations of the City, and the costumes of the Mayor and aldermen.[6] While he did so, Chapuys, who had been told to remain in England, continued to plead for Katherine, as did Dr Ortiz from the Vatican; this diplomat took the reports of the preparations for the coronation to be those for the wedding, and described Henry as 'feeling his way towards marrying this Ana publicly'.[7] Chapuys, better informed, remonstrated with the Council, who told him that the 'late' Queen was now known as the Lady Katherine. When Henry refused him an audience, he wrote imploring him to preserve the Queen's right, and for better treatment for her and the Princess Mary. Receiving no answer, he approached Cromwell, with whom he had always been on friendly terms, and who was now Henry's chief minister. Although amiability itself, that functionary could not supply any details about the King's marriage. Still Chapuys anticipated rebellion; but presently he had to admit that Henry appeared 'absolutely serene ... There is little hope', he told the Emperor, 'of bringing him to reason,' adding that informers were being employed to report any objections made by the people about the King's plans.[8]

In the week preceding the coronation Cranmer set up a court at Dunstable to put through the divorce, to which Katherine, who was living some four miles away, was called to appear. Realizing that if she obeyed, and referred her cause to Rome, as she was bound to do, she would be accused of high treason, she ignored the summons, and was declared contumacious by Cranmer, who, hurrying back to Lambeth, announced the legality of Henry's marriage to Anne on May 28th, four days before her coronation.

On the 19th of that month, Anne proceeded by water to the Tower, where custom decreed her remaining for a fortnight before she was crowned in Westminster Abbey.

King Henry, well aware that the Londoners' dislike of his Queen would be forgotten in their enjoyment of a show, had arranged for the Lord Mayor to fetch her from Greenwich in an elaborate and ingenious water-pageant, which resulted in the river being thronged by wherries and hoys. This dignitary, Sir Stephen Peacock, arrived at three o'clock in his state barge, preceded by a gunboat loaded with culverines; these surrounded an enormous dragon, so mechanized as to thrash its tail and vomit 'wild-fire' into the Thames; it was supported by a troup of men dressed as savages, dancing and yelling, while the cannon sounded so continuously that, according to an eye-witness, 'no glass was left, and it seemed as if the world was coming to an end'.[9] On one side of the mayoral barge was that of the bachelors, on the other, one bearing a party of young girls, sitting round a heap of red and white roses and singing the new Queen's praises; her emblem of a white falcon — crowned — had been placed on the top, a sceptre in its claw; on a scroll below was inscribed her new motto, 'Happiest of Women', in gold lettering.[10]

As the cannon ceased and the bells rang out Anne and her ladies entered the royal barge, which was followed by those of her father, of the Duke of Suffolk, and of other nobles. The musicians attendant on the Lord Mayor then struck up, and the order of the barges was reversed, so that hers came last, thus providing the climax of the procession when it cast anchor at the Tower some two hours later. Here, more cannons were shot off, while Norfolk and the Lieutenant of the Tower, Sir William Kingston, waited to conduct her to the King, who stood at the top of the main stairway.

She knelt before him. He raised and kissed her, placing his hands on her hips, so as to demonstrate her condition. After turning to thank the Mayor and aldermen, she and Henry, with their entourage, entered the royal apartments, where seventeen young noblemen were to receive the Order of the Garter.[11]

The six months of Anne's pregnancy had brought on the usual bouts of nausea and, what may have been even more taxing, those of salivation. Constantly forced to spit, she must have longed to retire; but Henry, 'with loving countenance', according to the chronicler, insisted on her presence at the banquet, which lasted some three or four hours; and for the rest of the night, music from the barges, interspersed with the hiss and crackle of fireworks and the sound of cannon, made sleep impossible. Yet she seems to have recuperated during the fortnight preceding her progress through the City.[12]

There was no rest for Cromwell, whose informers came to him with various reports of Anne's unpopularity. A merchant had been found displaying a caricature of her and Henry; examined, he said, 'I meant no harm, being commissioned by a Spaniard to bring it over from Antwerp.'[13] A prophecy was being circulated, announcing that a Queen would shortly be burned at Smithfield, and one Wendon, hearing it, had remarked, 'I trust it may be that whore and harlot, Queen Anne,' while a certain William Glover had been told by a spirit that her child would be a girl.[14] Finally, the Nun of Kent had received a letter from St Mary Magdalene — written in gold ink — telling her that the King was about to lose his power and authority.[15] She then wrote to Clement VII, ordering him to do his duty, and adding that if he did not, God would destroy him in a few days.[16] She was also writing to the Princess Mary, in the intervals of expeditions, organized by angels, to the Courts of Heaven. These had been interrupted by Satan's attempts on her virtue; his demonstrations of virility, duly reported in detail, were unsuccessful.[17]

Unfortunately for Anne, her stay in the Tower gave the people of London time to consider and so to renew their hostility. On her progress through the City the streets were lined with men who kept on their caps, and angrily staring women; no one cheered, or asked God to bless her.[18]

The procession opened with the Lord Mayor and aldermen in crimson, the French Ambassador's retinue in blue, and the Knights of the Bath in violet trimmed with miniver, all on horses trapped in velvet. They were followed by abbots, barons, bishops, earls and marquesses, riding in pairs. After these, the Lord Chancellor rode alone; behind him came the Venetian Ambassador, Cranmer in his episcopal robes, and the officers of the Queen's household, who escorted Suffolk as Lord High Constable of England. Last of all, came two gentlemen in blue and gold, representing the thirteenth-century English dukedoms of Normandy and Aquitaine.[19]

Queen Anne now appeared in an open litter of cloth of gold drawn by four white palfreys. She wore white cloth of silver, an ermine mantle and a circlet of diamonds. Sitting in her chair, a bunch of flowers in her hand, and a string of pearls, 'larger than chick-peas', round her neck, she turned, smiling and radiant, from one side to the other; and presently her looks called forth a few murmurs of approval.[20]

At the first triumphal arch, designed by Holbein, she halted to hear Apollo and the Muses greet her with music and song. Opposite, was another, less pleasing display, that of the Hispano-German merchants, who, forced to contribute to the celebrations, had revenged themselves by putting up a structure surmounted with the arms of Aragon and Castile and the imperial eagle of the Hapsburgs; below these were the dun cow and hawthorn bush of the Tudors, and, still further down, was Anne's white falcon.[21] She received the insult without comment, and the procession moved on to Leadenhall Street, where the merchants of the Staples had, as they thought, suitably, placed the figure of St Anne, the Mother of the Virgin—who had produced one child only, and that a girl. An attendant then stepped forward and recited a speech about fruitfulness. This rather unfortunate effort was partially remedied by another display, in which the white falcon was crowned by an angel, descending, 'with great melody', from a painted sky.[22] At the next stop, in Cheapside, the Recorder presented Anne with a purse containing a thousand gold marks, which she received gracefully, 'with many goodly words',[23] and so passed on to St Paul's, where the Three Graces, supported by two hundred 'well apparelled' children, saluted her in Latin verse. Finally, after pausing for similar shows at Ludgate, Fleet Street, St Martin's and Charing Cross, she reached Westminster Hall, descending to sit under her canopy of state, where she was served on the knee with spiced wine, sugar-plums and little cakes. And then, at last, she could withdraw.[24]

Henry was waiting for her. He said, 'How liked you the look of the City?' 'Sir,' she replied, 'I liked the City well enough—but I saw a great many caps on heads, and heard but few tongues.' She then told him that her fool, walking near her litter, had shouted to the crowds, 'I see you all have scurvy heads, and dare not uncover!' and that the people had yelled, 'French dog! Whoreson knave!' at the Sieur de Dinteville, Francis I's newly accredited Ambassador, whom Henry was particularly anxious to honour. She had not observed that, seeing the letters 'H.A.' prominently displayed, certain citizens had exclaimed, 'H.A.? Ha! Ha!' loudly, and at frequent intervals.[25]

After supper, Norfolk and George Rochford came to take leave before departing on an embassy to France. Anne, who knew that the Duke had done nothing to forward either her marriage or her coronation, drew his attention to her stretched gown. He made no comment. She said, 'I am in better condition than you would have desired'—and so they parted.[26]

At eight o'clock the next morning, Anne, robed in purple velvet and ermine, with a circlet of rubies, stood on the dais in Westminster Hall to receive the dignitaries of the Abbey. The procession then formed. Walking under a canopy carried by the Barons of the Cinque Ports, she was preceded by the Marquess of Dorset bearing the sceptre, the Earl of Oxford with St Edward's crown, and Lord Arundel with the ivory rod of peace. The Dowager-Duchess of Norfolk carried her train, and the lappets of her robe were held up by two bishops. Her ladies, in scarlet velvet barred with ermine, followed her until she was seated facing the high altar.[27]

The service, conducted by Cranmer, lasted some eight hours; a semi-private ceremony, it was less taxing than the progress of the previous day, and she sustained it without difficulty till the Archbishop set on her head the great crown of St Edward. It was too heavy for her slender neck, but she managed to support its weight while receiving the sceptre and the rod, and during the singing of the *Te Deum*. Then Cranmer, seeing her distress, removed it, and substituted a smaller crown, especially made for her, which she wore during the Mass, the *Agnus Dei* and her reception of the Sacrament; but she had to withdraw to a 'little place' prepared for her behind the shrine of the Saint, while the nobility put on their coronets. As soon as she was ready, the procession re-formed and, supported by her father on one side and Lord Talbot on the other, she walked back to Westminster Hall, where she had to withdraw again before returning for the banquet.[28]

As she took her place, the doors were thrown open to admit Suffolk, who, in crimson velvet sewn with pearls, rode into the Hall on a courser trapped with cloth of gold, together with Anne's uncle, Lord William Howard, whose horse was housed in white and purple. These noblemen escorted the twenty-seven knights chosen to wait on Anne, each of whom carried a smoking dish. Sir Thomas Wyatt then mounted the dais with ewer and basin, and she washed her hands. Lord Dorset was her cup-bearer, Lord Essex her carver, and the Earl of Arundel her chief butler, while the Lord Mayor had charge of the buttery bar.

By this time, the smells of food and wine had begun to affect her rather disagreeably; so the Countesses of Worcester and Oxford sat on either side of her, holding up a cloth, in case she 'listed to spit, or do otherwise [vomit?] at her pleasure'. As two more ladies sat under the table at her feet, it can only be presumed that heat and fatigue had caused incontinence.[29] But the procedure of the banquet could not be shortened; nor could she leave the Hall till the last course — 'subleties [sweets] of ships ... marvellous and gorgeous to behold' — [30] had been placed before her, while Suffolk and Howard rode up and down, 'cheering the lords and ladies, and the Lord Mayor and his brethren'.[31]

Somehow, Anne got through this seemingly interminable feast. Then she rose, washed her hands, which were stained and greasy with the remains of such food as she had been able to swallow, grace was said and the surnap ceremoniously removed. Yet this was not the end. The Earl of Sussex came forward and, kneeling, presented 'a goodly spice-plate' heaped with comfits. He was followed by Sir Stephen Peacock with the gold cup of assay. After she had drunk she gave it him, with a short speech of thanks. Then she walked from the Hall under the canopy, which she presented to the Barons of the Cinque Ports, 'with great thanks for their services'.[32] It was now six o'clock. She had been on show for nearly twelve hours. Next day Henry, who, with de Dinteville and the Venetian Ambassador, had watched the banquet from a latticed window, joined her for the jousts in the tiltyard of the Palace of Westminster. On the following morning she entered her barge for the return to Greenwich.[33]

Chapuys took this opportunity to complain once more on Katherine's behalf. Her arms, he told Cromwell, had been torn from the royal barge, to make way for those of the Boleyns. Cromwell replied that this must have been the work of some over-zealous subordinates, for whom neither he nor the King was responsible — and with this hollow excuse the Ambassador had to be satisfied; but he was very indignant, the more especially because he had just been officially informed that Henry was no longer bound by any laws issuing from outside the kingdom, and that Queen Katherine (as he continued to call her) had no right of appeal against the divorce.[34]

A fortnight after the coronation Clement VII issued a threat of excommunication, adding that any child of Anne's would be proclaimed illegitimate. A few days later, Chapuys, complaining to Henry's Council that no notice had been taken of this warning, was told, 'There cannot be two Queens in England.' He protested, pleading for Katherine, but had to admit that the Emperor did not intend to make war on his aunt's behalf. The Ambassador's only consolation was that a priest had been heard to announce that the new Queen was a whore.[35] On July 11th, he was further gratified by His Holiness declaring that Henry's marriage was null and void; Clement then held up the excommunication till September.

In August, Henry told Anne to leave the comparative quiet of Greenwich for Windsor. Her complaints of the pro-Spanish, Hanseatic merchants, who had anchored opposite the palace, and hoisted banners inscribed with the imperial eagles to the sound of trumpets, were disregarded by the King; he said that he could not afford to quarrel with them.[36] At Windsor, she and Henry were reported to be 'in good health and merry', while making preparations for her to lie in at Greenwich.[37] All bad news — the reports from the Vatican, and that of 'a lewd and naughty priest' exclaiming, 'As for Nan Bullen, who the devil made her Queen?'—were kept from her by Henry, who held his Councils at Guildford, returning to find her in a highly nervous state.[38]

She may have doubted the soothsayers' assurances that she was carrying a son; and then Henry, who was also under considerable strain, began what seems to have been a mild flirtation with one of her ladies. When she upbraided him, he turned upon her. 'You must shut your eyes and endure,' he shouted, 'as have more worthy persons. You must know', he went on, 'that it is in my power to humble you again in a moment—more than I have exalted you.' Although she does not appear to have been intimidated, they were not on speaking terms for several days.[39] Then he allowed her to send to Katherine for the royal christening robe—which was in fact Crown property. The ex-Queen refused to give it up 'for so horrible and abominable a case'.[40] Henry tried to atone for this rebuff by giving Anne a wonderful French bed for her lying-in. He was quite sure that the child would be a boy—the astrologers and white wizards had been unanimous—but he could not make up his mind whether it should be called Edward or Henry.

On the morning of September 7th Anne's pains began. Between three and four in the afternoon, after fearful suffering, she gave birth to her child. It was a girl.

NOTES

1. Scarisbrick, *Henry VIII*, p. 326.
2. *L. & P.*, Vol. VI, p. 163.
3. Ibid., p. 171.
4. Ibid., 179.
5. Ibid.
6. Ibid., p. 151.
7. Ibid., p. 198.
8. Ibid., p. 224.
9. *Spanish Chronicle*, pp. 12–13.
10. Hall, *Chronicle*, p. 798.
11. Ibid.
12. Ibid., p. 801.
13. *L. & P.*, Vol. VI, p. 224.
14. Ibid., p. 665; Elton, *Police and Policy*, p. 58.
15. Scarisbrick, op. cit., p. 361.
16. Froude, *History*, Vol. I, p. 199.
17. Ibid.
18. *Spanish Chronicle*, p. 14.
19. *L. & P.*, Vol. VI, p. 181.
20. *Spanish Chronicle*, p. 14.
21. Friedmann, *Anne Boleyn*, Vol. I, p. 207.
22. Ibid., p. 208.
23. Hall, op. cit., p. 801.
24. Ibid.

25. *Spanish Chronicle*, p. 14.
26. *L. & P.*, Vol. VI, p. 240.
27. Hall, op. cit., p. 798.
28. Ibid., p. 799.
29. Ibid., p. 801.
30. Ibid.
31. Ibid.
32. Ibid.
33. Ibid., p. 802.
34. *L. & P.*, Vol. VI, p. 240.
35. Ibid., p. 300.
36. Friedmann, op. cit., Vol. I, p. 431.
37. *L. & P.*, Vol. VI, p. 431.
38. Ibid., p. 417.
39. Ibid., p. 453.
40. Ibid., p. 397.

III

Metamorphosis

THE disappointment was not, after all, so very great. That the miscalculations of the astrologers and soothsayers shocked and disgusted Henry is shown by his ceasing to patronize them; thenceforth, he relied on his own judgment — and on the Deity who alone must direct him. The setback caused by the birth of an unwanted daughter which so rejoiced his antagonists was not irrevocable, or even very serious. Anne was capable of bearing other children; and this one, whom Henry decided to call Elizabeth, after his mother, was lively and robust. He therefore planned an elaborate christening, and issued orders for bonfires, fountains running wine and free meals. Bells were rung and the streets illuminated.[1]

Chapuys thought that the people's enjoyment of these amenities was the result of their pleasure in the new Queen's failure to produce an heir; he misunderstood their readiness to celebrate an event which enabled them to drink, eat and dance without cost to themselves; nor did he grasp the ancient, deeply rooted belief that Henry might have been as much to blame as Anne for her not giving birth to a son. '*I* would have gotten a boy,' one John Erley exclaimed, 'or else I would have so meddled with [the Queen] till my eyes did start out of my head.'[2] And the Ambassador's report of the christening as 'cold and disagreeable' is not borne out by Hall's account of that ceremony, which took place on September 10th, 1533, in the church of the Greyfriars (then part of the Palace of Greenwich) with great splendour.

'The little bastard' — as Chapuys called the child who, fifty-five years later, was to bring the pride of Spain to the dust — was wrapped in purple velvet with a train so long that three noblemen had to hold it up, and carried by the Dowager-Duchess of Norfolk walking under a canopy to the silver font presented by Francis I. She was baptized by Longland, Bishop of Lincoln, and sponsored by Cranmer, the Dowager-Duchess and the Marchioness of Dorset. Then the trumpets sounded, the Garter King-of-Arms cried, 'God of His infinite goodness send a prosperous life and long

to the high and mighty Princess Elizabeth of England!'[3] The procession of nobles and City dignitaries carrying the christening gifts
and attended by five hundred torch-bearers, then escorted the
Princess to her mother's bed-chamber, where both parents waited
to receive and bless her. A few weeks later, the succession was
settled on her, and Mary declared illegitimate.

The effect on Anne of what many looked on as a defeat was not
immediately apparent. She was fertile, and must therefore have
counted on conceiving again very soon. Her relations with Henry,
although sometimes stormy, were not seriously impaired; and as a
crowned and anointed Queen, who had born a healthy child, she
could look forward to a more stable career than that begun nearly
seven years ago.

Presumably Anne was aware that Chapuys continued to accuse
her and all her family of Lutheranism; for she countered this
charge by adding to the number of her chaplains, and giving each
of them a little book of devotions in Latin, printed on vellum and
bound in gold, with a ring attached, so that it might hang from
their girdles. She increased her charities, including those to
scholars, by some £2,000 a year, and inaugurated a school of
needlework, which produced clothing for the poor, and which she
supervised herself.[4] By the middle of October she had recovered,
the little Princess continued to thrive, and she and Henry were in
excellent spirits;[5] so she could afford to ignore the story, origin-
ating from the Vatican, that she had given birth to a monster, and
that Henry was tired of her.[6]

These rumours were encouraged by Chapuys — who was not
asked to visit the baby — and whom Henry, not unnaturally, refused
to see. The Ambassador turned to Cromwell, imploring him to influence his master. Elizabeth, that child of sin, was illegitimate, and
should not succeed. When the minister replied that Henry was now
lawfully married, and dismissed the Pope's pronouncement as invalid, he was supported by the French Ambassador, who described
Clement's threat of excommunication as unjust.[7] Cromwell then
invited Chapuys to a hawking party, and the Ambassador's hopes
rose. He had told the Emperor that Henry regretted marrying
Anne; but one of her ladies-in-waiting told him that the King,
hearing this rumour, had declared that he would 'sooner go begging
his bread from door to door than abandon her', and Cromwell
added that his love for her was undiminished.[8]

Yet Chapuys continued his fight for Katherine and her daughter. His reports grew longer and more censorious, as he refused to admit that Henry had carried 'iis people—some, the minority, unwillingly—with him, and that the Restraint of Appeals, Anne's coronation and Elizabeth's legitimacy amounted to a *fait accompli*. He could only fall back on encouraging the Lady Mary, as she was now called, to defy her father.

As before, Chapuys did not perceive the pattern of English behaviour. He still believed that the people, supported by the merchants and nobles (with whom they were generally at odds), would rise against the King, restore Katherine and give her daughter the right of succession. Also, he was totally unaware— perhaps he preferred to be—of the nature of Henry's power, or of his use of it. That the King's combination of subtlety, cunning, boldness and intuition amounted to genius, was beyond Chapuys's comprehension. He never, for a moment, became aware either of Henry's alertness or his empathy with his subjects. They might grumble, abuse Anne, and shrink before the prospect of excommunication; but Henry knew that their chief desire was to be let alone, while disregarding all political issues, and getting on with the struggle of daily life. Even if this attitude had been explained to the highly educated, cosmopolitan Savoyard, who thought and acted in a world ruled by emperors, kings, theologians and diplomats, he would have dismissed the notion. Nor did he grasp— although he was in a position to observe it every day of the week —the effect of the Supremacy on Henry's character, or of its result on the actions of Charles V and Clement VII.

Chapuys's vast reports—did his overworked master's heart ever sink at the sight of them?—were based on a rather peculiar process of reasoning. The King of England's new laws were heretical, illegal and unjust: therefore they were evil: therefore they could not succeed; and when, as was inevitable, they failed, then papal authority would be reinstated. The present outlook was black; but right must prevail, as long as those who supported it persevered. And Chapuys did persevere, daily, hourly; nothing would stop him.

His reports of his talks with Henry have a refrain of 'I pointed out', 'The King repeated', 'He laughed', 'I was firm', 'He contradicted me', 'I reminded him', interspersed with fears for Katherine's and Mary's lives; for he was quite sure that Henry intended to poison one or both, and his warnings about this contingency caused them much unnecessary suffering. However harsh Henry might be — and he meant what he said when he threatened to send Mary to the Tower — he had a horror of secret assassination, quite apart from the fact that he knew what the effect of such an action would be on his reputation; for he was still a popular hero, and determined to remain so.

Finally, Chapuys, while ceaselessly buttonholing and nagging (as Henry called it, 'stinging') the King and his ministers, avoided all contact with Anne. If he had to kiss her hand, or exchange a few words with her at a public reception, that was all he allowed himself; and at this time he took care never to mention such formalities to his master. So he was unable to see the situation as a whole, and Henry's gradual change of attitude was hidden from him. Some contact, however superficial, with the hated Concubine, might have been immensely enlightening; but scorn and loathing fatally limited the influence of which the Ambassador was so proud.

Anne had not yet felt any real danger to herself from Henry's moods, partly because an apparent tolerance — very noticeable in his talks with Chapuys — seems to have disguised his realization that he could now exercise a different kind of power: one that was to become absolute (yet deceptively constitutional) when the Restraint of Appeals had been finalized in Parliament. From the spring of 1533 until January 1534 he knew that he could look forward to complete jurisdiction in all spiritual issues. This awareness, which might have overset the prudence of many rulers, made Henry more careful, and quicker to respond to national feeling. His cautious attitude was perfectly exemplified by his partially complying with Anne's suggestions about the position of the Princess Mary (whom she saw as the potential destroyer of her own daughter's status), and also by his decision to expose the Nun of Kent in such a manner as to prevent her, temporarily, from achieving martyrdom.

At the beginning of November Elizabeth Barton was arrested, brought before the Council and examined by Cranmer about her prophecies, voices and visions. She admitted that she had helped to organize a conspiracy to overthrow the regime and deprive Henry of his throne. At this point, the audience, a large one, broke into cries of 'To the stake!'[9]

But Henry knew better than to destroy a popular celebrity whose reputation was that of a saint. Elizabeth Barton was imprisoned, but not tortured. Desired to confess, she did so from a raised platform at Paul's Cross. Standing there, with the monks and friars who had abetted and partially inspired her ravings, the poor creature announced, 'I ... most miserable and wretched person, have been the origin of all this mischief, and by my falsehood have deceived all these persons, and many more.'[10] She then begged for the King's mercy, and was taken back to the Tower, while Cromwell assessed the guilt of those connected with her schemes. The charge of misprision (concealment) of treason was proved against Father Bocking and the other monks; Henry's Plantagenet cousins, the Marchioness of Exeter and the Countess of Salisbury, were also implicated; but the Nun's efforts to involve Katherine and the Princess Mary had been unsuccessful. More had dismissed her; Fisher had 'wept for joy' on hearing her messages, and by her advice had corresponded with the Emperor about a Spanish invasion.[11] The capital charge of high treason (of which she was certainly guilty) was not pressed; and so Henry's tactics of drawing back in order to spring were once more exercised – as was his response to Mary's defiance of his command that she should acknowledge the validity of his marriage and Princess Elizabeth's legitimacy. He merely reduced his elder daughter's household to a minimum, and warned her that she would have to share that of her half-sister in a few weeks' time.

Anne, aware that for reasons of hygiene, Elizabeth would soon be moved out of London, to an establishment of her own in the country, would not let her out of her sight. Placing her on the floor on a cushion, she spent hours watching her.[12] In December Elizabeth, accompanied by Mary, was conducted to the manor of Hatfield. Both parents visited her there, sometimes taking her with them to Eltham, or back to Greenwich. On these occasions, Mary was told to stay in her room; an extra allowance was arranged for her upkeep, as her appetite was very large.[13] When desired to pay her respects to the baby Princess, she replied that she knew of no Princess in England but herself, and burst into tears.[14]

Chapuys blamed Anne for this bullying; Henry, he told the Emperor, 'is bewitched by this cursed woman ... does all she says, and dares not contradict her,' adding that Anne intended to poison her stepdaughter. He repeated this rather absurd analysis of the situation to Cromwell, who replied that pressure of business prevented his dealing with it for the moment.[15]

For both he and his master had many problems to consider. The Nun's conspiracy had been widespread, involving some hundreds of discontented persons, who were not, however, prepared to work together in order to form a united front against the King. Like Chapuys, de Dinteville was misled by the free talk of the English people; in his long report to one of Francis I's ministers, he described a rebellion on Katherine's and Mary's behalf as imminent, the wool trade in danger, and Henry completely subjugated by another lady.[16]

There was a modicum of truth in all these statements but the last. A large number of people who had never met Anne continued to dwell on her failure to keep her husband's love; those who did meet her noted her hold over him. Henry's 'new fancy', as the French Ambassador called her supposed rival, was one of many ladies made momentarily conspicuous by the King's easy gallantries. De Dinteville, accustomed to continental manners, looked on this light-hearted parry and riposte as the prelude to adultery. If it had been so, the news that Henry had set up a mistress would have been known in all the Courts of Europe. Chapuys, who had no illusions on this point, would have been the first to report that Henry was unfaithful.

This diplomat's hopes were now transferred to the future effects of the excommunication (it had been postponed again) and what he construed as Francis I's betrayal of Henry's cause at the Vatican. When the marriage contract between the Duc d'Orléans and Catherine de' Medici was signed, it seemed to Chapuys, as it did to many others, that Clement and Francis were about to join forces with the Emperor against England. According to de Dinteville, the Princess Mary's betrothal to the Dauphin was in abeyance, and he believed that Anne was responsible. 'Should the King be unwilling,' he wrote, 'and should his wife's persuasions still have influence with him, he will hesitate before he will defy, for her sake, the King of France and the Emperor united. His regard for the Queen ... diminishes every day.'[17]

Anne had no influence over Henry in matters of this nature; and she might have been relieved to see her dangerously popular step-daughter settled in France. As neither she nor Henry expected Francis to keep his promise of supporting their marriage at the

Vatican, they were surprised when he informed them that Clement had described the English King's cause as good, adding that he would issue a proclamation to that effect if Henry, in his turn, acknowledged the authority of the Holy See.[18] But six years of Italian acrobatics had shown Henry the worth of such advances; he had made his own arrangements; and he refused to subscribe to Clement's proposal. This displeased Francis, who begged him to co-operate by appearing to plead his cause at Cambrai, and who was also denied. 'God and truth', Henry told de Dinteville, 'are on my side.'[19] He added that the country was fully prepared to resist an invasion; but he did not say that he could count on all classes combining against a foreign enemy, perhaps because he preferred to leave both the French and the Spanish Ambassadors to their illusions.

National resentment of Clement's policy — if his activities can be so described — was expressed by one of the most orthodox and eminent Catholic noblemen. 'The Pope', Norfolk said to Chapuys, 'is a wretch, a bastard, a liar and a bad man. I would stake my wife and children, and my own person, to be revenged on him,' adding that, by order of the Council, Clement would henceforth be known as the Bishop of Rome.[20]

While Anne and her uncle hated one another as only those closely related can hate, they were united in their detestation of the Curia; and most English people, although practising Catholics, felt as they did. This was an attitude visiting foreigners could not understand. Anyone who abused Clement or supported Henry against him must be, simply, a heretic, preferably a Lutheran. In fact, Anne and her family were meticulously strict in their observance of all the rites and ceremonies of the faith in which they had been brought up, as became the favoured subjects of a King whose Catholicism was unaffected by his war against the Papacy. Anne herself, while patronizing certain Lutherans for political purposes, was more sincerely Catholic than her relatives; her life with Henry no doubt strengthened her religious belief, for in this, as in other matters, she was ruled by him. Chapuys's picture of her dominating the King in political matters was totally false, and resulted from the Ambassador's resentful interpretation of her success. In any case, Chapuys inclined to describe all those he disliked, or was shocked by, as Lutherans; it became a generic term of abuse.

The French envoys were less fanatical than those employed by

Charles V, and clearer-headed. Their master's rather uneasy alliance with Henry produced a certain tolerance towards English inconsistencies, and thus towards the Norfolk–Boleyn faction, whose support was necessary to them. Yet many of Henry's elderly courtiers treated them as representatives of the traditional enemy. When Cardinal Jean du Bellay returned to London in December 1533, his welcome from the King and Queen did not protect him from old Lord Shrewsbury's furious outburst at a banquet given by the Council in the Ambassador's honour. At some moment, du Bellay remarked that Shrewsbury's ignorance of French showed a lack of breeding — and the taunt was translated. The ancient warrior then stood up, clapped his hand on his sword, and shouted, 'Saith the French whoreson so? Marry, tell the French dog again, by sweet Saint Cuthbert, if I know one pestilent French word in all my body, I would take my dagger and dig it out before I rose from table!' Du Bellay, much embarrassed, subsided, drinking 'wondrous oft', while Shrewsbury continued to mutter about 'tawny whoresons' and 'French knaves'.[21]

Henry was noted for his easy-going way with such old-fashioned patriots. There is a story, unfounded but characteristic of his reputation in this respect, of a ninety-year-old supporter of the ex-Queen telling him to take her back. The King described this aged critic as 'like a child', and refused to penalize or even reprove him.[22] During this year, his decision to keep the annates — taxes paid to the Vatican — had increased his popularity; and his abuse of Clement enhanced his subjects' satisfaction in their independence of the Holy See. His General Council publicly denounced the Pope's 'pomp, pride and ambition', while one of Cromwell's agents remarked that the Bishop of Rome might as well 'wipe his arse' with his briefs of excommunication as trouble to send them into England.[23] But this was not a popular view.

At this time, the King's most urgent problem was that produced by Anne's fear of the Princess Mary. Knowing that he was still very fond of her, and dreading her reinstallation, she begged him to punish his undutiful daughter, and succeeded in establishing two of her aunts, Mrs Shelton and Lady Alice Clere, as her guardians; they were to box her ears if she persisted in speaking of herself as the Princess of Wales, and prevent her corresponding with Charles V, the Exeters and her other Plantagenet cousins.[24] But Mrs Shelton and Mary got on very well together — so well that Henry became suspicious. He decided to go to Hatfield and reason with the Princess himself, as soon as the Christmas and Twelfth Night revels were over. This further alarmed Anne, who turned for help to Cromwell. He agreed to follow his master and persuade him not to interview Mary. The result of his expedition was rather surprising.

NOTES

1. Hall, *Chronicle*, p. 801.
2. *L. & P.*, Vol. VI, p. 471.
3. Hall, loc. cit.
4. Wyatt, *Anne Boleyn*, p. 19.
5. *L. & P.*, Vol. VI, p. 523.
6. Ibid., p. 431.
7. *Span. Cal. B.*, Vol. IV, pt. 2, p. 124.
8. *L. & P.*, Vol. VI, p. 556; Friedmann, *Anne Boleyn*, Vol. I, p. 232.
9. Froude, *History*, Vol. I, p. 408.
10. Ibid.
11. Scarisbrick, *Henry VIII*, p. 336.
12. *Spanish Chronicle*, p. 42.
13. Froude, op. cit., Vol. I, p. 409.
14. Parmiter, *The King's Great Matter*, p. 258.
15. *L. & P.*, Vol. VI, pp. 611, 628; Parmiter, op. cit., p. 259.
16. Froude, *History*, Vol. I, p. 406.
17. Ibid., p. 407.
18. Ibid.
19. Thomas, *The Pilgrim*, p. 19.
20. *Span. Cal. P.*, Vol. IV, pt. 2, p. 875.
21. Bowle, *Henry VIII*, p. 172.
22. *Spanish Chronicle*, p. 43.
23. Bowle, op. cit., p. 172; Pocock, *Records of the Reformation*, Vol. II, p. 523.
24. *L. & P.*, Vol. VII, pt. I, p. 31.

IV

The Two Princesses

ANNE'S New Year present to her husband was the work of an artist who might have been the pupil of Cellini. Inside a golden basin lined with rubies and pearls stood a fountain containing patterns of diamonds; this was supported by three naked nymphs whose breasts spouted water over the jewels, thus giving them an unearthly radiance.[1]

The splendour of this production seems to symbolize the giver's apotheosis: for a week or two later, talk of her pregnancy reached Chapuys, who told the Emperor that God had abandoned the English people.[2] The Ambassador added that their secession from the Holy See had been confirmed by Henry sending embassies to several Lutheran rulers, and by Cromwell's arrangement for the translation of Marsiglio's *Defensor Pacis*. The Pope's inertia, Chapuys concluded, had caused these deplorable actions; that the educated classes were beginning to be interested in the Marsiglian principles, and that Wolsey's six-year-old description of Anne as sober, womanly and chaste had been sent to the Dukes of Saxony and Bavaria, all formed part of the general degradation.[3] Worse still, it was now treason to impugn Henry's second marriage or the legitimacy of Elizabeth. Indeed, Latimer glorified this Act at such length that Cranmer warned him not to preach for more than an hour and a half — 'Else', he explained, 'the King and Queen may wax weary, and so leave.'[4]

In the second week of January 1534 Cromwell overtook Henry on his way to Hatfield, and interviewed the Princess Mary. He began by urging her to renounce her title, and when she refused, warned her that if she remained obdurate, she would not be received by the King. Mary said that she wanted only to kiss her father's hand and ask his blessing; this, replied the minister, could not be, unless she submitted, at which she withdrew to her own apartments.[5]

Henry, with his nobles, then arrived, and spent some time with the baby Princess, while Cromwell told him what Mary had said.

As he rode out of the courtyard he looked up – and there she was, on the leads, kneeling, her hands clasped. On such occasions, Henry's respect for the conventions generally prevailed. He reined in his horse, lifted his cap and bowed; his astounded courtiers followed suit before the cavalcade moved away.[6]

When this incident was reported to Anne, she told Henry that his elder daughter should be more closely guarded; she added that Mary's latest letter to him, describing herself as his lawful heir ('If I agreed to the contrary, I should offend God,' it concluded), must have been dictated, possibly by Katherine.[7] But Mary was merely subscribing to the Tudor ethos, and thus unconsciously repro-ducing Henry's affiliation with the Deity – who had always told her, too, what she should do. Naturally, Anne saw Mary as an obstacle in her own daughter's path, in spite of the fact that in de-fault of sons, Elizabeth's inheritance to the throne had been made statutory. Mary seemed to her far more dangerous than Katherine, whose illness was reported to Henry soon after he returned from Hatfield. If only, he said to Chapuys, she would die; but she re-covered, to declare, once more, that if she were to be executed (this baseless rumour came from the Ambassador), it must be publicly.[8] She seems to have longed for martyrdom; and indeed, the un-happy woman, often ailing and permanently separated from her daughter, had not much to live for, although she continued to fight for her reinstallation as Queen of England.

Then someone in Chapuys's entourage told Anne that the Princess Mary might be recalled to Court.[9] She was soon reassured by Henry, and set herself to entertain and allure Castillon, the newly accredited French Ambassador, who had just replaced de Dinteville. Castillon reported her and Henry as being on excellent terms and in high spirits, although the King, annoyed by the Orléans–Medici alliance, suspected Francis I of abandoning his cause, and proposed a meeting to discuss this and other matters, later in the year; he received a noncommittal reply.[10]

It was rather difficult for those wishing to ingratiate themselves with the new Queen to find out what New Year present they could give her that she did not already possess. At last Lady Lisle, advised by Elizabeth's Governess, Lady Bryan, ventured to add to Anne's collection of pets with the gift of a little dog, 'which she liked so well' that she took it from the messenger's arms without waiting for him to beg her acceptance of it.[11] At such moments,

Anne's liveliness and gaiety charmed those hoping for her favour, and the haughtiness complained of — and doubtless caused — by Chapuys, had no place. Yet she remained a prey to moods, bursting into tears at the news of the death of Hawkins, Henry's envoy at the French Court, and then eagerly planning a two-day visit to Hatfield. These alternations struck Chapuys as unseemly and ill-bred; he recorded them in weary disgust.[12]

Anne returned from Hatfield to find Henry more than ever en-raged with Mary, to the point indeed of tears, during a talk with Castillon, who had begun to praise the Princess. 'She inherits her obstinacy with her Spanish blood,' he said, and refused to consider marrying her to anyone.[13] His decision to separate Mary from Katherine was based on the belief that the ex-Queen encouraged her daughter to defy him; Mary would have rebelled in any case, not only on religious grounds, but because she was increasingly aware of the people's adherence. She may even have heard that one John Snap, drinking after market, had declared, 'If I had twenty thousand pounds, I would bestow my life and all I have upon my Lady Mary's title, against the issue that come of the Queen.' To his companions' horrified cries of 'Fie, Snap, fie! No more of these words!' he merely repeated the challenge, which in due course reached Cromwell's rather sinister list of 'remembrances',[14] to-gether with the report of a friar, who had hoped to see Henry 'suffer a violent and shameful death', and his Queen, 'that mis-chievous whore', burned at Smithfield.[15] In fact, nothing ever could — and perhaps never will — prevent one of the most vociferous races in Europe from bursting into incriminating speech on all occasions, no matter what the danger. And at this time, those failing to report such utterances might themselves be found guilty of misprision of treason by yet others, who, in their turn, were supposed to inform the local magistrates of failure to repeat all dis-loyal remarks. Cromwell, controlling and aiming to perfect this system, was neither greedy nor bribable; a cold man, whose only ideal was that of service to the state, he eventually perished because he served it too well.

He served Anne as long as it suited Henry that he should do so — as did du Bellay, now in Rome, who reprimanded Dr Ortiz for speaking of Katherine as the true Queen, and warned Clement VII that other countries (he meant his own) might follow England's example and secede, while remaining Catholic.[16]

Meanwhile, Chapuys was always in touch with the Princess Mary, who told him that Norfolk and George Rochford had sent for Lady Alice Clere and reprimanded her for being too indulgent. Lady Alice replied that she and Mrs Shelton had no intention of ill-treating their charge, upon which Chapuys told the Emperor that Anne would surely 'revenge herself' upon her stepdaughter.[17] Mary maintained her defiance by refusing to accept a much-needed replenishment of her wardrobe, because the chests were not labelled with her title as Princess of Wales.[18] This was the result of Katherine bidding her 'show her teeth' to Henry, whom Chapuys now approached with a rather strange request. He wished to appear at the bar of the House of Lords in order to speak for Katherine and Mary. 'I desire', he said, 'to present my remonstrances on their behalf.'[19]

Calmly, Henry replied that his marriage to Anne was lawful adding that Mary was illegitimate and disobedient. A long argument ensued, during which the King kept his temper, offered to send Chapuys certain books which proved his case, and pointed out that it was not the custom in England for foreigners to take part in Parliamentary debates. As Chapuys continued to insist, Henry told him that the Pope had now no jurisdiction in his kingdom, and that the Princess Elizabeth was next in succession, until a son — 'which I hope soon to have' — was born. Still the Ambassador persisted, on the grounds that Anne so hated Mary that she might order her assassination. Henry, apparently unmoved by this impertinence, replied that he, and not Chapuys, was responsible for Mary's welfare. He then said, 'You should be satisfied with the patience with which I have heard you,' and dismissed him.[20]

In the first week of March Henry and Anne decided to adopt a different tone with the Princess, presumably in order to show that she had brought her father's displeasure on herself, and that he was perfectly willing — on certain conditions — to receive her. So it was arranged that on her next visit to Hatfield Anne should send for Mary, and make a friendly advance.

She began by inviting her stepdaughter to come to Court, 'and visit me', she went on, 'as Queen.' This opening was irresistible. Mary replied, 'I know no Queen in England but my mother. But if you, Madam, as my father's mistress, will intercede for me with him, I should be grateful.'

With unusual self-control, Anne pointed out the impossibility of this request, and repeated her offer of friendship. Mary refused to answer – so she told Chapuys – and Anne left in a rage. 'I intend to bring down this unbridled Spanish pride!' she exclaimed: and thenceforth she made no secret of her hatred, enhanced by fear, of the Princess. She told Henry that he should punish the girl; but he was too busy with his new book, and with arrangements for the attainder of Elizabeth Barton and her accomplices, to attend to the matter. He seems to have soothed Anne's fears, and to have ignored such disturbances as Mary was able to create.[21]

Anne then poured out her grievances to her brother, who warned her not to attack Mary; he may have known that Chapuys had told the Emperor that she meant to assassinate the Princess.[22] The Ambassador chose to believe this rumour, and, with unconscious cruelty, persuaded Mary to do so; this caused her to refuse to leave Hatfield for The More, when the order came for her and Elizabeth to change households. Fearing the worst, she struggled and fought, until she was seized and dumped down in her litter, opposite Lady Alice Clere, who managed to reassure her.[23] So Chapuys was able to send off another horrifying report to the Emperor, adding that Mary's distress had made her very ill. He admitted that Henry had sent Dr Butts to look after her; it was, of course, the Concubine who was threatening the Princess's life, and urging Henry to execute her and her mother.[24]

The attainder of Elizabeth Barton and five friars was followed by their execution on April 21st, while Fisher and More, who had refused to take the oath acknowledging Henry's Supremacy, were sent to the Tower for misprision of treason. Anne's intercession for the other conspirators resulted in their being pardoned.[25] (Chapuys was careful not to mention this in his reports to the Emperor.) As 'the most dearly and entirely beloved wife' of Henry VIII, Anne was acknowledged as Queen in Parliament, and her marriage as 'true, sincere and perfect, ever hereafter'.[26] In the same week, news came from the Vatican that the King of England was to be excommunicated from the Church, and had forfeited his subjects' allegiance.[27]

Henry's Supremacy may have been unwillingly accepted by many of his people; but, to Chapuys's amazement and disgust, the first attempts at rebellion – in one of which the Earl of Northumberland was momentarily involved – faltered and failed. This submission changed Henry's attitude towards his ministers, his enemies – and his wife. Henceforth, his will must be paramount, his statements unchallenged and his power absolute. A monolithic steadfastness characterized all his actions. His reply to the announcement of the excommunication was one of Olympian indifference. Some time ago, he had told Clement that if his marriage to Anne was accepted as valid, then, he would, in return, acknowledge the authority of the Holy See in spiritual matters. Now, it was too late for any agreement. He would have nothing to do with Francis I's suggestion of 'winning over' the Curia. 'I now have perfect knowledge', he wrote to one of his agents in France, 'of the Pope's indurate heart ... and malicious attempts,'[28] adding that all contact between himself and the Curia was at an end. A month later, Clement postponed the excommunication again, on the grounds that Henry, 'from his love to Anna de Boulans', had probably become 'more insolent than before', and repeated that their marriage was invalid.[29] Henry, supported by Parliament and his Council, disregarded both pronouncements, and returned to the revision of his anti-papal treatise.

But had he triumphed within his own kingdom? Until Anne justified that six years' struggle – and her own existence – by the birth of a son, he could not be sure. And so the burden of producing an heir fell more heavily on her. In April, Henry invited Castillon and his subordinate, La Pommeraye, to inspect the little Princess Elizabeth, and she was shown to them 'in very rich apparel, in state and triumph as a Princess'. Then, so that they would be able to deny any pejorative rumours about her physique, she was undressed, and they saw her naked. They asked to visit Mary, but this was not permitted.[30]

Anne's second pregnancy, accepted as a fact by Chapuys in January, seems to have been a rumour; or, having conceived in that month, she may have miscarried, conceiving again shortly afterwards. If the miscarriage had taken place within a few weeks of conception, she might have been able to conceal it: although her circumstances would have made this very difficult, if not impossible. On February 25th, Henry's statement to Chapuys that he was hoping for a son, indicates that he believed her to be pregnant at that date. Did she therefore miscarry in March, and, as it were, retrieve the situation in April? In fact, her condition in the first three months of 1534 cannot be accurately defined and still remains mysterious. Chapuys, who dreaded the birth of an heir, announced what may have been a third pregnancy in July, together with the comment that Anne was 'oppressing' the English nation.[31] So it must be presumed that that of January was false, or that it had ended in disaster. In any case, Anne and Henry were both in excellent spirits in April, when she was once more stated to be with child.

In May they moved to the medieval palace of Eltham, sending for Elizabeth to stay with them. Henry never tired of carrying her about and playing with her; while the Princess Mary, left at The More, was told that he had ceased to trouble about her marriage, and did not care what happened to her.[32] He and Anne returned to London to preside at a banquet given at Whitehall in honour of Castillon, to which the public was admitted. Henry concluded the feast by rising to drink the health of Francis I, and thanking God for their alliance, which was to be celebrated at Calais in June.[33] He then left Anne at Greenwich, and went on progress; that she did not accompany him seems to show that she had been advised to take special care of her health; for it is clear that she had fallen into the habit of miscarrying.

Whatever her state, she appeared outwardly cheerful; her appetite for rich food increased, and became the subject of some talk, eventually reaching the assiduous Lady Lisle, who, through George Rochford, sent her eighteen dotterels, a species of plover, then a great delicacy; they were eaten in batches of six, over a period of three days. Lady Lisle followed up her success with the gift of a linnet in a cage.[34]

It was better for Henry to go on progress alone; for then his popularity was unmarred by his subjects' resentment of Anne, whom some blamed for the execution of Elizabeth Barton and the friars, and the imprisonment of More and Fisher. His gift for the common touch, combined with the formidable graciousness then expected of majesty, ensured a rapturous acclaim whenever he appeared. He returned to find Anne holding court with success; her talks with travellers from abroad showed her as lively and informal;[35] and she was momentarily free from worry about Mary, whom Henry had apparently cast off, giving all his love and care to the baby Elizabeth. Then trouble broke out again, in Ireland and the North, just as he was preparing to leave for France. He seems not to have realized until later on that Chapuys was trying to organize a conspiracy on a large scale.

By the middle of June the situation had become so serious that
he decided to stay in England. His Council informed Francis I that
His Grace must postpone their meeting till the following year,
since Katherine and Mary, 'bearing no small grudge against his
most entirely beloved Queen Anne, might perchance in his absence
take occasion to ... practise ... matters of no small peril to his royal
person, realm and subjects.'[36]

The Irish rebellion, led by the usual murderous scoundrel, a
Fitzgerald, known as 'silken Thomas', who seized the opportunity
to affiliate himself with the Papacy, lasted just over a year, ending
with his capture, imprisonment and execution. It had little or
nothing to do with that begun by Sir Thomas Dacre of Naworth
and supported by Chapuys and the Scottish Border nobles. Dacre
was captured at Carlisle, brought before the Privy Council and
prosecuted by Cromwell on a charge of high treason. For seven
hours he defended himself — so ably, that the Lords, determined to
rebuff the upstart minister, acquitted him, with one dissentient
voice, that of Norfolk, who saw in this verdict an attempt to bring
down Anne's power, with that of his own faction.

Katherine's part in Dacre's unsuccessful effort to destroy the
regime had been put forward in a letter to Chapuys, in which she
desired him to tell the Emperor that the time had come 'to use
stronger remedies', adding that she dared not say more, in case her
letter was intercepted, but that speedy action was essential.[37]
Charles did not reply to this covert demand for an invasion,
although Chapuys had assured him that if Henry left England,
Anne, as Regent, would execute both Katherine and Mary. On this
point, the Ambassador's zeal and his imperfect understanding of
English — as of English law — led him into misapprehension, when
he heard Wiltshire, and, on another occasion, Cromwell, say that if
only Katherine and Mary were dead (they had both been ill) peace
would follow.[38]

Anne, too, longed for them to die; but she had no intention of
bringing about their deaths; in any case, she had not the power to
do so, quite apart from the fact that a secret attempt on their lives
would have wrecked her relationship with Henry, which had once
more become precarious; for at the beginning of September what
seems to have been her third miscarriage was followed — and
perhaps caused — by his pursuit of another lady.

A furious scene ensued, in which her reproaches and Henry's

disappointment and rage were violently expressed. He did not trouble to tell her that he was already tired of her rival, merely saying, 'You have good reason to be content with what I have done for you—and I would not do it again, if the thing were to begin. Consider from what you have come.'[39] Her situation had apparently deteriorated; but she remained indomitable—and ingenious; for, a few days later, Chapuys was gloomily reporting that the Concubine 'knew how to manage' her husband, and that their quarrel had been made up.[40] This was not all the truth: nor even half of it; for Henry was not manageable. He might divert himself; but he still loved—he may also have pitied—his dark lady.

Yet the cloud that had appeared no bigger than a man's hand at the birth of Elizabeth was coming nearer—and beginning to spread across her mother's horizon.

NOTES

1. *L. & P.*, Vol. VII, pt. 1, p. 4.
2. Ibid., p. 6.
3. Ibid., p. 10.
4. Ibid., p. 15.
5. Ibid., p. 31.
6. Ibid.
7. Ibid.
8. Ibid.
9. Ibid., p. 48.
10. Ibid., p. 68.
11. Ibid., p. 36.
12. Ibid., p. 68.
13. Ibid.
14. Prescott, *Mary Tudor*, p. 52.
15. Elton, *Policy and Police*, p. 24.
16. *L. & P.*, Vol. VII, pt. 1, p. 37.
17. Ibid., p. 85.
18. Froude, *Divorce*, p. 262.
19. *Span. Cal. P.*, Vol. IV, p. 59.
20. Ibid.
21. *L. & P.*, Vol. VII, pt. 1, p. 127.
22. Friedmann, *Anne Boleyn*, Vol. II, p. 10.
23. Prescott, op. cit., p. 52.
24. Ibid., p. 56.
25. Froude, *History*, Vol. I, p. 426.
26. Ibid.
27. Ibid.
28. Parmiter, *The King's Great Matter*, p. 267.
29. *L. & P.*, Vol. VII, pt. 1, p. 195.
30. Ibid., p. 191.
31. Ibid., p. 372.
32. Ibid., p. 204.
33. Ibid., p. 253.
34. Ibid., p. 240.
35. Ibid., p. 371.
36. Froude, op. cit., Vol. I, p. 435.
37. *Span. Cal. P.*, Vol. V, p. 153.
38. Ibid.
39. *L. & P.*, Vol. VII, pt. 2, p. 463.
40. Ibid.

V

Distant Thunder

HENRY VIII had now been King of England for twenty-five years; and the Queen's enemies considered that, through her predominance, his Court had changed for the worse.

In a practical sense, this was not so; for Cromwell was managing, although with difficulty, to put down some of the waste and exploitation created by a number of idle hangers-on and privileged nobodies, whose rank had given them nominal but well-paid situations, principally in the Privy Chamber, where Henry's daily routine began and ended with a series of ritualistic ceremonies.

These long overdue reforms enraged those who now found themselves unemployed; but their hatred of and attacks on the reformer failed to destroy Henry's dependence on him; and because Cromwell had temporarily allied himself with Anne, she had some support from the circle immediately surrounding the King.

Yet that circle had deteriorated since his youth. It might be compared to one in the *Inferno*; for it contained both sin and punishment, differing only from those described by the poet, in that its inhabitants were in perpetual conflict with each other, as with those below them, and in deadly fear of losing their power. Thus sycophancy and intrigue combined to produce a miasma of creeping suspicion, crude flattery and ill-concealed spite, chiefly centring on Anne, who at this time had only two steadfast adherents—her brother and her stepmother. But Rochford, although loaded with honours and places—he had recently been made Warden of the Cinque Ports—was not really influential; and Lady Wiltshire counted for nothing, in spite of the fact that Anne was very fond of her.

So, beneath the glitter and the magnificence, the cloth of gold and silver, the jewels and the embroideries, the velvets, the ermine and the miniver, their wearers stalked to and fro, like beasts of prey, waiting for a chance to tear one another to pieces, while perfecting a falsity of behaviour that deceived and sometimes bewildered those fancying themselves secure and popular. Such persons were generally unaware that they were treading on a bog which might, at any moment, give way, and bring them down to disgrace and death.

Three actors in this drama of violence and cruelty—played to the music of lutes and virginals—were undeceived and on the alert: Henry, Anne and the Duke of Norfolk. The King knew that he could control it; Anne's hope of doing so was founded on the birth of a son; and Norfolk's gift for unscrupulous manipulation and barefaced lying, added to his prestige as the minister whose power was second only to Cromwell's, enabled him to penetrate and sometimes expose the convolutions of treachery and spying that lay behind the gorgeous façade of Court life.

In fact, Norfolk alone of these three could afford to utter what most of his contemporaries felt when, in the first week of October 1534, news came that Clement VII was no more. 'The Great Devil is dead,'[1] he remarked, while Henry and Cromwell began to establish what promised to be very satisfactory relations with Clement's successor, Paul III, formerly Cardinal Farnese, who had voted for the invalidity of the Aragon marriage at several Consistories. The Roman citizens shared Norfolk's view of the late Pope. Bursting into the death-chamber, they snatched his body from the bier, and were about to dismember it, when the Papal guard intervened. No one of importance mourned the poor old man: not even Charles V, whom he had tried so hard to placate.[2]

Meanwhile, the new Pontiff's advances to Henry were genial and immediate, greatly disconcerting the anti-Boleyn groups, and adding to the confused yet murderous strife surrounding Anne. Her position became increasingly tenuous as she waited, it seemed vainly, to conceive again, and bear the heir that Henry needed—although for different reasons—as much as she did. She was like someone whose house is surrounded by floods, and who climbs, ever more desperately, from one floor up to the next, finally reaching the roof-top to see the waters still rising; and on the crest of the wave was the King, serenely breasting the current of revolution, and pausing, every now and then, to embrace a younger woman. So her rivals, attended by a galaxy of courtiers, rose with him, if only for a time.

Henry's relations with these ladies are not easily defined. From October 1534 to January 1536, certain continental Ambassadors spoke of him as having acquired yet another mistress; and their reports have produced what may be a legendary reputation; for in the sixteenth century the word 'mistress' was used to describe a woman courted by a man who might or might not become her lover in the modern sense. The formal publicity of Henry's daily life was such that, in order to spend the nights with Elizabeth Blount, he had had to establish her in a house some way out of London; and while all his associates, Cromwell specifically, knew what his connection with Mary Boleyn had been, there is no surviving record of how he arranged to see her privately.

On the other hand, his relations with his six wives were ceremoniously effected, and known to everyone, both in his palaces and beyond them. His bedchamber, in which two of his gentlemen slept on palliasses, was separated from that of the Queen by a series of ante-rooms and passages. When he decided to visit her, the curtains of his bed were drawn back, his night-robe was sent for and put on, and an escort consisting of pages and Grooms of the Bedchamber, two of whom carried torches, was summoned. Thus accompanied, he would proceed to his wife's apartments, the purpose of his descent on her being one of national, and therefore public, concern.

Finally, his attitude towards the pleasures of the alcove seems to have been that of a man who likes to be surrounded by pretty faces, while creating an impression of concupiscence. On several occasions, he is reported as being 'on the water with ladies'. In the royal barge, watched and cheered from the banks by his subjects, who commented, without regard to delicacy, on his habits, he appeared as an insatiable pursuer of women, while confining himself to jokes, compliments and flirtation; and, on such expeditions, the Queen might sometimes be one of the party.

So it was that when Anne's nervous irritation and fluctuating condition caused temporary estrangement, Henry's frequentation of other women (not all their names have come down to us) was generally described as adulterous; and she, knowing this, was further exacerbated. When his intentions were serious, and designed to culminate in marriage, his behaviour was quite different and extremely circumspect; it bore no resemblance to his approach when he was momentarily attracted by some Court lady.

In such matters, therefore, no definite pronouncement can be made; but it may be suggested that when Henry seemed to have tired of Anne—as in October and November 1534—he was merely escaping from her moods. For at this time, they were both hoping, and no doubt assuming, that her miscarriages would cease. Whether these were partially caused by the almost unbearable strain of her situation must also remain a matter of conjecture. She was physically robust; but for seven years she had been living on the edge of a precipice, hated by many, unsupported by all but one of her male relatives, and unable to rely on the King, who, as her self-control began to fail, seemed, every now and then, to be moving away from her, while openly deprecating her origins. On this point, an expert and famous historian has observed that Henry VIII, although every inch a king, never attained the stature of a gentleman.[3] But Tudor manners so differed from those of today as to appear incomprehensible.

At this time, Anne could not afford to disregard the gossip arising from the casual attentions Henry was paying to an un-known lady—whom Chapuys described as beautiful and intelligent—because it reached the Emperor and Francis I. Her distress gave Jane Rochford the opening she had been denied by the husband who would not let her share his privileges; for they had long detested one another, and she was therefore excluded from Henry's private circle. She now suggested to Anne that she should intrigue against the young woman, Anne consented, and her sister-in-law put in hand a plot of which the details are not extant. The scheme was reported to Henry, who banished Lady Rochford from Court in the second week of October, with the result that Anne's prestige was considerably lowered in the eyes of his courtiers; one of them told Chapuys that the new favourite had promised Princess Mary that she would effect a reconciliation between her and her father.[4]

A week later, Anne, attended by Suffolk, Norfolk and several other courtiers, went to Richmond, where Mary and Elizabeth were now established. She had no sooner entered her daughter's apartments than she became aware that the two Dukes, with their attendants, had left her and were paying court to Mary, who remained closeted with them till her stepmother's departure.[5]

Henry ignored her complaints, as he and Cromwell did those of Chapuys, who told the minister that Anne had insulted the Princess by not visiting her. Cromwell replied sharply, 'I have done all in my power on Madam Mary's behalf,' and refused to discuss the matter further.[6] Anne's relations with Henry then improved, partly through the consent of Parliament to the Treason

Act in November. This strengthened her position by making it a capital offence to impugn their marriage, or to speak of the King as heretic or schismatic; but some time passed before she and Henry made up their dispute; then, in December, Chapuys was forced to admit that the King's so-called love for the pretty lady was not serious; although he had complained of Anne as 'vexatious and importunate', they were once more on good terms.[7]

The meticulous but violently prejudiced reports of this Ambassador are partially accounted for by Sir William Paget, one of Henry's secretaries, a perceptive and comparatively unbiased statesman, who came to know Chapuys very well indeed. 'I never took him', Paget recalled, 'for a wise man, but for one that used to speak ... without respect of honesty or truth, so it might serve his turn ... He is a great practiser [plotter] ... tale-telling, lying ... and flattering.'[8]

Chapuys's loyalty to his master increased his spite against Anne; with her marriage and the birth of Elizabeth, his reports became less reliable; he was further chagrined when he realized that she and Henry had simply had another 'lovers' quarrel', and that Francis I had publicly maintained the legitimacy of the Princess Elizabeth.[9]

Anne was thereby sufficiently reassured to send her own doctor to Mary when the Princess fell ill; she then took sides with Henry over a family matter, that of her widowed sister's love-match with Sir William Stafford, which was clandestine, neither their father's nor the King's permission being asked. Wiltshire expressed his disapproval by cutting off his daughter's allowance, on the grounds that she had become pregnant before the marriage, and that Sir William, although a gentleman-usher and well connected, had no fortune. Lady Stafford then pleaded for herself and her husband with Cromwell. 'I had rather beg my bread with him', she wrote, 'than be the greatest queen christened,' following up this hit at Anne with one at Henry. '*My* husband', she went on, 'would not forsake *me*.' The King refused to intervene on his ex-mistress's behalf, and the Staffords retired, disgraced, to the country.[10]

As this scandal darkened Anne's reputation, Francis I instructed his new envoy, Admiral Chabot, to emphasize his disapproval by pointedly disregarding her existence. Having been received by Henry, Chabot made no inquiries for the Queen; two days passed without his even mentioning her name. When Henry suggested that he should wait on her, he coldly replied, 'As it pleases Your Highness,' and asked leave to visit the Princess Mary. This request was refused; but the Admiral let it be known that he had made it, and told everyone that his master was arranging an alliance between the Dauphin and the Princess. Henry then told him that Mary was illegitimate, and proposed that Francis's third son, the Duc d'Angoulême, should be betrothed to Elizabeth. Chabot replied noncommittally.[11] On December 1st, 1534, at a Court ball, he was invited to sit on the dais, with Henry and Anne, to watch the dancing.

Turning to Anne, Henry reminded her that she had not yet received Monsieur Palamède Gontier, Treasurer to the French Embassy, and, instead of sending a page to fetch him, left the dais and himself made his way down the room. Anne, watching his progress, suddenly burst into wild laughter. 'What, Madame,' Chabot offendedly inquired, 'do you laugh at me?' She continued to laugh; then she managed to say, 'The King told me that he was going to ask your Secretary—to divert me—but on the way, he met a lady who made him forget the matter.' Chabot made no comment, and gradually Anne regained her composure. News of this incident did not reach Chapuys till the New Year, when he reported it in great glee.[12]

Meanwhile, Chabot told Gontier to find out whether Henry was pursuing the lady he had spoken to at the ball. On February 4th, 1535, Cromwell conducted the Treasurer to Anne's apartments. The King was there, talking to some courtiers a little distance away, when she drew Gontier aside and began, 'The alliance between the Princess Elizabeth and the Duc d'Angoulême must no longer be delayed,' adding, 'The Admiral must apply some remedy and act towards the King so that I may not be ruined—and lost.' As Gontier said nothing, she rushed on, 'I am very near that—and in more grief and trouble than before my marriage.' Glancing about her, she continued, 'I cannot speak as fully as I would, on account of my fears—and the eyes which look at me—my husband's—and the Lords' here.' At this point Henry began to move towards her. She had just time to whisper, 'I cannot write—nor stay longer—nor see you again'—and left the room.[13]

The young woman singled out by Henry at the ball was succeeded by Anne's cousin, Margaret, or Madge, Shelton, Mrs Shelton's daughter. This girl's attraction for him did not last; but the fact that she was one of Anne's ladies-in-waiting increased her mistress's fears. If only she could become pregnant again—but nothing happened. And then, once more, Henry's caprice took another turn.

He was beginning to feel his age. The headaches that had plagued him since his youth became worse; and the first signs of the occluded sinus on his leg, which eventually caused his death through osteomyelitis, made it difficult for him to take the exercise he needed. In fact, his days of gaiety—those jocund days, when he and his courtiers had ridden out to bring in the May, picnicking in the woods of Paddington, those days of masques and jousts and tennis—were coming to an end. Now, physical pain, and anxiety about the succession made him irritable, morose and suspicious. Anne, who had shared so many of his troubles, ceased making jealous scenes. She could still divert him; and she did so, effectually enough. But her life was, as ever, a see-saw, jerked up and down by a moody Titan, whose whims were unpredictable. Sometimes he behaved as if she were purposely failing him; then her hold over him would be renewed. Surrounded by spies and rivals, she struggled on, apparently undefeated, while Cromwell's record of her detractors steadily increased. In Cambridge, an ostler, discussing politics with a groom, was heard to say, 'This business had never been, if the King had not married Anne Boleyn,' and when the other disagreed, 'they fell together by the ears'. And in Oxford, a drunken midwife was called before the magistrates for describing the Queen as 'a whore and a bawd'.[14]

These and many other insults were poured forth by persons who had never seen or spoken to Anne, and knew nothing of her situation. She was the scapegoat, blamed for the new laws resented by those who thought of Henry as misguided and bewitched; his adherence to her during the years of the divorce had given her what would now be called a bad press, one that she could neither escape nor refute. Thrust into a glare of ill fame that continued to intensify and which Henry did nothing to subdue, she was the victim of his love, as of his determination to break the powers that withstood him; and her reputation, even among the historians of today, is that of an unscrupulous, coarse and evil woman. Certainly, she was no angel; nor was she the devil of the English Reformation.

In the spring of 1535, the indefatigable Chapuys, who had been assured by Cromwell that the King really preferred Mary to Elizabeth,[15] still declared that Anne's enmity would cause her stepdaughter's death. He was then distracted by the reappearance of Northumberland in Court circles; he reported the Earl as bitterly hostile to the woman he had once loved, and taking the Duke of Norfolk's side against her.[16]

So Norfolk and Northumberland became allies. The Duke told Northumberland that if the Queen did not soon conceive, Henry would make the Princess Mary his heir. Anne, hearing of this, turned upon her uncle in a fury. 'She heaped more injuries upon him', the Earl told Chapuys, 'than upon a dog.' Norfolk, equally enraged, left the room, muttering, 'Great whore.'[17] But Anne had regained Henry's favour. One of Chapuys's spies heard her tell him, 'You are more bound to me than man can be to woman—for I delivered you from a state of sin—and without me, you would not have reformed the Church, to your great benefit, and that of all the people.'[18] Henry did not object to this kind of comment; he was less pleased when Anne repeated that Katherine and Mary should be punished for their resistance to his orders. She may have hoped for their imprisonment in the Tower; Henry, having once considered this step, had now rejected it; for he still thought that Mary might be persuaded—or threatened—into obedience. He sent for Lady Alice Clere, and asked if the Princess's spirit was subdued. When told that it was not, he said that Katherine must be responsible, and that all intermediaries between Mary and her mother were to be dismissed. A maid was sent away; but the correspondence continued through Chapuys.[19] Mrs Shelton then warned Mary that she would be charged with high treason and executed unless she took the oath acknowledging Elizabeth's succession—or so the Ambassador told his master, blaming, naturally, the Concubine for this new assault. His report came neither from Mary nor from Mrs Shelton, but third-hand, through a servant. He chose to believe it, and set about a scheme for Mary's escape to Spain; for he was sure that if it succeeded, the Emperor would be forced to invade.[20] It did not occur to him that such an attack would result in the English people uniting in their King's defence, and thus enhancing Anne's powers.

As her relations with Henry continued smoothly, Chapuys became more gullible, delightedly reporting anything he heard, no matter how improbable, to her discredit. In March, he was told that she had bribed a local prophet to announce that while Katherine and Mary lived she would never have another child; and the Ambassador solemnly passed on this story to his master.[21] During April and May, his hope that Henry had tired of her was disappointed; for the King's attentions to other ladies ceased; and so it began to dawn on the Ambassador that Henry, although appearing to play the Sultan, had no seraglio in the accepted sense of the word. While the tale of Anne's miscarriages proved his frequentation of her bed, none of the women he singled out conceived; and thus his reputation as a great lover—one that would not have displeased the King himself—is without foundation. He was often irritated with Anne, and much tried, not only by her failure to bear a son, but also by her bursts of temper, and her too constant demands for harsher methods with Katherine and Mary. The days when he had thought of life with her as bringing him 'heart's ease and quietness of mind' were gone for ever.

As her power was maintained, and seemed, during the summer of 1535, to increase, those competing for her favour continued their offerings. Lady Lisle, who was about to give her another dog, and hearing that she did not want one—her Italian greyhound, Urien, was a favourite, but most of all she loved a spaniel, Little Purkoy—[22] suggested the present of a monkey. Henry VII, Margaret Tudor, Katherine of Aragon and, later, Edward VI were all painted carrying these fashionable pets; and Lady Lisle set about obtaining one for the Queen. Just in time, she was told that Anne had a horror of them, and so had to try and think of some other novelty; she does not appear to have succeeded.[23]

In the first week of June, Rochford, returning from an unsuccessful conference in Calais about the alliance between Elizabeth and Angoulême, saw Anne before making his report to the King. It was observed that she sent all her attendants away, and that they remained alone together for a long time.[24] Jane Rochford, who had set spies about her husband, in the hope of finding out how best to revenge herself on him, seems to have been given information of this and similar interviews. As Rochford remained in high favour, she could not use it; so she stored it up, with a view to the future. Her hatred of him now spread to Anne, whom she longed to destroy—as did a woman reported to Cromwell as saying, 'Since this new Queen was made, there was never so much pilling and polling in this realm. A vengeance on her!'[25] Lady Rochford and her unknown ally had less than a year to wait.

A week later, Henry decided that More and Fisher must

acknowledge his Supremacy. Paul III chose this moment to make Fisher, then in his eighties, a Cardinal, thus ensuring his fate. Henry's threat to send the old rebel's head to Rome for the hat[26] was not carried out; but neither would Fisher abandon his principles. His and More's executions, preceded by those of nine Carthusian monks, took place in June and July respectively; and so what are now known as the Catholic martyrdoms began.

Inevitably, these horrors were attributed to Anne's influence. More's son-in-law and biographer, William Roper, describing Henry's long friendship with Sir Thomas, recorded the King as saying to her, 'Thou art the cause of this man's death.'[27] In fact, Roper, who was never at Court, had simply repeated an apocryphal anecdote. More's fate was the result of Henry's rage at his old friend's refusal to support him; his determination that the ex-Chancellor should die overrode all Cranmer's and Cromwell's efforts to save him. More's denial of Anne's and her daughter's rights, as passed by Parliament, could not be forgiven; and it is clear, from Henry's comments at the time, that his decision was untinged by the faintest hesitation or regret. Yet Roper's story has been repeated by several of Anne's biographers.

The suggestion that these, or any other executions, appalled the English people did not arise, even when they considered them unjust, as many did those of Fisher and More. Such events were part of everyday life. Shortly after these two celebrities went to the block, Henry pointed out that they had been mercifully treated, in that he had ordered them to be beheaded, instead of hanged, drawn and quartered, as the Carthusians were. A fortnight after their deaths, he and Anne, then at Windsor, were told that a strolling company had put on a play entitled *The Apocalypse*, in which an actor dressed as the King was shown cutting off the heads of the clergy. Henry, superficially disguised, at once set off to see this performance, joined in the applause, roaring with laughter, and was thus 'discovered', to the delight of the audience. He returned to tell Anne that she should have been there to enjoy it with him.[28]

But such entertainments, however popular, could not compete with the sight of an actual execution, whether by burning, hanging or beheading, partly because the latter was free, while those watching a play were charged a penny entrance fee, at least, for a poor imitation of the reality; to this, they could bring their children, and come away with souvenirs of bloodstained handkerchiefs, charred wood, or, if they bribed the hangman, a bit of rope, after what was known as the 'casting' of a criminal. Etiquette forbade the presence of the sovereign, or of any lady of rank at such exhibitions. It was the duty of Henry's bastard son, Richmond, of his brothers-in-law, Suffolk and Rochford, and of many other distinguished and privileged noblemen, to attend them, and to stand next to the scaffold. No record exists of these persons being disturbed, or in any way inconvenienced, on such occasions; and indeed there is no reason why they should have been; hideous and ghastly spectacles were part of the background of the age, then, and for centuries to come. The administration of the rack was differently organized, taking place in private, perhaps because its use was unofficial.

Paul III viewed the condemnation of Fisher as a personal affront, and began to reconsider issuing Henry's excommunication. This added to the difficulties of Anne's position, which were further increased by Cromwell's tentative plan to make Princess Mary her father's successor. Anne, already suspicious of his friendship with Chapuys, heard of it, and charged him with betraying her. A violent quarrel ensued, during which she so lost control of herself as to exclaim, 'I would wish your head off your shoulders!' Cromwell reported this remark to the Ambassador, calmly adding, 'I trust so much my master that I fancy she cannot do me any harm.'[29] Then, the most alarming rumour she had yet heard reached Anne—that Henry had expressed 'a secret wish' to discard her.[30] And she knew that, had he done so, he would have had his people behind him.

But no one knew what the King's intentions were. He gave nothing away; and his understanding of his subjects' dislike of innovations temporarily halted his altering the ritual of the Mass. In fact, he was planning changes in all services later on, and, with Cromwell's help, to 'reform'—his and the minister's ingenious euphemism—the monastic institutions. These schemes must wait —as Henry waited to decide what he should do with Anne. Meanwhile, the Venetian Ambassador, Capello, describing Henry as 'unpopular, but with rare endowments of mind and body, personal beauty, genius and learning', thought that he was wearied of Anne, 'to satiety'.[31]

On June 15th, knowing that she had now reached the extreme verge of disaster, she gave a banquet, followed by a play and various 'mummeries', for Henry, at which Chapuys was present. Next day, he despairingly reported that 'the King dotes on the Concubine—more than ever'.[32]

A week later, the blow fell. Anne became pregnant again.[33] But there was always the hope, in view of her past miscarriages, that fate might yet overtake her.

July and August came—and autumn, and winter; and her state remained healthy. By the end of the year, Chapuys realized that she had been saved. The child was due in the spring; and it might be a boy.

NOTES

1. Froude, *Divorce*, p. 291.
2. Pollard, *Henry VIII*, p. 258.
3. Ibid., p. 268.
4. *L. & P.*, Vol. VII, pt. 2, p. 485.
5. Ibid., p. 495.
6. Ibid.
7. Ibid.
8. Froude, op. cit., p. 112.
9. *L. & P.*, Vol. VII, pt. 2, p. 578.
10. Ibid., Vol. IV, Preface, p. ccxxv.
11. Friedmann, *Anne Boleyn*, Vol. II, p. 43.
12. *L. & P.*, Vol. VIII, p. 15.
13. Ibid., p. 58.
14. Elton, *Policy and Police*, p. 278.
15. *Span. Cal. P.*, Vol. V, p. 295.
16. Ibid., p. 355.
17. Ibid.
18. *L. & P.*, Vol. VIII, p. 251.
19. Prescott, *Mary Tudor*, p. 54.
20. Ibid.
21. *Span. Cal. P.*, Vol. V, p. 433.
22. *L. & P.*, Vol. XI, p. 335.
23. Ibid., Vol. VIII, p. 425.
24. Ibid., p. 112.
25. Ibid., p. 321.
26. Ibid., p. 345.
27. Strickland, *Queens of England*, Vol. II, p. 237.
28. Bowle, *Henry VIII*, p. 373.
29. *Span. Cal. P.*, Vol. V, pt. 1, p. 484.
30. Friedmann, op. cit., Vol. II, p. 138.
31. *Ven. Cal. P.*, Vol. V, p. 26.
32. *L. & P.*, Vol. VIII, p. 345.
33. Ibid., p. 361.

VI

Wolf Hall

'AMONG others who entered England with William the Conqueror, or soon after,' writes an eighteenth-century genealogist, 'were those of the name of Seymour ... [which] name was anciently written St Maur.'[1]

In the fourteenth century the descendant of this Norman knight was established at Wolf Hall in Wiltshire, and had become Ranger of Savernake Forest. His guardianship was symbolized by a vast, ivory hunter's horn, bound with silver, and still in the possession, as is the post of Ranger, of his successors. This gentleman's descendant, Sir John Seymour, inherited the title in the reign of Henry VII, and had six sons and four daughters; two of his children — Edward and Jane — acquired fame and distinction under Henry VIII.

Edward, the heir, who had fought in France with the Duke of Suffolk, became Squire of the Body to Henry in 1524; his father entertained the King in the summer of 1535; and so it was that Henry renewed his acquaintance with Jane, Sir John's eldest daughter, who had been one of Queen Katherine's ladies and was now in her twenty-sixth year. No marriage had been arranged for her, partly because her portion was not large; and her looks were insignificant. Diminutive, pale and shy, she had long been ruled by Edward, a handsome, ambitious and accomplished courtier. On his first visit Henry is said to have been attracted by this rather colourless young lady.

When he came to hunt from Wolf Hall in the following September and October, Anne, who did not accompany him, was pregnant for the fourth time, and had every hope of bearing the child that Henry believed would be a boy. She herself dared not count on this solution, and could only repeat that her 'greatest wish' was for a son.[2] Henry took pains to please and distract her — he gave her the Carthusian monastery of Sion as a country palace —[3] and they were happy together. His attentions enabled her to withstand, if not to ignore, the abuse heaped on her in France and Spain and by her own people.

Cromwell, now Viceregent and Vicar-General, recorded and assessed some of the national criticisms. The indiscreet jokes of Henry's jester, Will Somers, about the Princess Elizabeth's legitimacy, so enraged his master that he threatened to send him to the Tower on a capital charge. He was removed from Court, remaining in retirement for a year; by the time he returned, Anne was dead, Elizabeth had been declared illegitimate, and he and the King grew old together.[4] Every now and then, fear of the law produced a hasty assertion of loyalty. 'I pray every Sunday for the King, the Queen and the Princess Elizabeth, and I am willing to declare the usurped power of the Bishop of Rome,' wrote a repentant preacher.[5] Reports from overseas show the extent of Cromwell's power. One of his agents, hearing a priest at Antwerp compare Henry and Anne to Herod and Herodias, frightened the man into telling the congregation, 'I am sorry that I ever spoke such words of so noble a prince,' and into taking off his cap whenever he uttered Henry's name.[6]

But nothing could silence the thunders from the Vatican. 'The blood of the martyrs', Ortiz exclaimed, 'calls to God for justice. La Ana', he hopefully informed the Empress, 'is said to be very ugly. The English people are frightened, Francis I has deserted the King, leaving him hanged, [i.e. excommunicated] and the Concubine, that kitchen-wench, is unwillingly called Queen.'[7]

Cromwell agreed with Chapuys that Henry and Anne were afraid of those supporting Paul III, and that a rebellion might result; his intention was to soothe and please the Ambassador, who told his master that the King and Queen had been so 'astounded' by the news of his victories over the Turks that they were 'like dogs falling out of a window'.[8] Cromwell was secretly planning to change the English alliance with Francis for one with the Emperor; he knew that Charles was not in a position to invade, and that he could provide a steadier and richer interchange of trade, which would remove all danger, temporarily at least, of civil war. His greatest problem was the bad harvest of August 1535, for which Henry was blamed. 'It is all along of the King that this weather is so troublous and unstable,' said a Worcestershire labourer, 'and I ween we shall never have better weather whilst this King reigneth, and therefore it maketh no matter if he were knocked and patted on the head.'[9]

Such comments seem to support the Venetian Ambassador's

belief in Henry's unpopularity. In fact, the King was loved, detested, admired and feared; those who had never seen or spoken to him were ready to rebel, or thought they were; when he appeared, however briefly, his effect was unfailing—and he took care to maintain it by going on progress at regular intervals. His magnificence, his train of splendidly attired nobles, his recklessness (so coolly calculated), his defiance of the Curia and his dealings with two great empires, his jovial yet awe-inspiring response to the tributes and greetings of his subjects, were seen as those of a conqueror. He had become a tyrant and a despot; but such a king, alarming, then suddenly kind, appeared irresistible; that he might be, and often was, merciless, had long been as much a part of his legend as were his flights into stern yet fatherly oratory. Above all, while nailing his colours, startling though they were, to the mast, he could be trusted to avoid shipwreck, whatever the hazards, whether of invasion or excommunication.

Francis I, already afflicted with the syphilis which killed him twelve years later, told Norfolk that Anne 'had not always lived virtuously', and encouraged the Duke's plan of marrying his eldest son, the poet Surrey, to the Princess Mary, thus enabling him to claim the throne.[10] Francis then sent de Dinteville to ask Henry for a subsidy, in the event of war between himself and the Emperor. This was an attempt at blackmail, reinforced by the Pope's having forbidden all Christian princes to associate with Henry, and desiring them to combine against him. The King refused to grant the subsidy; and when de Dinteville spoke of the marriage long agreed on between Mary and the Dauphin and asked to see her, forbade him to do so. The Ambassador ignored the prohibition; but when he arrived at Eltham, Mrs Shelton told him that the Lady Mary had been locked in her room, and that he must wait on the Princess Elizabeth, then just eighteen months old.[11] De Dinteville, angry but helpless, later heard that Mary continued to speak of the Dauphin as her husband; when Mrs Shelton told her that he was betrothed to a Spanish princess, she replied that no one could have two wives, and that hers was the prior claim.[12]

The situation created by Mary's and Katherine's efforts to regain their former positions as Princess of Wales and Queen of England respectively, was very serious; the so-called cruelty of Henry's treatment of his ex-wife and their daughter was that of a ruler trying to prevent a civil war, while allowing those at its focus important advantages. For both Mary and Katherine were living in comfortable circumstances — Mary as a princess, and Katherine in a manor-house, served by some twenty attendants, including her favourite ladies — and were able, without very great difficulty, to correspond with Henry's enemies at home and abroad, whom they advised and supported. Katherine, while continuing to protest her love for the King, was now urging his excommunication and a Spanish invasion; in other words, she threatened him with eternal punishment in the next world, and a revolution, which might cause his death, in this one — an odd kind of affection, which he could not be expected to appreciate. The solution was, of course, the imprisonment of both women, which he had so far refused to contemplate, in spite of Anne's begging him to do so; for as long as Katherine and Mary remained under the present mild restraint, both she and her child — and Henry — were in danger.

Some time ago, Henry had ordered Mrs Shelton to tell Mary that she was his worst enemy, and that, through her, he was at odds with most of the princes of Christendom.[13] When he realized that the Princess — who continued to assure him of her obedience in all but 'matters of conscience' — was still corresponding with his adversaries, he summoned his Council, and announced that sterner measures — i.e. imprisonment — must be taken with Katherine and Mary. The Marchioness of Exeter, an ingenious and active conspirator, hearing of this meeting, told Chapuys that the King had expressed his intention of 'getting rid' of both mother and daughter: that several Councillors had burst into tears, and that Henry had said, 'This is not a matter to cry, or to make wry faces, for if I were to lose my crown for it, I would persevere in my purpose.'[14]

From this second-hand report, Chapuys saw, or thought he did, a way to victory. He did not care what happened to Mary and Katherine themselves; what he hoped for was their deaths, or, as he would have put it, their martyrdoms, which he believed would bring about the end of the Tudor dynasty through revolution; then Spain would invade, and colonize England. Fortunately for the Ambassador's hosts, among whom he had many friends, including Cromwell and the King himself, the Emperor did not subscribe either to his prophecies or his schemes. When Chapuys told him that Henry had threatened to execute Mary and Katherine, Charles V, a sensible and practical man, replied, "The threats you speak of can only be designed to frighten them ... but if they are really in danger ... you may tell them from me that they must yield.'[15]

Meanwhile, Paul III was preparing the ground for the issue of Henry's excommunication. Without the support of Spain and France, it would have little or no effect, and he had not yet received this; so he sent his son, Pier Luigi, to ask Charles for his co-operation; the young man was to assure the Emperor that Francis I had already promised his backing. But Charles insisted on a written assurance from the slippery Roi-Chevalier, which was not forthcoming. Nevertheless, a rupture between France and England seemed imminent, until Charles announced that he could not treat with Henry as long as he remained in his 'abominable position' with regard to the divorce.[16] Francis I then warned Henry that the Emperor was preparing to invade, and had promised to restore Katherine. Chapuys assured Cromwell that this was not so, and that his master had refused to subscribe to Paul III's proposal of excommunication.[17]

Throughout October Henry and Anne were on progress, 'merry, in good health and hawking daily,[18] and the reports, circulated by Chapuys, that the King was about to arraign his ex-wife for high treason, were denied.[19] While he and Anne were amusing themselves (there was some fear for her condition in the second week of this month, which was remedied by prescriptions from a 'book of physic' from one of Cromwell's agents),[20] that minister had begun his assessment of monastic and ecclesiastical property with his compilation of the *Valor Ecclesiasticus*, aimed at the dissolution of the monasteries.

The annual income from the 563 religious houses came to £800,000. Within the next four years, all were dissolved, and their inhabitants—7,000 monks and 2,000 nuns—pensioned off and absolved of their vows. The men, many of whom accepted dean-eries, or became parish priests, settled down more easily than the women. Their respective establishments were, on the whole, neither dens of iniquity nor temples of holiness; economically and nationally, they had outlived their justification, and except in Lincolnshire and the northern counties, were not regretted. Anne was blamed for the first dissolutions, although she had no direct share in the profits accruing to the state, and no interest in the reports made by Cromwell's famous Visitors, all of whom were brutal and corrupt. Their glee in the exposure and destruction of

relics that had brought comfort to generations of simple people —
St Elizabeth's girdle, Our Lady's milk, Christ's blood and His tears
(in separate flasks), the remains of the Last Supper — was ill concealed by a highly dramatized horror of such pandering to superstition; these agents revelled in their discoveries of sodomy, fornication, drunkenness, embezzlement and bastard children. Such
details did not interest the Vicar-General so much as the wealth
collected (and greatly needed by the exchequer), any more than
the irreparable loss of the monastic libraries. He paused in this
enormous task to order the removal of Sir Thomas More's and
the Carthusians' heads from London Bridge — they had turned
black — [21] and to give one of Chapuys's secretaries leave to visit
Katherine, now dying of cancer, at Kimbolton.

In November 1535 Henry and Anne returned from Winchester
to London to find her attendants in great distress. Her favourite
dog, Little Purkoy, was dead, as the result of a fall, and none of
them dared tell her of this disaster. Finally, they decided to approach
the King; he broke the news, and Little Purkoy was replaced.[22]

In December a more cheering report came from the Vatican. At
a Consistory, Paul III, declaring his intention of proscribing and
excommunicating Henry, had not been supported by the Cardinals,
and he was forced to fall back on yet another warning; this made
him very angry, especially with Francis I. Cardinal du Bellay, who
was present at the debate, informed his master that 'It is long since
there was a Pope less loved by the College, the Romans, and all the
world.'[23] So it seemed that Henry and Anne could embark on the
Christmas revels with light hearts, for she was still in excellent
health. She had already accepted Jane Seymour's appointment as
her lady-in-waiting.

In the Queen's intimate circle — one of gallant young men and
sophisticated married women, whose chief interests were those of
music and dancing — this quiet girl became a background figure,
demure, silent, inconspicuous. Their free and easy manners, their
gifts and graces, were not shared by her; and their allusive
language and private jokes may have been beyond her understanding. Of these, one, apparently originated by Anne, survives, that
of a French phrase for bewilderment, or, as would be said now, for
being all at sea. This — 'dans la forêt de Fontainebleau' — had been
transposed to 'in the forest of Windsor', and was used to describe
a credulous person circulating false news.[24] Outsiders took it literally.

Among the younger men in this set, a great favourite of Henry's, now one of his Gentlemen of the Bedchamber, was Sir Henry Norris; Sir Francis Weston, a married man, was the richest, and Sir William Brereton the best looking; all these gave place to George Rochford, Anne's only confidant. Lady Worcester, who, with Lady Oxford, had held the napkin before the Queen's face at the coronation banquet, was still in her service, and in touch with Jane Rochford and Anne's aunt, Lady William Howard; all three were secretly supporting the Princess Mary through Sir William Fitzwilliam, Treasurer to the Household. A lesser, but much-favoured and highly skilled attendant, was a lutanist, Mark Smeaton. He, Weston and Norris professed, and may even have felt, something more ardent than the then modish and permissible *amour courtois* for Anne, who enjoyed and sometimes provoked their declarations. In fact, 'Pastime in the Queen's Chamber', as Cavendish had once called it, was that of a group who played at flirtation, and chose to see themselves as stricken with unrequited yearnings expressed in music and verse. In these exchanges, neither Lady Worcester nor Jane Seymour took part; for the Countess was middle-aged and pregnant, and little Mistress Seymour ill at ease with bold young men; later on, she acquired a certain technique in slyly alternating the repulse and encouragement of improprieties.

The general atmosphere of this inner circle bore a synthetic resemblance to that centring on Francis I and his celebrated sister; its conscious and rather amateurish daring amused Henry, whose own accomplishments were therein eagerly sought and graciously displayed. Meanwhile, Anne, now reaching a matronly stage, increased her financial support of the needlework guild, made Bishop Latimer, formerly imprisoned on a charge of heresy, one of her chaplains, and at about this time became the patroness of Coverdale, whose translation of the Bible had been licensed by Parliament. (Her copy, inscribed 'Anna Regina Angliae', is in the British Museum.) During this Christmas week, she was occupied with the replenishment of Princess Elizabeth's wardrobe; for in her third year, the child had to be dressed as became her rank in the garments of a grown person. Kirtles of white damask, various pairs of sleeves trimmed with fur, a set of coifs, black satin mufflers for out of doors, and velvet shoes, were ordered; her bed was hung with red damask at five shillings and eightpence a yard.[25]

These arrangements involved frequent visits to Eltham, where both Princesses were now established; and after one of them Anne went to Mass in the oratory. At the end of the service she was told that the Lady Mary had curtsied to her as she went out. 'If we had seen it,' said the Queen, 'we had done as much for her,' and desired one of her ladies-in-waiting to make her stepdaughter an offer of friendship. This approach was of course disingenuous; it was the result, either of orders from Henry, or of Anne's intention to show him that she herself was not to blame for Mary's hostility. Her messenger, having caught up with the Princess, began, 'The Queen salutes Your Grace with much affection, understanding that at your parting from the oratory you made a courtesy to her, which, if she had seen, she would have answered you with the like,' adding that her mistress desired Mary's good-will. The Princess replied, 'It is not possible that the Queen can send me such a message, Her Majesty being so far from this place. You should have said', she continued, 'the Lady Anne Boleyn—for I can acknowledge no other Queen but my mother.' She then pointed out that her reverence had been made to the altar—'to her Maker, and mine; and so they are deceived who can tell her otherwise.'[26]

Anne, enraged, left the palace—only to realize, during the week after Christmas, that her efforts to achieve a relationship with this insolent young woman must be renewed at the risk of yet another rebuff; for although the King was still very angry with his elder daughter, he seems to have hoped to make peace with her—through Anne—on condition that she acknowledged his Supremacy and her half-sister's rights. The occasion for Anne's next approach arose with the news of Katherine's death, which arrived on the afternoon of January 9th, 1536.

Henry cried a little when he read her letter of farewell;[27] he made no attempt to conceal his relief. 'God be praised,' he said to Chapuys, 'we are free from all suspicion of war,' and he put on white mourning for that day, and commanded a banquet and ball in the evening. He and Anne both appeared dressed in yellow—Henry transported with joy, according to the Ambassador, with a white feather in his cap. After supper, he sent for the Princess Elizabeth. She was brought in to the sound of trumpets, and taken up by her father, who carried her round the hall, showing her off to his courtiers.[28] The little girl rose to this, as to other such occasions, with delight. At two years old, says a contemporary, she 'walked and talked like a child of four'.[29]

Henry's choice of colour was not openly criticized; Anne replied to the censure made on hers by pointing out that yellow was Spanish mourning. Such retorts did her nothing but harm, although they may have amused the King. But now, in the seventh month of her pregnancy, she believed—rightly, as it happened—that she was carrying a male child; and this made her next advance to Mary more sincerely gracious: for she was once again in a strong position. 'She hath as fair a belly', reported Sir William Kingston, 'as I have seen.'[30] 'If you will obey your father,' she wrote, 'we will be like another mother to you ... and if you will come to Court, you need not carry my train' (it was customary for junior royalties to do this), adding that Mary's precedence would immediately follow her own, and come before that of the Princess Elizabeth. Mary showed the letter to Mrs Shelton, who begged her to accept the offer. The Princess refused; Mrs Shelton, bursting into tears, renewed her persuasions, to which Mary replied that such an action would be 'against my honour and conscience', the Pope having denied Anne's rights as Queen-Consort. This alarmed Chapuys, who had been told by Cromwell that Katherine's death would enable Henry to make an alliance with the Emperor, and he bribed Mrs Shelton to persist;[31] but Mary remained adamant, thus further infuriating Henry, who gave orders that Katherine should be buried as Princess-Dowager with the minimum of ceremony.

Anne then resolved to abandon all attempts at friendship with her stepdaughter. She instructed Mrs Shelton 'not to move the Lady Mary towards the King's Grace more than as it pleases herself'. Neither she nor Henry, she went on, 'care what road she takes ... for if I have a son, as I hope shortly, I know what will happen to her, and therefore, considering the word of God to do good to one's enemy, I wished to warn her beforehand [i.e. of severer treatment] ... She ought clearly to acknowledge her error ... She will see nothing', Anne concluded, 'but what pleases herself.'[32]

Mary ignored this warning. She sent Anne's letter to Chapuys, who forwarded it to Charles V on January 29th. On the same day, that of Katherine's funeral in Peterborough Cathedral, the first stage of Anne's destruction, long ordained, some said, by a jealous God, was dramatically effected.

Henry celebrated Katherine's interment by a joust, during which he ran many courses. Then he was thrown; and his horrified courtiers saw him lying where he had fallen. He was raised, and his armour removed; he remained unconscious for two hours. As soon as he came round, he desired Norfolk to tell Anne what had happened, and that all was well.[33]

The news of Katherine's death had been brought to Anne when she was washing her hands; and she had expressed her thankfulness by giving the messenger the gold basin and ewer.[34] Now, three weeks later, she realized that her situation had changed for the worse; for in the eyes of Europe and of many of his own people, Henry was a widower—and unless she gave him an heir, he might discard her for what would be generally looked on as a second marriage. And if, in one of the jousts in which he still persisted and which his infected leg made increasingly dangerous, he was killed before the birth of her child, both she and Elizabeth would be set aside, and Mary accepted as Queen. So it was that when Norfolk abruptly announced that the King had been thrown and temporarily incapacitated, she gave way to hysteria.

She then fell into labour; and, after long and terrible suffering, gave birth to the baby who, living, would have saved her. It was a boy: and it was dead.

NOTES

1. Collins, *Peerage of England*, Vol. I, p. 139.
2. *L. & P.*, Vol. IX, p. 127.
3. Ibid., p. 99.
4. Baldwin Smith, *Henry VIII*, p. 90.
5. *L. & P.*, Vol. IX, p. 29.
6. Ibid., p. 110.
7. Ibid., pp. 84–96.
8. Ibid., p. 120.
9. Ibid., p. 74.
10. Ibid., p. 390.
11. Ibid., p. 123.
12. Ibid., p. 125.
13. Friedmann, *Anne Boleyn*, Vol. II, p. 142.
14. Ibid., p. 148.
15. Froude, *Divorce*, p. 366.
16. *L. & P.*, Vol. IX, p. 225.
17. Ibid., p. 187.
18. Ibid., p. 173.
19. Ibid., p. 187.
20. Ibid., p. 243.
21. Wriothesley, *A Chronicle of England*, Vol. I, p. 27.
22. *L. & P.*, Vol. IX, p. 335.
23. Froude, op. cit., p. 370.
24. Cavendish, *Life* (Singer's edition), *Addenda*, pp. 451–61.
25. Loke, *Materials*, p. 22.
26. Clifford, *The Life of Jane Dormer*, p. 81.
27. Ibid., p. 77.
28. *L. & P.*, Vol. X, p. 47.
29. *Spanish Chronicle*, p. 42.
30. Bowle, *Henry VIII*, p. 179.
31. *L. & P.*, Vol. X, p. 47.
32. Ibid., p. 69.
33. Ibid., p. 102.
34. Strickland, *Queens of England*, Vol. II, p. 151.

VII

Jane Seymour

HENRY VIII's entertainment value may be partially accounted
for by his marrying six times; and present-day interest in his story
has been further enhanced by the contrasts his wives provided.
Whether they were chosen for him, as in the case of Katherine of
Aragon and Anne of Cleves, or whether he selected them himself,
as he did the other four, no faintest resemblance can be traced
between any of these women.

The appearance and character of Jane Seymour so differed from
that of Anne Boleyn as to give the impression that Henry was
drawn to her simply because she gave him everything her predecessor had never possessed. Her humility, shyness and acquies-
cence entranced him, in spite of the fact that she was quite plain
and rather dull. The motto she adopted as Queen – 'Bound to
Obey and Serve' – while emphasizing her attitude towards him,
does not describe her temperament or her impact on his associates.
She was by no means as subservient as she chose to appear; and
her influence was that of the cool-headed observer, who stands
away from the position she intends to occupy as soon as she can do
so without having to struggle for it. It seemed to those who came
to know her during the first period of Henry's courtship that her
modest reserve and maidenly respectability were inspired by
Edward Seymour's advice, and that he was using her to advance
his own interests. Certainly he achieved his power through her;
but Jane was neither characterless nor negligible; in the final
months of her life she so influenced the King as to surprise and
disconcert his courtiers. And when her hold over him was established through Anne's last and fatal miscarriage, her attitude, perfectly calculated and exquisitely sustained, was that of the gentle
yet unobtrusive ministrant to a disappointed, anxious, angry
sovereign, to whom she owed obedience in everything but the loss
of her 'honour' – a word very effectively produced at this point in
their relationship.

As lady-in-waiting, Jane Seymour did not attend her mistress's confinement; that was the business of the midwives and bed-chamber women, several of whom were paid by Chapuys to report Anne's conversation, both with them and with Henry. But as Jane was privy, if only at second-hand, to any significant comments, whether made by Anne or the King, she must have realized, in the hours immediately following the miscarriage, that Anne was not yet defeated, and that she herself must now face a time of suspense, withdrawal and circumspection.

Some days went by before Chapuys was able to send a full report of what passed between Henry and Anne when the King came to visit her after the disaster. One of his spies was in attendance as Henry walked up to her bed. He said, 'I see clearly that God does not wish to give me male children.' Anne protested that Norfolk's abrupt announcement of his fall was responsible for the hysteria which had caused her miscarriage; she added that she loved him more than Katherine ever had. 'My heart was broken when I saw that you loved others,' she began. Henry interrupted with 'You shall have no more boys by me. I will speak to you again when you have recovered' — and left the bedchamber. A few hours later, she was told that he had left Greenwich for Westminster.[1]

He was further enraged by Anne's reference to his pursuit of other women; in his mind, such fault-finding amounted to *lèse majesté*; so Chapuys reported to the Emperor, adding that on the day of his return to Westminster Henry said to one of his courtiers that he had been forced into marriage with Anne through her 'sorceries', and that as God had once more showed His displeasure by denying him an heir, he was entitled to take a third wife. 'This', Chapuys exclaimed, 'is almost incredible!' noting that Anne was in great fear.[2]

Whatever her terror, she concealed it by telling her attendants to stop crying and condoling. 'It is for the best,' she said. 'I shall soon be with child again, and the son I bear will not be doubtful like this one, which was conceived during the life of the Princess-Dowager.' Chapuys considered that in this way she came near to acknowledging the illegitimacy of her own daughter; and he told his master that when Anne recovered she kept a watch on Jane Seymour, whom she dared not dismiss; if she had, Henry would either have reinstated her, or have followed her to the country.[3]

While continuing to court Jane, Henry's anger with Anne diminished. When she discovered that he had given Jane a locket, she tore it from her rival's neck, so violently that she wounded her hand;[4] this scene, followed by what an observer described as the 'bye-blows and scratchings' Anne inflicted on Jane,[5] changed Henry's mood. He said to Anne, 'Be at peace, sweetheart, and all shall go well for thee.'[6] But his attitude towards her did not change his intentions.

Meanwhile, Cromwell told Chapuys that in the event of a divorce His Grace would be kinder to the Princess Mary. 'I hope it may be so,' the Ambassador told Charles V, 'and that no scorpion lurks under the honey.'[7] He then decided to support Jane Seymour, who was much courted by Henry's circle, and praised for her 'even and constant temper', the 'pleasing sprightliness' of her manners and her taste in dress. 'The richer she was in clothes,' one observer recalled, 'the fairer she looked; the Other, the richer she was apparelled, the worse she looked.'[8]

In the last week of March 1536 Henry followed up his gift of a locket with the more compromising present of a purse filled with gold pieces; when his gentleman brought it to Jane, with a note from the King, she knelt, kissed the letter and returned it unopened, with the purse. Then she said, 'There is nothing I value so much as my honour. If the King's Grace wisheth to send me a present of money, I humbly ask him to reserve it for such a time as God will be pleased to send me an advantageous marriage.'[9] This practical suggestion delighted Henry. 'I praise her virtuous behaviour,' he said, and desired Cromwell to vacate his suite of rooms at Westminster for the Seymours.[10] Thus chaperoned, Jane received the King with complacent propriety, while Anne remained at Greenwich. Edward was made Gentleman of the Bedchamber, and, watching over his sister, advised her to hint at the Queen's tendency towards Lutheranism.[11] Still Henry made no definite move about a divorce; on certain occasions he and Anne appeared together as usual, and the rumours of her being discarded died away. This encouraged Lady Lisle to obtain her favour by the present of a cloth of gold kirtle.[12]

Between the end of March and the beginning of April, Henry's conscience, that delicate instrument, began to trouble him again, although hesitatingly. It did not, as in the last period of his marriage to Katherine, work quite so smoothly, and rather resembled an ancient clock, gathering itself to strike with creaks and jerks, as if its strength were failing. That Anne's hour would be struck seemed doubtful to all but Cromwell, who suggested that Henry's confessor, Bishop Longland of Lincoln, should be consulted about a divorce.[13] But the King did nothing, and no one could be certain what he meant to do.

By April 1st Chapuys was getting impatient. He asked Cromwell point-blank, 'Is His Majesty about a new marriage?' as they stood apart in the embrasure of a window, hastily adding, 'I admit that the Queen hath never harmed me.' Cromwell replied that he had 'smoothed the way' towards Henry's marriage with Anne. Then he said, in what Chapuys described as a cold, detached tone, 'I believe that His Majesty will now live honourably and chastely, notwithstanding he is still inclined to pay attention to—other ladies.' Pausing on this reference to Mistress Seymour, he leant against the window, his hand over his mouth, as if to conceal a smile.[14]

Chapuys took the hint. He was greatly relieved—for he had been afraid that Henry contemplated marrying a French Princess—and so could assure his master that such an alliance was not in question, adding that Edward Seymour and his wife were now both chaperoning Jane, and urging her to 'hold out' for marriage.[15] He later described her as the sister of a 'certain Edward Semel', and the daughter of 'Sir John Seamer. She is of middle height,' he went on, 'and nobody thinks that she has much beauty. Her complexion is whitish.' He then threw doubts on Jane's virtue. 'But if she were still a virgin,' he added, 'this King will be rather pleased, for he may marry on [that] condition ... The said Semel is not very intelligent, and is said to be rather haughty ... She seems to bear great goodwill and respect to the Princess [Mary].' Hearing that Henry still refused to receive Mary, the Ambassador wrote advising her to submit to him.[16]

By this time, Henry's attachment to Jane Seymour had become common talk, and ballads were being circulated about her and the King, with the result that she, her brother and his wife withdrew to the country. Henry wrote to reassure Jane in a respectfully chivalrous strain, addressing her as 'My dear Friend and Mistress', referring to himself as her 'entirely devoted servant' and promising to send her 'the things ye lacked' as soon as they could be obtained. This letter, which was accompanied by 'a token of my true affection' and mentions Jane's 'sincere love' for the writer, seems to indicate that their marriage was in sight. Its tone is in marked contrast to the agitated and passionate missives sent to Anne seven years earlier.[17]

When the news of her miscarriage and of Henry's advances to Jane Seymour reached the Continent, Francis I began to consider abandoning the English alliance, and recalled Anne's chief supporter, du Bellay, from Rome: while Charles V assumed that Henry, having divorced her, would be reconciled both to himself and to the Holy See. On April 18th Chapuys was told that the King would receive him at Greenwich in order to open negotiations. He was first greeted by George Rochford, and then by Cromwell, who asked him to wait on Anne, 'to do pleasure to the King. Nevertheless,' he added significantly, 'I will leave it to you.'

Chapuys did not need to be further enlightened. He replied, 'For a long time my will has been that of the King, and to serve him it is enough to command me. But I think, for several reasons, which I will tell His Majesty another time, that such a visit would not be advisable — and I beg you to excuse me.'[18]

The Ambassador was then attended to Mass by George Rochford. He took up his position behind the door, so that, when Anne entered, he would not be obliged to salute her. As the whole Court waited to see how she would deal with this rebuff, she came in, paused — and turned round to face Chapuys. He was forced to make a low bow; she curtsied and, with Henry, moved to her place.[19]

After the service the King, as was his custom, joined Anne for dinner, together with a number of foreign envoys. Perceiving that the most important of these was not among them, she asked, 'Why does not Monsieur Chapuys enter, as do the other Ambassadors?' Henry's reply made her situation ominously clear. 'It is not', he said, 'without good reason.' So Anne faced the fact that she had lost her status as an international figure.

Without a change of countenance, she began to criticize the policy of Francis I, thus indicating that she was ready to transfer her allegiance. But as Henry did not pursue the subject, she was further — and publicly — relegated.[20] Although she may have guessed that his next step would be towards a divorce, she remained as undaunted as when she had told her attendants that her miscarriage would shortly be remedied. She did not realize that a greater, an almost superhuman courage would be required of her within the next ten days.

Chapuys now made a point of flattering Edward Seymour, who seemed to be replacing Cromwell as Henry's adviser. This so enraged the Vicar-General that he was unable to conceal his chagrin when he and Chancellor Audley disagreed in the King's presence. Chapuys and Seymour, watching all three, could not hear what was said; but they saw Cromwell turn away, walk the length of the room and, red and sweating, sit on a coffer, calling for drink.[21] Next day Henry, discussing the imperial alliance with Chapuys, also lost his temper. He was not a child, he said, to be cajoled one minute and ordered about the next; if the Emperor made the first advance, then he would consider his proposals.[22] Cromwell, who had been working for this agreement, spoke of his disappointment to Chapuys, who told him that even if the Queen did produce an heir, his master would not acknowledge the legitimacy of any of her children.[23]

Still appearances had to be maintained. On April 23rd Chapuys was required to offer Anne a candle during the celebration of Mass. He did so, reporting the gesture to his master as the last he need make to that 'she-devil', and adding that the King was 'sick and tired' of her; also that Henry had refused to give Rochford the Garter—another public slight.[24]

After some consideration, it became clear to Cromwell (so he later told Chapuys) that Henry could be freed from Anne, and that he himself must bring their marriage to an end. He began by consulting the Bishop of London about a divorce. That cleric replied, 'I will not give any opinion but to the King himself—and before doing so, I would know His Majesty's inclination. I heartily repent', he added, 'supporting his divorce from the late Queen.'[25] Other advisers considered that the King could obtain a divorce only through reconciliation with the Curia and restoration of the abbey lands; these conditions were of course out of the question. Finally, Cromwell came to the conclusion that, even if she were divorced, Anne, as Marquess of Pembroke, with a great fortune and her brother's support, would become as dangerous an enemy to himself as she had been to Cardinal Wolsey.

He then saw that if he were to maintain his position and serve his master, he must work fast—not for a divorce, which might entail innumerable delays before Henry could marry again, but for the elimination of Anne. He had been ill: yet he set about his plans with characteristic efficiency and speed.

When the King joined Anne at Greenwich, he held his Court apart from her; and there, the hinges of the trap began to close.

NOTES

1. *L. & P.*, Vol. X, p. 134; Heylyn, *History of the Reformation of the Church of England*, p. 15.
2. *Span. Cal. P.*, Vol. V, pt. 2, p. 28.
3. *L. & P.*, Vol. X, p. 134.
4. Heylyn, op. cit., p. 5.
5. Clifford, *Jane Dormer*, p. 41.
6. Wyatt, *Anne Boleyn*, p. 443.
7. *L. & P.*, Vol. X, p. 102.
8. Heylyn, op. cit., p. 15.
9. *Span. Cal. P.*, Vol. V, pt. 2, p. 54.
10. Ibid., p. 85.
11. Ibid.
12. *L. & P.*, Vol. X, p. 201.
13. Ibid., p. 315.
14. Ibid., p. 243.
15. Ibid.
16. Ibid., p. 374.
17. Halliwell, *Letters of the Kings of England*, Vol. I, p. 350.
18. *L. & P.*, Vol. X, p. 390.
19. Ibid.
20. Ibid.
21. Ibid.
22. Ibid.
23. Ibid.
24. Ibid., p. 303.
25. Ibid., p. 315.

VIII

Courtly Love

CROMWELL could not collect the evidence he needed for Anne's destruction until the third week of April 1536, three months after her miscarriage. Not only had the question of divorce to be considered, but also, in this as in other crises, Cromwell faced the fact that Henry VIII would keep his own counsel. Having accused the Queen of witchcraft, he left her alone.

At Greenwich, she held her private Court as usual. Although she was aware of Henry's desire to discard her for Jane Seymour, she seems to have thought of their estrangement as temporary; and she may not have realized that illness and anxiety had affected her looks. She found distraction in the rivalry of Norris and Weston for her preference; and in this mock duel, both young men behaved as aspirants, despairing one moment, over-bold the next. Their advances and Anne's reproofs had become automatic through constant practice. And when these two courtiers perceived that Henry had virtually deserted her, their approaches bordered on insolence.

Sir Henry Norris was betrothed to Anne's cousin, Madge Shelton; but she had begun a flirtation with Weston, whose wife was one of the Queen's attendants. With a view to rousing Mistress Shelton's jealousy, Norris made a great parade of his attentions to Anne, who asked him, 'Why do you not go through with your marriage?' 'I would tarry a time,' he replied. Her comment, one of almost crazy indiscretion, was the result of her own misery, and of her fear of Henry's death in a joust: for she had not recovered from the shock that had caused her miscarriage. 'You look for dead men's shoes,' she burst out, 'for if aught came to the King but good, you would look to have me,' upon which Norris exclaimed, 'I would rather my head were off!'[1]

In her later description of this scene, Anne recalled her anger and fear. 'I could undo you if I would,' she said, implying that she might complain to the King. Norris, equally annoyed and alarmed, replied as violently. Anne then required him to report their quarrel

to her almoner, Skip, and to clear her character, which he did.[2]
When Sir Francis Weston heard of this dispute, he said to her,
'Norris comes more to Madge's chamber for you than for Madge.'
'You love my kinswoman?' Anne asked. Weston replied, 'I love not
my wife,' adding, 'I love one in her household better than both.'
'Who is that?' Anne pursued, and Weston said, 'It is yourself.'[3]

According to her own account, Anne, enraged and frightened,
'defied' Weston, forbidding him such dangerous familiarity; she
did not know that Lady Worcester was presently informed of these
and other conversations with Norris and Weston, and also of those
with Sir William Brereton. Anne was reassured by Skip, who told
her that Norris had said, 'I would swear that the Queen is a good
woman.'[4] So it seemed to her that although these young men had
broken the rules, she had safeguarded herself by putting them in
their places. She and they had of course taken fearful risks; but
this quasi-audacious interchange was part of the process of Courtly
Love as they understood it, and as they had always practised it
before Anne lost the powers which may have been enhanced by
Henry's awareness of her attraction for other men. Himself an
accomplished amateur of gallantry and compliment, Henry had
tolerated, and might even have approved, the tributes called forth
by a Queen who had flouted the conventions so strictly maintained
by her predecessor.

Neither Anne nor any of her friends seems to have realized that
her unpopularity and Henry's pursuit of Jane Seymour had combined to change his courtiers' attitude towards her disregard of the
formalities. A story began to circulate that a Privy Councillor
(unnamed) had rebuked a lady for her 'light behaviour' — to which
she replied that it did not compare with that of the Queen.[5]

Such rumours grew out of the knowledge that Henry no longer
loved Anne and was openly courting a woman who would make a
much more suitable wife; and the general public, having accepted
one divorce, was ready to tolerate another. Only Cromwell rejected
this solution. But he knew better than to inform his master of the
alternative. His plan was to frame a case against the Queen which
would bring upon her a charge, not only of high treason, but of
crimes designed to amaze and horrify all Europe. Having done so,
he intended to present Henry with well attested and irrefutable
evidence against Anne, which would enable the Privy Council to
arrest and condemn her.

At about this time, Anne sent for the Princess Elizabeth. As the King neither visited her nor called for the child, she decided to approach him without asking leave to do so. Carrying the little girl, she waited in the courtyard below his apartments until he appeared at an open window. She then held up their daughter, and, according to a witness of the scene, 'entreated him'. Embarrassed and annoyed, 'though he concealed his anger wonderfully well', the King made some excuse and turned away.[6] It was Anne's last throw; yet even now she did not give up hope: for Henry remained at Greenwich.

On April 30th Anne, who spent the greater part of the day in the park, playing with her dogs, came upon Mark Smeaton standing in the window of her presence-chamber. They were alone: and as he turned towards her, she asked, 'Why are you so sad?' He replied, 'It is no matter.' She then, recollecting the familiarities of Norris and Weston, and fearful of the musician's emulating their approaches (for she seems to have guessed that he was in love with her), decided to warn him. She said, 'You may not look to have me speak to you as I should to a noble person, because you be an inferior person.' Sadly, Mark reassured her. 'No, no, Madam,' he said. 'A look sufficeth me—and thus fare you well.'[7]

Some days earlier, Cromwell had begun to collect and then collate the necessary evidence. He worked unceasingly and in secret through a combination of bribery and threats, beginning with Lady Rochford, Lady Worcester and the latter's maid, Nan Cobham, thence descending to the lowest section of the Queen's entourage. One of the last to be arrested and terrorized was Smeaton. Threatened with torture and promised freedom if he confessed to 'carnal knowledge' of the Queen, he signed the paper prepared by the Vicar-General, and was later imprisoned—as he believed, temporarily—in the Tower.[8] His statement was then added to those of the other informers, whose names are no longer extant; for in Queen Elizabeth's reign all these documents were destroyed.[9]

Cromwell's task was made easier by the laws then obtaining in cases of high treason. The accused had no counsel and was not allowed to question the witnesses produced by the Crown. At the trial, their statements were read out—they themselves might not even have to appear—and the prisoner, who had not seen the evidence, but had already been cross-examined *in camera*, was desired to answer, point by point, in his or her defence. The jury, faced with signed declarations made on oath, had then no choice but to give a verdict of guilty. As in other governments of more recent date, the ethical aspect of this procedure was based on the assumption that the State (in this case the monarch) was incapable of injustice or error; so that, once a charge of high treason had been decided on, no escape was possible, unless the person organizing it was overthrown through a palace revolution before trial and execution took place. The juries were not bribed, but packed, in the sense that they knew that if they dared to question the evidence, their punishment—a crippling fine or a long imprisonment-- would follow that of the accused. (This procedure was slightly modified a few years later; in the reign of Edward VI the defendant was confronted with, and allowed to interrogate, two witnesses.)

As he saw it, Cromwell's duty was to establish the succession by enabling Henry to beget the son Anne Boleyn had failed to provide; and he knew that the King would consider no wife but Jane Seymour. Finally, this arrangement must be effected quickly, and in such a way as to show that Henry was the injured party. All the minister had to do, therefore, was to prove Anne's adultery; this charge was synonymous with high treason. But here, one lover was not enough; she must be presented to the English public, and to the Courts of Europe, as a wanton—a Messalina, as Chapuys put it—[10] whose insatiable lust had long been known by those in her service; so Chapuys's spies and Cromwell's informers were merely earning their salaries when they provided the evidence—subjoined by dates—of her intercourse with Norris, Brereton, Weston and Smeaton. (Her actual contact with Brereton had been negligible; Cromwell seems to have added his name to the list for good measure.) Her other attendants, those not in the Vicar-General's or the Ambassador's employ, were terrorized into subscribing to the charges. It was all quite simple. And Anne's unpopularity made it simpler still.

Cromwell himself gained nothing, in a material sense, in setting up the case against the Queen, although his prestige was there- by much enhanced. And he made it clear, to Henry, to the Privy Council and to the foreign Ambassadors, that he had been appalled and amazed by these discoveries.

He had, however, to protect himself; and on this point, Lady Rochford was his most important witness; for as an injured and neglected wife, she was best able to inform on the relations between Anne and her husband. Rochford must not survive; if he did, he would avenge his sister by attacking Cromwell. Jane Rochford was more than willing, eager indeed, to provide evidence of incest — another capital charge, and one that fitted admirably into the general scheme of blackening Anne's character, and was to prove a double triumph for the prosecution.

Cromwell presented Henry with the evidence of Anne's adultery and incest after consultation with the Privy Council, who were thus ready to carry out the King's orders for the arrest of the four courtiers, her brother and herself. It was said that Henry heard the news of her crimes with horror, but not with surprise; for he later admitted to having had 'doubts and strange suspicions' as long ago as January 1535.[11] Whatever his feelings, he remained at Greenwich for several hours after receiving Cromwell's first report — which was compiled between the 24th and the 30th April — and on May 1st, a Sunday, desired Anne to accompany him to the joust in which Norris and Rochford were to compete. Cheered by this gesture of kindness, she appeared at his side, and for the greater part of the display, which took place in the morning, after the celebration of Mass, they watched it together.

The ambivalence of Henry's attitude exactly reproduced the pattern followed seven years earlier, when, in the palace of Bridewell, he had told his audience that if his marriage to Katherine of Aragon were 'proved good', he desired nothing better than that they should be reunited. Cromwell had informed him that Anne not only hoped for his death, but was planning to bring it about, and so free herself to marry Norris — whom the minister seems to have presented as the chief offender; for he knew that as Henry had always 'greatly favoured' Norris, the news of that gentleman's intimacy with Anne would ensure the King's revenge on them both. And Henry, as a devout and orthodox Christian, was even more enraged and shocked by the thought of her relations with Rochford. The result — that her death would free him to marry Jane Seymour — had nothing to do with the tragedy in which he must appear as, and felt himself to be, the wronged husband, the sad cuckold.

So it was that, halfway through the joust, Henry VIII, unable to endure the proximity of the woman who, he was convinced, had heartlessly betrayed him, gave way to rage and despair. He started up, left the pavilion, and summoned Norris to ride with him to Westminster. (The story of his departure having been caused by the Queen's dropping her handkerchief as a love-token for Norris is a later invention, disproved by Henry's first biographer.[12]) Anne, apparently bewildered rather than alarmed — for surely Henry would not have desired her to attend the joust with him if she were still under his displeasure — returned to the palace.

Henry, who was attended, and presumably overheard by, six gentlemen, accused Norris of fornication with the Queen; that fearless and haughty young man indignantly denied the charge. The King persisted; he said that Norris would be pardoned if he confessed, thus implying that he could save himself by sacrificing Anne. Norris continued his refusals until they reached London, when he was arrested and sent to the Tower. There, his chaplain was allowed to see him, and under the seal of the confessional desired him to tell the truth. Norris said, 'I would rather die a thousand deaths than betray the innocent,' and the chaplain, as instructed, repeated his reply to Sir William Fitzwilliam, one of Cromwell's witnesses. Henry, enraged by the obstinacy and in-gratitude of this privileged courtier, exclaimed, 'Hang him up, then!' and Cromwell arranged with Fitzwilliam that Norris's chaplain should produce a confession of guilt.[13]

Meanwhile, Anne, having dined, went to watch a bull-baiting in the park. In the afternoon orders came from the King that she was to retire to her rooms and remain there. So she began to realize her position; presently she knew herself trapped and helpless. She seems to have been alone, but for a few pages and bedchamber women; for Lady Worcester, Nan Cobham and 'many other wit-nesses', according to Chapuys, were in conference with Cromwell at Westminster.[14] They were joined by Lady Rochford, who des-cribed her husband's meetings with his sister. Having sent all her attendants away, Anne sometimes received him after she had gone to bed. On several occasions he had been seen leaving her room in his night-robe.[15] Lady Rochford added other details, which Cromwell decided to produce at the public trial.

The Vicar-General then spent some hours with Henry, who ordered the arrest of Weston, Rochford and Brereton, and, later, that of Sir Thomas Wyatt, on the grounds that he had been Anne's lover before her marriage. The King's mood changed from fury to lamentation as the hours went by. That evening the Duke of

Richmond, as was his custom, asked to be received in order to say goodnight to his father. He found Henry in floods of tears. Embracing the young man (Richmond was already infected with the tuberculosis of which he died three and a half months later), the King declared that he had been bewitched. Then, the memory of all he had endured—in vain—for the woman he had so passionately loved overcame him. 'You and your sister', he exclaimed, 'are greatly bound to God for having escaped the hands of that accursed whore who had determined to poison you'—and Richmond was dismissed.[16] Meanwhile, the news of the Queen's downfall spread throughout the Court and thence to the city, before Anne herself knew of what she was accused.

On the morning of May 2nd she was told of the arrests. This news was followed by the arrival of the Privy Council. Headed by Norfolk and Cromwell, and attended by their secretaries, they first interviewed her household, who confirmed and added to the statements already made to the Vicar-General. Then the Queen was summoned, and charged with adultery, incest, and intent to murder her husband. No record survives of how she received these assaults; her denials were met with harsh incredulity. 'I was cruelly handled,' she said afterwards, recalling the contemptuous hostility of her uncle Norfolk, who, shaking his head, replied with 'Tut, tut, tut,' to all her answers. The only Councillor who treated her fairly was the Marquess of Winchester, Henry's Lord Treasurer and Controller of the Household. He alone seemed puzzled by the discrepancies in the evidence, and doubtful of its veracity. Anne appears to have comforted herself with the belief that Henry had commanded the examination in order, as she said later, 'to prove me'.[17] She thought then that she would eventually emerge from this hideous ordeal, because it seemed unbelievable that the King could doubt her feeling for him; her misery when he turned to other women was caused, not only by jealousy and wounded pride, but by her dependence on his love. She was bound to him, as so many were with whom he had to do. She now begged to see him; but this was impossible. Those accused of high treason could not be received by the monarch until their innocence had been proved.[18]

She was then told to make ready to leave for the Tower. Four ladies—her aunt by marriage Lady Boleyn, Mrs Cousins, Mrs Shelton and Mrs Stonor, all in Cromwell's pay—were to attend her. When she entered her barge at two o'clock, Norfolk, Cromwell,

Lord Audley, Lord Oxford and Lord Sandys, with an escort of
guards, accompanied her. By this time, the news of her arrest had
spread from the palace to the neighbourhood, and the banks were
lined with staring people. The party disembarked beneath
Traitors' Gate at five o'clock. There, Sir William Kingston was
waiting to receive them.[19]

NOTES

1. *L. & P.*, Vol. X, pp. 340–47;
   Cavendish, *Life* (Singer's edition), *Addenda*, pp. 451–61.
2. Cavendish, loc. cit.
3. Ibid.
4. Ibid.
5. Cavendish, op. cit., p. 428.
6. Jenkins, *Elizabeth the Great*, p. 12.
7. *L. & P.*, Vol. X, pp. 340–47.
8. Ibid.
9. Burnet, *The History of the Reformation of the Church of England*,
   Vol. I, pp. 196–7.
10. *Span. Cal. P.*, Vol. V, pt. 2, p.
    120.
11. Froude, *History*, Vol. I, p. 146.
12. Herbert of Cherbury, *Henry the
    Eighth*, p. 446.
13. *Archaeologia*, Vol. XXIII, pp.
    64–6; Godwin, *Annales of
    England*, p. 81.
14. *Span. Cal. P.*, Vol. V, p. 107.
15. *Spanish Chronicle*, p. 65.
16. *L. & P.*, Vol. X, p. 376.
17. Williams, *All the Queen's Men*,
    p. 51; Cavendish, op. cit.,
    pp. 451–61.
18. Burnet, op. cit., Vol. I, pp. 196–7.
19. Cavendish, loc. cit.

IX

Preparation

THIS was the second time that Anne had been received by Kingston in his official capacity as Lieutenant of the Tower. Three years ago, standing beside Henry VIII at the principal entrance, he had waited to kiss her hand while the King raised and embraced her. Now, posted above the black and dripping jaws of Traitors' Gate, he waited again. Followed by Norfolk, Cromwell and her ladies, she walked up the stairs towards him.

As they faced one another, whatever courage had sustained her during the examination and her three hours' journey suddenly failed. She fell on her knees, crying, 'O Lord, help me – as I am guiltless of this whereof I am accused!' Sir William, accustomed to such collapses, said nothing, and she went on, 'Master Kingston, shall I go into a dungeon?' 'No, Madam,' he replied reassuringly. 'You shall go into your lodging that you lay in at your coronation.' She began to weep, sobbing out, 'It is too good for me – Jesu have mercy on me!' Then, as the grim irony of the situation struck her, she broke into wild laughter. At last she got up, and turning to Norfolk and Cromwell, repeated, 'God help me, as I am not guilty! I desire you to beseech the King to be good to me.'[1]

Once more, there was no answer, and as the ministers withdrew, Kingston escorted her to her rooms. There, he stood ready to hear – and to report to Cromwell – any remarks, significant or otherwise, that she might let fall. Regaining some measure of calm, she asked the King's leave for the Sacrament to be placed, and later administered, in her bedchamber – 'That I may pray for mercy,' she explained, 'for I am as clear from the company of man as I am clear from you – and I am the King's true wedded wife.' The Lieutenant remained silent, and she went on, 'Master Kingston – do you know whereof I am here?' 'Nay,' Kingston replied. 'When saw you the King?' Anne pursued. 'I saw him not since I saw him in the tiltyard,' Kingston said, apparently referring to the joust at Greenwich. Lady Kingston then joined Anne's ladies – she too had been ordered to report the prisoner's conversations – and the

Lieutenant retired. That evening, he set down all that had passed in the first of his letters to Cromwell.[2]

The Vicar-General later collated this report with the Council's private examination of Smeaton, Norris, Weston and Brereton, when they were summoned to answer to the charge of fornication with the Queen. Relying on Cromwell's promise of freedom, Smeaton acknowledged his own guilt and reported that of the three courtiers, who all declared their innocence.

Rochford was then called to reply to the charge of incest. His closest friend, Sir Thomas Wyatt, later recorded the evidence as having been supplied by 'his wicked wife', who desired his death, 'and so accused him'.[3] Rochford's denial having been noted, he was informed that his public trial would take place, with that of the Queen, on May 15th, three days after those of the other prisoners. So he had a fortnight to prepare his answers; he was not shown his wife's letter to the Council.

On the following morning, May 3rd, Cranmer, then at Lambeth, was told what had happened, and determined to plead for the Queen, in whose guilt he could not bring himself to believe. He wrote to condole with Henry, humbly and at length, adding, 'If it be true that is openly reported of the Queen's Grace ... I am in such perplexity that my mind is clean amazed; for I never had better opinion in woman than I had in her; which maketh me to think that she should not be culpable ... Next to Your Grace, I was most bound to her of all creatures living ... I ... wish and pray for her that she may declare herself inculpable and innocent ... I loved her not a little for the love which I judged her to bear towards God and His gospel.' The Archbishop went on to say that if Anne were guilty, she deserved punishment 'without mercy ... to the example of all other'. He then reminded the King of God's grace, adding with uncharacteristic boldness, 'But Your Grace, I am sure, acknowledgeth that you have offended Him,' and concluded with a prayer that Henry might be preserved 'from all evil', i.e. from unjust condemnation of the Queen.[4]

Before Cranmer dispatched this letter—he may have hesitated to do so—he was summoned to the Privy Council, who had been ordered by Henry to show him the evidence of Anne's guilt. Returning to Lambeth, he added a postscript to his defence. 'I am exceedingly sorry', he wrote, 'that such faults can be proved by the Queen, as I heard of their [the Council's] relation.'[5]

That same day, Anne asked Kingston, 'I pray you to tell me where my lord Rochford is.' The Lieutenant replied evasively, 'I saw him before dinner, in the court.' Anne insisted with 'O where is my sweet brother?' 'I left him', said Kingston, 'at York Place' [Whitehall]. 'I hear say', she went on, 'that I shall be accused with three men. I can say no more but nay,' she added, 'without I should open my body' — and here she parted the skirts of her gown. Then she burst out, 'O Norris! Hast thou accused me? Thou art in the Tower with me, and thou and I shall die together — and Mark, thou art here too. O my mother — thou wilt die for sorrow!'

As if to distract her, Lady Kingston intervened with some comment on Lady Worcester's miscarriage, adding, 'What should be the cause?' 'For the sorrow she took for me,' said Anne. Turning to the Lieutenant, she asked, 'Master Kingston — shall I die without justice?' Solemnly, Kingston replied, 'The poorest subject that the King hath, has justice.' The reproof — for how could His Majesty's goodness and mercy be questioned? — destroyed such composure as Anne had achieved. She burst into screams of laughter — peal upon peal — and Kingston withdrew to make his next report to Cromwell.[6]

By this time, a quantity of anecdotes about the Queen and her lovers — collected by an anonymous Spaniard, possibly a merchant, who was not in Court circles — had grown into a saga. Some of his stories resemble the equally baseless reports of royal persons still produced by certain continental and transatlantic journalists. Yet, in this case, a thread of truth may be discerned here and there, as in the report of the locket Henry gave to Jane Seymour; for in the enclosed world of sixteenth-century London his courtiers often gossiped with friends and acquaintances outside his entourage. So it was that this writer placed fictional characters in authentic settings, and interspersed their remarks with the talk of real persons, whose conversations are verifiable.

A favourite theme was that of Mark Smeaton's intimacy with the Queen. He was represented as handsome, talented and such a graceful dancer that Anne paid him a large salary. A mythical go-between, 'old Margaret', was accustomed to summon him to her mistress's bed when Anne called to her, 'Bring me a little marmalade.' (This confection, originally made of quinces, did not reach England from Spain till the reign of Queen Elizabeth.) Anne, it was said, rewarded the musician with presents of plate, rich clothes and a horse. Smeaton had then been arrested, and made to confess through torture; this scene was supposed to have taken place in Cromwell's presence as the Vicar-General finished his supper. The legend of 'old Margaret' presently became entangled with the torture and confession of a non-existent Lady Wingfield, later burnt for her co-operation in Anne's affairs with Weston, Brereton and Norris. Another story described Sir Thomas Wyatt as having warned the King that Anne was 'a bad woman'; it was said that their love scenes had been interrupted by the sound of 'stamping overhead'. This anecdote seems to have arisen from Wyatt's pursuit of Anne before her marriage; his departure on a mission to Spain was now attributed to Henry's jealousy. All these tales but that of Anne's relations with her brother were eagerly accepted. Their incest was rejected on the grounds that Rochford was said to have declared, 'I am blameless, and never knew that my sister was bad,' when interviewed by the Privy Council.[7]

When Anne told Mrs Cousins that Sir Henry Norris had sworn that she was a 'good woman', that lady inquired, not unnaturally, 'Madam, why should there be any such matters spoken of?' — upon which Anne repeated her conversation with Norris about his intention to 'have her' if anything happened to the King, which had caused a falling-out between herself and Sir Henry and, later, her angry rejection of Sir Francis Weston's advances. Sir William Kingston reported these remarks to Cromwell on May 4th.[8]

Anne did not then realize that Mrs Cousins and her companions, who all slept in her room, were repeating everything she said to them, to the Lieutenant; nor did she understand that Lady Kingston's bed had been placed outside her door for the same purpose. This carelessness was partly the result of her anxiety about her brother, whose arrest and imprisonment were suspected by but concealed from her till May 5th, when Sir William's first interview with him took place.

Kingston brought Rochford a message from the wife who had engineered his fate. She wanted to know, Sir William said, 'how he did', and was pleading for him with the King. Rochford, unaware that it was she who had accused him of incest, sent her his thanks, and went on, 'When shall I come before the King's Council?' Before the Lieutenant could reply, he added, 'For I think I shall not come forth till I come to my judgement' — and broke down.[9]

Some rumour of this interchange reached Anne, who at once

sent for Sir William. She began, 'I hear say my brother is here.' 'It is truth,' he replied. She said—it seems calmly—'I am very glad that we should be so nigh together.' Kingston then told her that Weston and Brereton were also in the Tower, as were Sir Thomas Wyatt and the poet's friend Sir Richard Page. This news was re-assuring—for it did not occur to her that five out of the seven men accused with her were doomed—and she said, 'I shall desire you to bear a letter from me to Master Secretary.' Kingston, who had no intention of approaching Cromwell unless the Vicar-General sent for him, replied, 'Madam, tell it me by word of mouth, and I will do it.'

Anne thanked him; then she raised another point. 'I have much marvel', she said, 'that the King's Council comes not to me.' Receiving no answer, she went on, 'We shall have no rain till I am delivered out of the Tower.' Kingston replied satirically, 'I pray you it may be shortly, because of the fair weather.' As she seemed to ignore his mockery, he added, 'You know what I mean'—and left to make his next report to Cromwell.[10]

In the evening of the same day Kingston saw Anne again. She now knew that she was surrounded by spies, and she greeted him angrily. 'The King wist not what he did,' she began, 'when he put such about me as my lady Boleyn and Mrs Cousins, for they can tell me nothing of my lord my father, nor nothing else—but I defy them all!' Lady Boleyn said severely, 'Such desires as you have had hath brought you to this,' and Mrs Stonor, hoping to find out what Anne felt for Smeaton, put in, 'Mark is the worst cherished of any man in the house, for he wears irons,' adding spitefully, 'That is because he is no gentleman.'[11]

Anne, aware that she was being tested, replied, 'But he was never in my chamber but at Winchester—and there I sent for him to play, for there my lodging was above the King's.' She added that she had not spoken to Smeaton again till they were at Greenwich, when she had warned him not to approach her as the other courtiers did.[12]

Kingston subjoined an account of this rather unsatisfactory interview to his letter of the 5th, upon which Cromwell ordered another agent, Sir Edward Baynton, to obtain confessions of criminal intercourse from the male prisoners. The result was not what the Vicar-General had hoped for, in that—as had been agreed—Smeaton alone acknowledged having had relations with the

Queen, while the courtiers stuck to their original declarations of
innocence. Nevertheless, Sir Edward hastily added, he himself was
sure of their guilt.[13] Cromwell, who had been summoned by
Henry to Hampton Court to arrange the details of their trials, was
disappointed but resolute, in spite of what Kingston described as
Anne's 'obstinacy'.[14]

It was then decided not to issue the bills of indictment till May
10th, so as to give the informers more time to collect further
evidence. Another agent, George Constantine, was sent to interview
Brereton and Sir Henry Norris. Brereton, prepared to die, said
merely, 'No way but one, in any matter,' and Norris, once more
affirming his innocence, later told Kingston that he was ready to
suffer, 'if it be the King's pleasure'.[15]

Cromwell and Henry then decided that Norris, Weston,
Brereton and Smeaton must be tried in Westminster Hall, and that
Anne and her brother should be judged in the Tower by the grand
jury of Kent, the two petty juries of Middlesex and all the members
of the Privy Council. Thus their defence would be heard by
seventy-six persons. At this point, Chapuys, informing the
Emperor that the King had 'determined to get rid of Anne', even
if her guilt was not proved,[16] was disturbed by the news that she
had pleaded a pre-contract with the Earl of Northumberland, in
the hope of nullifying her marriage to Henry. When Northumberland denied this charge (as she once had), her fate seemed assured.[17]
George Constantine then told his employer that there was 'much
muttering' about the way the preliminaries for the case were being
handled; later, he confided to a friend that he himself was not
convinced of the Queen's guilt.[18]

After Henry's consultations with the Vicar-General he ordered
Norfolk to preside over Anne's trial. Meanwhile, her behaviour
puzzled Kingston, who reported her as 'one hour determined to
die, the next much contrary to that'. She asked Lady Kingston,
'Does anybody make [approach] your bed?' 'Nay, I warrant you!'
was the indignant reply. 'They might make ballads,' Anne pursued, 'but there is none better that can do it.' 'Yes—Master
Wyatt,' said Lady Kingston, hoping for some kind of confession,
but Anne merely answered, 'You say true,' and returned to the
question of the Sacrament and her almoner, 'whom I suppose', she
added, 'to be devout.'[19]

During May 9th and 10th the Lieutenant was too busy with

arrangements for the trials to interview Anne, and had to rely on his wife's and the other ladies' reports. They found her changes of mood inexplicable. When he asked Lady Kingston, 'How hath she done this day?' he was told, 'She hath been very merry, and made a great dinner – and yet, soon after, she called for supper.' At Kingston's next visit, Anne began, 'Where have you been all day?' – almost as if in idle curiosity. 'I have been with the prisoners', he replied. Suddenly remembering Winchester's doubts during her first examination, Anne asked to see him, and was told that he had not come to the Tower. Reverting to the private language of her circle, she described the Lord Treasurer as 'in the forest of Windsor' -- in other words, bewildered by the evidence brought against her, adding, 'He is a very gentleman.' She went on angrily, 'I to be a queen, and cruelly handled as never was seen!' This recollection, combined with hopes that she must have known to be fallacious, was too much for her, and she burst into shrieks of laughter, coldly noted by Kingston, who remained silent till she repeated, more calmly, 'I shall have justice.' 'Have no doubt therein,' he assured her, seemingly in the expectation of some useful confession. 'If any man accuse me,' she continued, 'I can say but nay – and they can bring no witness.' Sir William then left, and turning to Mrs Cousins, she declared, 'I knew at Mark's coming to the Tower that night I received [the Sacrament], and I knew of Norris going to the Tower,' apparently to show that she was not to be fooled. A few minutes later, her thoughts still on the lack of evidence in her favour, she said, 'If it [any statement proving her innocence] had been laid [before the Council] I had won.'[20]

Next day, Kingston found her defiant and enraged. 'I would I had my Bishops,' she told him, 'for they would all go to the King for me – for all England prays for me – and if I die, you shall see the greatest punishment within this seven year that ever came to England – for I have done many good deeds in my days. But I think the King put such about me as I never loved.' Pained by this criticism, Kingston protested, 'The King takes them to be honest and good women.' 'But I would have those I favour most,' Anne persisted, and the Lieutenant, despairing of any further information, went away.[21] This conversation seems to have taken place just before the trials of the four courtiers.

This hearing was a disappointment, in that, while Smeaton kept his promise of admitting to fornication with the Queen, the three gentlemen still maintained their innocence. Both their declarations and that of the musician were similarly received. All were sentenced to death. On the 13th, Weston wrote to his wife asking her to forgive him any sins he had committed against her (presumably with Madge Shelton), and this letter was held back and preserved as proof of his relations with Anne.[22] In Court circles her and Rochford's guilt was assumed; those nearest the King took care to denounce her evil ways.[23]

Yet until Anne and her brother had been proved guilty, Cromwell could not be absolutely sure of the outcome. On May 14th he sent Bishop Gardiner a letter which, hurriedly written, was meant to be shown to the King as an official statement. 'The Queen's incontinent living', he wrote, 'was so rank and common that the ladies of her Privy Chamber could not conceal it.' He himself, he added, had 'quaked' when the Council told him of her shameless and unbridled promiscuity.[24] But Kingston's reports of Anne's hysterical outbursts and wild chatter fell far short of the Vicar-General's expectations. That she was, although intermittently, in a state of shock, which prevented her visualizing the full horror of her situation—for burning to death was the punishment for adultery—bewildered Cromwell's informers. They could not foresee that her public trial would re-create the stubborn courage and resolute coolness that had enabled her to face disaster in the past. The Vicar-General feared that this might happen; for he had always—as he later told Chapuys—secretly admired her ability to rise to a crisis.[25]

It was especially disconcerting that, out of all her talk to her courtiers, as reported by herself, only one outrageously rash remark—that to Norris, about his hopes and the possibility of Henry's death—could be regarded as compromising. Cromwell's carefully prepared case, to be conducted by himself as the King's counsel, might yet be defeated, not only by Anne, but also by her brother, whose audacity equalled hers, and was enhanced by his determination, already shown, to defend himself, single-handed, by categorically denying a series of charges obtained from a number of suborned witnesses. In the last resort, the crime of incest could be resolved only by Jane Rochford's evidence—and was she entirely dependable?

NOTES

1. Cavendish, *Life* (Singer's edn), *Addenda* pp. 442, 451–61; *L. & P.*, Vol. X, pp. 340–47; Wriothesley, *Chronicle*, Vol. I, p. 36.
2. Cavendish, *Life*, loc. cit.
3. Ibid., p. 442.
4. *L. & P.*, Vol. X, p. 333.
5. Ibid.
6. Cavendish, *Life*, loc. cit.; *L. & P.*, Vol. X, pp. 340–47.
7. *Spanish Chronicle*, pp. 55–69.
8. *L. & P.*, Vol. X, pp. 340–47.
9. Ibid.
10. Ibid.
11. Ibid.
12. Ibid.
13. Ibid.
14. Ibid.
15. *Archaeologia*, Vol. XXIII, pp. 64–6.
16. *Span. Cal. P.*, Vol. V, pt. 2, p. 107.
17. Collins, *Peerage of England*, Vol. II, p. 137.
18. *Archaeologia*, Vol. XXIII, pp. 64–6.
19. *L. & P.*, Vol. X, pp. 340–47.
20. Ibid.
21. Ibid.
22. Ibid.
23. Ibid., p. 351.
24. Ibid., p. 359.
25. *Span. Cal. P.*, V, Vol. pt. 2, p. 125.

X

The Trials

ON May 13th Cromwell ordered the Queen's household to be broken up, and arranged for her and Rochford to be separately tried two days later. The question then arising of Lord Wiltshire being cited as one of the Privy Council to judge his son and daughter, he was told that he might be excused. He assured the King and the Vicar-General of his willingness to appear; for he feared that if he did not, he would be suspected of family loyalty, and thus deprived of some, or even all, of his properties and places at Court.[1] It was decided that his presence was not necessary; the attendance of his children's other relatives—that of their uncle Norfolk and their cousins, the Earls of Surrey and Maltravers— came under the heading of those gentlemen's service to the state.

Some two thousand spectators were assembled in the King's Hall, where a great scaffold had been erected for the Privy Council. The juries had taken their places when Norfolk as Lord High Steward and Earl Marshal of England entered at the head of the Council, carrying his white wand of office. Surrey, holding a gold staff, then sat at his father's feet. The Duke of Suffolk was placed on Norfolk's left and Lord Chancellor Audley on his right; the other Councillors were disposed according to their rank. Cromwell, as the King's Advocate, stood apart. In the centre of the Hall a chair for the accused faced the judges.[2]

After a short interval, the doors were flung open, and the Queen, attended by her ladies, escorted by Sir William Kingston and the Constable of the Tower, Sir Edmund Walsingham—and followed by the headsman carrying the axe with its edge turned away from her—made her entrance. She curtsied to the Council and sat down. Several observers reported her as perfectly composed—'as unmoved as a stock'—of proud bearing and richly dressed.[3]

After the juries had been sworn and the authority of the Privy Council attested, Cromwell read out the charges. They ran as follows: for three years and more, the Queen, 'despising her marriage and entertaining malice against the King and following daily her frail and carnal lust, did falsely and traitorously procure, by base conversations and kisses, touchings, gifts and other infamous incitations, divers of the King's servants to be her adulterers ... so that several ... yielded to her vile provocations.' Then came the supporting evidence. (1) On October 6th, 1535, she had 'procured' Sir Henry Norris, Gentleman of the Bedchamber; (2) on November 2nd and 27th, 1535, 'her own natural brother George Rochford violated her, her tongue in the said George's mouth and the said George's tongue in hers'; (3) on December 8th, 1534, she had had carnal relations with Sir William Brereton gentleman; (4) on May 8th, 1535, with Sir Francis Weston gentleman; and (5) on April 12th, 1536, with Mark Smeaton, musician. 'These lovers,' the prosecution continued, 'being jealous, gave her presents, she being jealous of them and any other woman ... and gave them great gifts to encourage them in their crimes.' It was further stated that, with them, she had conspired the King's death and agreed to marry one of them when he died. The signatures of the witnesses to these acts were affixed to all six charges. They themselves were not present. The fact that four out of these five seductions were reported as taking place during her last pregnancy was ignored.[4]

The Queen then replied to the accusations in such a manner as to convince a spectator whose account has survived, that she was innocent. She made, he says, 'so wise and discreet answers to all things laid against her, excusing herself with words so clearly, as though she had never been guilty of the same'.[5] She admitted to having given Smeaton and Weston presents of money and medals; these last had probably been struck to celebrate her coronation.[6] To the charge of her incestuous relations with Rochford, she replied as she had to Norfolk at her first examination — 'If he has been in my chamber, surely he might do so without suspicion, being my brother,' and denied that of criminal intercourse with him. She categorically refuted the charges of adultery with Smeaton, Weston, Brereton and Norris, and added that neither she nor they had plotted the King's death; nor had she entered into an agreement of marriage with any of them.[7]

The juries and the Privy Council were then desired by Norfolk to give their verdict. In view of the sworn evidence of the witnesses, their reply was unanimous and inevitable. The Queen was pronounced guilty of incest, adultery and high treason.[8]

Norfolk then rose and said, 'Because thou hast offended our Sovereign Lord the King's Grace, in committing treason against his person, and art here attainted of the same, the law of the realm is this: that thou shalt be burnt here, within the Tower of London, on the Green—else to have thy head smitten off, as the King's pleasure be further known of the same.' He added that she would be deprived of all her titles.[9]

At this point, there was some disturbance in the ranks of the Privy Council, of which the Earl of Northumberland was a member. He had not dared ask leave of absence from the trial—and now found himself unable to endure the victimization of the woman he had once loved; he fainted, and was carried out of the Hall.[10]

Anne was then asked whether she had anything to say. She replied, 'I am ready for death. I regret that of innocent persons.' She went on, 'There is some other reason than the cause alleged. I have always been faithful to the King. I willingly give up my titles to the King who gave them.'[11] She curtsied and, followed by her ladies, Kingston, Walsingham and the executioner, who now turned the edge of the axe towards her, left the Hall.

The trial of Rochford was then delayed, because Norfolk had begun to cry.[12] As soon as he recovered, his nephew was brought in, the juries were sworn a second time, and Rochford was charged with incest.

Cromwell, aware that this accusation would be denied, then read out others, which, although comparatively trivial, would ensure the King's signing the young man's death warrant on the capital issue. Rochford and the Queen were charged with mocking Henry's verses, and making fun of his dress and of his compositions. Rochford refuted all these accusations, speaking at some length, 'so prudently and wisely', according to the same observer, 'to all articles laid against him, that it was a marvel to hear. He never would confess anything, but made himself as clear as though he had never offended.[13]

Cromwell then gave Rochford a paper, telling him not to read it aloud. The prisoner ignored this order, and read out the following accusation, which was that Anne had told him that the King was impotent, and no longer had 'either vigour or virtue'. As Cromwell broke into furious protest, Rochford denied the charge, adding, 'I will not create suspicion in a manner likely to prejudice the issue the King might have from a second marriage.' He refused to consider the suggestion that the Princess Elizabeth was not Henry's daughter, and that she might be his.[14]

In the pause that followed bets were interchanged by the audience, the odds being ten to one in Rochford's favour. Cromwell, seeing the juries somewhat shaken, then produced Lady Rochford's letter, which stated her knowledge, presumably that of a concealed eye-witness, of her husband's incestuous relations with the Queen. This 'accursed secret' had been known only to her, and she now felt herself bound to betray it.[15]

The verdict of Rochford's guilt was then unanimously pronounced. Norfolk rose and said, 'You shall now go again to the Tower [prison] from whence you came, and be drawn from the said Tower of London through the City of London, there to be hanged and then, being alive, cut down — and then your members cut off and your bowels taken out of your body and burnt before you, and then your head cut off and your body divided into four pieces, and your head and body to be set at such places as the King shall assign.'[16]

Rochford, who perhaps counted on this sentence being commuted to beheading, remained unmoved and made no further defence. He was then taken back to his cell. Norfolk broke his wand of office in two, and dismissed the seventy-six judges, who followed him out in order of precedence. Cromwell at once took a boat to Westminster to report the course of the trials to the King.

By this time, it had been decided that Sir Thomas Wyatt was free from all suspicion of intercourse with the Queen, but that he must remain a prisoner until the sensation caused by her trial had died down. He had once been her ally; and now, because a number of people were beginning to pity her and censure the King, his release might endanger Henry's reputation, in the event of his publicly expressing his belief in Anne's innocence. For the revulsion of feeling in her favour (even from those who had been her bitterest enemies) was the next problem with which Cromwell had to deal. There was general dissatisfaction about the conduct of the trials; also, three of the men accused with the Queen — Norris, Weston and Brereton — were thought of as gallant gentlemen, whose statements were worth serious consideration.[17]

There was not the faintest doubt in Henry's mind that he had been infamously betrayed by the woman for whom he had defied the Holy See and convulsed his kingdom — the woman he had made

Queen of England in the face of his subjects' disapproval. The thought of her shameless abandonment to his courtiers' embraces — of her incest — of her mockery — of her attacks on his virility — of her murderous intentions — so appalled him that, having read and absorbed the list of her crimes, he collapsed and went to bed, refusing to see his ministers, or to make any of the decisions now urgently required of him.[18] Nevertheless, he owned himself impressed by her calm defence and fearless confrontation of her accusers. 'She has a stout heart,' he said, 'but she shall pay for it.'[19]

On May 16th Henry and Cromwell saw Sir William Kingston about the payment of Rochford's debts. A few hours later, the King ordered Cranmer to obtain from Anne the acknowledgment of her guilt under the seal of the confessional; the Archbishop must then declare the nullity of their marriage and the illegitimacy of the Princess Elizabeth. (The fact that this pronouncement would invalidate the charge of adultery was ignored.) Henry then commanded the execution — by beheading, for he was determined to be merciful — of Rochford, Brereton, Norris and Weston on Tower Hill for May 17th, while Smeaton, as became his rank, was to suffer the penalty of hanging, drawing and quartering on a separate scaffold. The arrangements for the nullity of the King's marriage resulted in the postponement of Anne's execution till the 19th. He now decided to make a final gesture on her behalf by sending for the headsman of Calais — long renowned for his skill with the sword, as opposed to the axe — to dispatch her on Tower Green in the presence of a selected number of privileged spectators.

Cromwell then took further precautions. He told Kingston to expel all foreigners from the Tower;[20] for their reports of the prisoners' last moments might well create censure among the King's continental allies, some of whom were already criticizing the ruthlessness of a monarch who, having divorced one wife, was now executing a second in order to marry a third. 'He may well divorce [Jane Seymour],' Chapuys told a French correspondent, 'when he tires of her.'[21] The Queen of Hungary's comment achieved the perfection of understatement. 'I think wives will be hardly well contented,' she remarked, 'if such customs become general.'[22]

The question of Anne Boleyn's guilt or innocence became a matter of dispute for the next four hundred years — and even now, remains partially unresolved. In the nineteenth century, a brilliant and distinguished historian pointed out that the unanimous verdict of seventy-six persons, the majority of whom were responsible and God-fearing men, proved that she must have committed some, if not all, of the crimes of which she was accused.[23] Certainly, she was guilty of indiscreet and, perhaps, unseemly behaviour with those courtiers who perished on her account. But, to become the mistress of four men, while at the same time indulging in criminal relations with her brother during pregnancy, in a Court where privacy did not exist—would have been, literally, insane; and at no moment did she show signs of mental disease. Also, the death of the King would have taken away her only powerful supporter. Finally, her judges—whether or not good men and true—were bound to accept the sworn statements which had been placed before them; that was the duty of every loyal subject. The summing-up of this, as of other cases, comes from an expert whose lifelong experience of sixteenth-century law was supreme and unquestioned. Cardinal Wolsey, reflecting on English justice as then exercised, remarked, 'If the Crown were prosecutor and asserted it, juries would be found to bring in a verdict that Abel was the murderer of Cain.'[24]

In fact, the State could not err, whatever the circumstances. And to dispute, or even criticize, the right to punish offenders, was another form of treason. Anne herself accepted this premise, as did those who died, with her, in the cause of national expediency. Their lives were forfeit. England, rather than Henry VIII, was the Moloch on whose altar they must be sacrificed.

On the evening of May 16th Anne was taken by water to Lambeth Palace. There, in the gloom of the crypt, she confessed to Cranmer, returning to the Tower for supper. The Archbishop observed the rule of the confessional; he kept her secret. He could only try to save her by declaring that, according to canon law, she and Henry had never been married, giving two causes for this decision—her pre-contract with Northumberland, which the Earl again denied, and her sister's relationship with the King. The illegitimacy of the Princess Elizabeth was subjoined to this announcement; and so it was thought, by the general public, and by Anne herself, that she would be exiled, to end her days in a nunnery. That night she said to her ladies, 'I shall go to Antwerp, in hope of life.'[25]

This hope did not last. Calmly, Anne prepared to die, sending for another of her chaplains, Matthew Parker, from whom she received the Sacrament in Kingston's presence. She seems to have

asked Parker to do what he could for her daughter, who made him
Archbishop of Canterbury soon after her accession. Anne then
spoke sadly of what she described as Mark Smeaton's false
evidence, 'His soul will suffer,' she said, adding that she would
have preferred to die on the same scaffold as her brother, 'so as to
go to Heaven with him'.[26] That same night Kingston came to
Rochford's cell and told him, 'Be in readiness to suffer tomorrow.'
The young man replied, 'I will do my best to be ready.'[27] The
Lieutenant was impressed by Rochford's courage, as by that of all
the prisoners, who were now composing their speeches from the
scaffold. Kingston deposited copies of these in the archives of the
Tower.

Several of Cromwell's agents attended the executions, so as to
report to him, and thus to the King, the prisoners' last words. They
themselves, knowing this, observed contemporary custom in
speeches that now seem to contradict their former declarations of
innocence. Smeaton, hoping for a reprieve, admitted his guilt to
the final moment of horror, when he concluded with, 'Masters, I
pray you all to pray for me, for I have deserved the death.'

According to Constantine and one or two other witnesses, the
behaviour of the courtiers varied, as did their speeches. But all four
united in submitting to the authority of the State, by whose laws
they had been condemned. It was assumed by them, and by those
who heard them, that the *cause* of that condemnation had nothing
to do with the fact that they were being penalized by an institution
which was faultless and all-powerful. In acknowledging, as they
always had, the right of the State to order their lives, it followed
that they owed it their deaths, if these were required of them; and
therefore, they were bound to ask forgiveness for the crimes of
which they had been found guilty — *even if they had not committed
them.* Furthermore, if they did not obey this unwritten but deeply
reverenced law, their families, and even their descendants, might
suffer for their foolish and supererogatory defiance. They must
leave the world in what religious circles later described as a state
of grace, i.e. as became believers in and supporters of a power
second only to God's: a sacred and inviolable authority.

So it was that Sir William Brereton, who 'died worst of all',
according to Constantine, in that he seems to have lacked physical
courage, said, 'I have deserved to die, if it were a thousand deaths.'
He could not, however, resist an oblique protest, when he added,

'But the cause whereof I judge not – but if ye judge, judge the best,' and repeated this statement three or four times. It was then Norris's turn. He spoke briefly of Henry's favour. 'I do not think', he said, 'that any gentleman of the Court owes more to him than I do, and hath been more ungrateful and regardless of it than I have' – and accepted the sentence of death, praying to God 'for mercy on my soul'. Sir Francis Weston, more explicit in repentance for all his sins, said, 'I had thought to have lived in abomination these twenty or thirty years, and then to have made some amends. I thought little it had come to this.'

Rochford's speech was lengthy, didactic and, in a sense, irrelevant. The rumours of his tendency to Lutheranism – and possibly atheism – seem to have preyed on his mind to the exclusion of all else, and he began, 'I desire you that no man will be discouraged from the Gospel at my fall. For if I had lived according to the Gospel – as I loved it and spake of it – I had never come to this.' He then spoke, loudly and repetitively, of the Law, to which 'I submit me,' and of 'the true word of God' (orthodox Catholicism) which he had ignored. He concluded with a breach of custom, by affirming that he had 'never offended' the King, and went on, 'As for mine offences, I cannot prevail you to hear them that I die here for, but I beseech God that I may be an example [of repentance] to you all. There is no occasion for me to repeat the cause for which I am condemned – you would have little pleasure in hearing me tell it.' He then asked the spectators' forgiveness, adding, 'I forgive you all – and God save the King.'[28]

As none of these men mentioned the Queen or their relations with her, they may be said to have maintained, through silence, their guiltlessness – with the possible exception of Smeaton, whose confession had already been publicized. All, in acknowledging the justice of England, died in a correct and orthodox manner. So none disgraced their name or their families. Honour – a word now so seldom used as to have become almost meaningless – was upheld, and shame eliminated.

The destruction of five persons of whose guilt he had been convinced was a great relief to Henry VIII, and he emerged from retirement in excellent health and spirits. His visits to Jane Seymour – whom Chapuys described as 'very commendable' – we reinterspersed with parties, banquets and expeditions on the river to the sound of music, some of which continued till the small hours.[29]

This shocked the Londoners; they felt that he should have waited to celebrate his freedom till after Anne's execution. Henry's empathy with his subjects resulted in his attempting to conceal his love for Jane. When Charles V proposed that his next wife should be a Portuguese princess, he received an amiably non-committal reply.[30]

Henry spent the evening of May 18th with the Seymours, bringing Jane, who was now 'very richly dressed', a present of jewels, and telling her about the new barge, modelled on that of the Venetian Bucentaur, which he had ordered for her first public appearance.[31] That young lady was sufficiently emboldened to take on the role of peacemaker; she pleaded with the King for the restoration of the Princess Mary, so as to establish 'the general tranquillity of the Kingdom'. 'You are a fool,' he told her. 'You should think of *our* children' — adding that he had no intention of legitimizing his elder daughter.[32]

He then left to attend a party given by the Bishop of Carlisle, taking with him the 'tragedy' he had just written about his betrayal by Anne Boleyn, which he gave to his host, remarking, 'For a long time I foresaw this.' Chapuys, who was one of the guests, reported that the Bishop gratefully received Henry's play, but did not read it. It has since disappeared.[33] Something was then said about the prophecy of the Queen's death in the book left on her table before her marriage — upon which Henry burst out, 'She hath procured a hundred men!' The Ambassador, much amused, told the Emperor, 'You never saw a prince — or a husband — wear his horns more patiently and lightly than this one does.'[34]

These conversations took place on the eve of the execution of the woman Kingston now described as 'unjustly called Queen'. Her life, the courtiers declared, had always been one of 'great infamy', while Henry, 'that noble prince', was 'unlucky' — but perhaps he should have paid more attention to Merlin's prophecy about the adultery of a Queen of England in his reign.[35] Kingston, meanwhile, was increasingly disheartened by Anne's steadfastness, and no longer hoped for a confession of guilt. 'I suppose', he resignedly told Cromwell, 'she will declare herself a good woman for all but the King.'[36] And some days later, when his anxieties were behind him, Cromwell told Chapuys how worried he had been during the trials, by the 'sense, wit and courage' of Rochford and the Queen.[37]

NOTES

1. *Span. Cal. P.*, Vol. V, pt. 2, p. 125.
2. Wriothesley, *Chronicle*, Vol. I, p. 36.
3. *L. & P.*, Vol. X, p. 428.
4. Ibid., p. 361.
5. Wriothesley, loc. cit.
6. Froude, *Divorce*, p. 424.
7. Wriothesley, loc. cit.
8. Ibid.
9. Ibid.
10. Collins, *Peerage of England*, Vol. II, p. 137.
11. *L. & P.*, Vol. X, p. 458.
12. *Archaeologia*, Vol. XXIII, p. 66.
13. Wriothesley, op. cit., Vol. I, p. 39.
14. *Span. Cal. P.*, loc. cit.
15. Nicolas, *Excerpta Historica*, p. 261.
16. Wriothesley, loc. cit.
17. *L. & P.*, Vol. X, p. 376.
18. Ibid., p. 361.
19. *Spanish Chronicle*, p. 65.
20. Friedmann, *Anne Boleyn*, Vol. II, p. 291.
21. Baldwin Smith, *Henry VIII*, p. 103.

22. *L. & P.*, Vol. X, p. 401.
23. Froude, *History*, Vol. II, p. 154.
24. Strickland, *Queens of England*, p. 256.
25. *L. & P.*, Vol. X, pp. 428, 471.
26. Ibid.
27. Ibid.
28. *Archaeologia*, Vol. XXIII, pp. 64–6; Bell, *Notices of Burials in the Tower*, pp. 94–108; *L. & P.*, Vol. X, p. 376; *Spanish Chronicle*, pp. 66–7; Nicolas, op. cit., pp. 261–5; Wriothesley, op. cit., Vol. I, p. 37; Thomas, *The Pilgrim*, p. 116.
29. *Span. Cal. P.*, Vol. V, pt 2, p. 125; *L. & P.*, Vol. X, p. 376.
30. *L. & P.*, loc. cit.
31. Ibid.
32. Ibid.
33. Ibid.
34. *Span. Cal. P.*, Vol. V, pt. 2, p. 120.
35. *L. & P.*, Vol. X, p. 382.
36. Ibid.
37. *Span. Cal. P.*, loc. cit.

XI

Tower Green

I N the late sixteenth century a letter from Anne Boleyn to Henry VIII was discovered which had apparently been written some days before her execution.[1] Neither the handwriting nor the style of this lengthy and eloquent epistle resembles hers; and it can now be linked up with the apocryphal anecdotes collected by the Spanish merchant which became, and still remain, a part of her legend. This anonymous chronicler reports her as saying to Cranmer, 'My lord Archbishop, waste no more time. I never wronged the King, but I know well that he is tired of me,' adding that Henry's love for Jane Seymour was the cause of her condemnation. And, in another interview, she is supposed to have said that her brother's execution was arranged, 'so that none should be left to take my part'.[2]

Although Anne might well have made these and similar comments, there is no authentic record of her having done so. They epitomize the view of those outside the Court circle, who felt, and even dared to say, that she had been unjustly condemned and who, in her daughter's reign, portrayed her as a tragic heroine; an attempted rehabilitation with which that supremely wise, cautious and tactful monarch would have nothing to do. Elizabeth was two years and eight months old when her mother was beheaded; and there is no report of when or how she received the news of that event, or what effect, if any, it had upon her. This very sharp child's comment on the verdict of her illegitimacy was made two years later, to Sir Francis Bryan. 'Why, Governor,' she demanded, 'how hap it yesterday my Lady Princess, and today but Lady Elizabeth?'[3]

Another story describes Anne kneeling before Lady Worcester — whom she did not see again after her arrest — and saying that she could have 'no quiet' in her conscience until she had repented of her 'severity' towards the Princess Mary, and received forgiveness for it.[4] Again, this invention can be connected with Anne's supposed statement that her stepdaughter would be 'the cause of my

death, unless I get rid of her first'.[5] Her only recorded judgment of
Henry's attitude comes from one of her ladies, who told Chapuys
that the Queen blamed him for the loss of her husband's love.
'From the very moment of his arrival,' she said, 'the King no
longer looked at me as before'—upon which the Ambassador
remarked, 'I was flattered by the compliment, for she would have
cast me to the dogs.'[6]

The last twenty-four hours of Anne's life were very busy ones
for Sir William Kingston, whose arrangements for the other
prisoners' executions had made it difficult to report her talks with
him as fully as he would have wished. In any case, he was no great
hand with the pen; and her distressingly unconventional behaviour
halted such eloquence as he could achieve. After she had received
the Sacrament for the last time, she appeared unrepentant, and,
worse still, cheerful and calm. He had never liked her; and now
she outraged his sense of propriety. 'I have seen many men, and
also women, executed,' he told Cromwell in his letter of May 18th,
'and they have been in great sorrow—and, to my knowledge, this
lady hath much joy and pleasure in death.'[7]

Yet he was doing all he could for her, rushed and fussed though
he was; he had arranged for one of her chaplains to be with her till
the end—but not on the scaffold, as she had never acknowledged
her guilt—and even, at her rather unreasonable request, had himself managed to take the Sacrament with her. If he had been allowed
a longer interval between the executions of the men and that of
this sensationally important prisoner—for the beheading of a
Queen of England was an historic and unprecedented event—he
could have seen to every detail with his usual efficiency. As it was,
he found himself harassed and confused by the orders from
Whitehall. The scaffold used for the courtiers would not do;
another must be built—'of such a height that all may see it'—and
so a posse of carpenters had to be engaged and set to work, hammering and sawing (at some cost, too), throughout the night of the
18th.[8] It then became clear that the final scene, which had been
fixed for nine o'clock, would have to be postponed until noon.
'What is the King's pleasure touching the Queen,' Kingston asked
Cromwell, 'as well *for her comfort*, as for the preparation of
scaffolds and other necessaries?'[9] This conscientious civil servant
seems to have been worried by there being no time in which to
obtain and put up the black draperies required for such an

occasion; and what with replacing one scaffold by another, and selecting the spectators—not more than thirty, he had been told, some of whom must be Court and others City dignitaries—he forgot to have the Queen measured for her coffin, or indeed to order that that necessary object should be placed in the chapel of St Peter-ad-Vincula. It was all very taxing; he could only promise to do his best. 'And', he added more confidently, 'I am very glad of the executioner of Calais—for he can handle the matter.'[10]

The choice of witnesses placed the Lieutenant in another dilemma; for the limitation of their numbers meant that certain notables would be left out, and thus mortally offended. However, those were His Majesty's orders. Chancellor Audley, the Dukes of Suffolk, Norfolk and Richmond, the Earls of Surrey and Maltravers, the Vicar-General and other members of the Privy Council were convened as a matter of course. The Lord Mayor, with the Sheriffs and Aldermen, must attend; and that left little room for the chief 'craftsmen' and the yeomen of the guard. After the headsman, the most essential functionary was the cannoneer; he was to stand on the battlements above Tower Green, his linstock lit and ready for the moment of death; and so his view of the scaffold must be unimpeded.[11]

Sir William had never before worked so continuously or at such pressure; but he knew his duty, and did not shrink from it. On the morning of the 19th, there was still so much to see to that he had to send a message to Anne that he would not be able to call for her till half an hour or so before midday; for the carpenters had to be paid off and dismissed, and the Frenchman received and entertained by the Lieutenant himself; such matters could not be left to an underling, however reliable. At last Sir William made time to visit the Queen and apologize for the delay. Before he could speak, she began, 'Master Kingston, I hear I shall not die afore noon—and I am very sorry therefore, for I thought to be dead, and past my pain.' 'It should be no pain, it is so subtle,' he replied. 'I heard say', she went on conversationally, 'that the executioner was very good—and I have a little neck,' and put her hands about it, 'laughing heartily'.[12] That terrible sound—one he could neither understand, nor pity, nor forgive—silenced him. Appalled and shocked, he left her to her ladies, who were now in tears.

For her alternations of mood, ranging from assured serenity to a frightful mirth, had been too much for them, coldly observant though they were. After it was all over, one repeated to Chapuys —who, quietly triumphant, reported general rejoicing at the Concubine's fate—her jokes about being remembered as Queen Lackhead, and her attempts to console them.[13] And this on the last, dreadful night, when sleep was out of the question, partly because the hammering and banging and the shouts of the workmen did not cease.

So she had time, during those hours, to recall the glories and disasters of her too short, too dramatic career. It seems unlikely, judging by her behaviour on the scaffold, that she felt anything but relief at having reached the end of the road that had led from the tranquil beauty of Hever Castle to the low-built lodgings—still known as the Queen's House—facing Tower Green. Nine years of splendour, triumph, anger, censure, notoriety and despair were about to end, as they had begun, in a glare of publicity: one she was perfectly qualified to sustain, and in which she prepared to dazzle and astound those waiting to watch her die.

Her farewell to the world had been composed some days earlier. Brief, orthodox and formal, it yet contained a rather strange tribute to her husband's 'gentleness and mercy',[14] which now reads like a bitterly satirical comment on the vengeful fury of a disappointed, faithless monster—but this was not the case. The lives of Henry VIII and Anne Boleyn, intertwined through his love and her subjugation to it, had drifted apart some time before that last miscarriage and her condemnation; and during those six years of struggle over the divorce he had endured her wild exasperation and her outbursts of temper with stubborn patience, even—although rarely—with a tolerant understanding that she did not deserve, and may not have appreciated then. Now, she could do so.

It was not her fault that she had failed him; but in that age of relentless cruelty, she expected, as all Henry's victims did, the punishment of failure. Living on the heights, loaded with honours, riches and power, she knew that the depths had always awaited her; therefore she nerved herself to enter them as became a queen. She accepted the decision that the 'little neck' which had been too slender to bear the weight of Edward the Confessor's crown, must be submitted to the sword.

Meanwhile, the most immediate consideration was that of her dress, chosen some days before. Her attendants put on her a robe of dark-grey damask, with a crimson underskirt, an ermine cape and a coif trimmed with pearls. The problem of her hair, which, freed from this, might inconvenience the headsman, was solved by a white linen cap, entrusted to one of her ladies, together with the embroidered handkerchief for binding her eyes, and the cloth to throw over her head when it fell.[15] She wore no other jewels — they had been sent back to the Keeper of the Wardrobe — and carried in one hand a little gold-bound prayer-book that she intended to send to Sir Thomas Wyatt, who (she may have guessed it) was going to watch her execution from the window of his prison.[16] It was the only tribute he could pay her. To attend, or to watch from a distance, the execution of a friend, was expected of those who were accustomed to look on violent death without horror or disgust. If any of the men ordered to stand beneath the scaffold had asked to be excused from such a spectacle, they would have been censured for attempting to evade a solemn duty.

Sir William Kingston's observance of the formalities was succinctly expressed when he came to fetch the Queen. 'Madam,' he began, 'the hour approaches — you must make ready.' She replied in the same manner with 'Acquit yourself of your charge — for I have been long prepared.'[17] Followed by her ladies, they then descended the stairs, pausing outside the doors for the guards to fall in before and behind them.

During that two and half minutes' walk, Anne, apparently aware that the Lieutenant's correctness barely concealed his disapproval of her character and behaviour, asked him not to prevent her repeating the speech of which she had given him a copy.[18] He would not have been permitted to do so, even if he had wished it, and she was reassured. As she had no money to fee the headsman, he had orders to give her £20 for that, or for any other legacies required of her.[19] At the Green, he handed her over to the Sheriffs who, with the Constable of the Tower, were waiting below the scaffold. They and he then stood back while she and her ladies mounted it — to be faced by the masked headsman, who, leaving his assistant to hold the sword, advanced to meet her. Kneeling, he said, 'Madame, I crave Your Majesty's pardon — for I am ordered to do my duty.' In the set formula, the Queen replied, 'Willingly,' and gave him his fee.[20] Then she turned and looked behind her, as if expecting some new arrival.

At this point, it was observed by more than one witness that she not only retained all her accustomed elegance, but was in great looks, and perfectly composed. As she moved towards the rail to address the spectators, she showed 'a cheerful and smiling countenance'.[21] When she began to speak, her voice was rather faint; presently, it became stronger, then very clear. She said, 'Good Christian people—I am come hither to die, for according to the law, and by the law, I am judged to die, and therefore will I speak nothing against it. I am come hither to accuse no man, nor to speak anything of that whereof I am accused and condemned to die. But I pray God to save the King, and send him long to reign over you —for a gentler nor a more merciful prince was there never; and to me he was ever a good, a gentle and sovereign lord. And if any person will meddle with my cause, I require them to judge the best. And thus I take my leave of the world, and of you all, and I heartily desire you all to pray for me.'[22]

By this time, her ladies, and some of the spectators, were crying. The Queen removed her cape; then she took off her coif, replacing it with the linen cap—and once more, she looked behind her. (It was later conjectured that she might have been hoping for a reprieve: but this seems unlikely.) She gave her prayer-book to the lady who was to convey it to Sir Thomas Wyatt, and who now bound the handkerchief over her eyes. As she stood there—'dazed', according to one observer—the headsman said, 'Madame, I beg you to kneel, and say your prayers.' Guided to the block, she obeyed, taking care to fold her gown about her feet. And then her voice, steady and penetrating, rose from the scaffold. 'To Jesus Christ I commit my soul. O Lord, have mercy on me. To Christ I commend my soul. Jesu, receive my soul!' At the same time, the headsman said quietly to his assistant, 'Bring me the sword.'

Now he was standing above her—and his skill did not fail. A single, hissing stroke sufficed. A small, round, white-capped object rolled over the straw. And the cannon sounded from the battlements.

He stooped and picked up the head, holding it out, to show that justice had been done. As he had no English, it was the duty of some other official to call out, 'So perish all His Majesty's enemies!'

One spectator, a Portuguese clerk from the Spanish Embassy, who had somehow managed to join those convened, afterwards reported that, as the head rose into view, the eyes and lips still moved. But then, he had never before seen a woman, much less a queen, executed; and this one's courage and beauty may have been too much for him.

As the head was dropped into the straw a lady stepped forward with the cloth. The dark-grey dress, the outstretched arms, the neck pouring blood, remained: exposed, obscene. The executioner and his assistant climbed down from the scaffold to join Sir William Kingston, whose business it was to give them drink, and set them on their way to the coast. Meanwhile, the spectators were moving slowly away, in order of precedence, and the Lieutenant was scribbling a last note to Cromwell. The Queen, he wrote, 'died boldly', adding, 'God take her to His mercy — if it be His pleasure.'[23]

All the ladies had disappeared. The Tower clock struck once — twice — three times. And still the head and body of her whose motto had been 'Happiest of Women' lay there, soaking into the straw.

Late in the afternoon, Kingston remembered that he had a final duty. He gave orders that the Queen's remains, duly covered and enclosed, should be deposited in St Peter-ad-Vincula. His assistants reported that no coffin had been provided — but, they added, they knew of an old elm arrow-chest that might serve. Kingston approved; and in a few minutes the decapitated corpse was shovelled into this receptacle, and carried to the chapel.

But where to place it? Kingston then recalled that Rochford had been buried beneath the altar. For the second time in three days, the stones were prized up, and the arrow-chest was pushed down beside the makeshift coffin of Queen Anne's brother. So her wish that they should be together in death was granted.[24]

NOTES

1. Burnet, *Collectanea*, Vol. I, p. 87.
2. *Spanish Chronicle*, p. 65.
3. Rutland MSS., Vol. I, p. 310.
4. Burnet, *History of the Reformation*, Vol. I, p. 204.
5. *Span. Cal. P.*, Vol. V, pt. 1, p. 551.
6. Ibid., pt. 2, p. 120.
7. *L. & P.*, Vol. X, p. 461.
8. Ibid., p. 274.
9. Ibid.
10. Ibid.
11. Froude, *History*, Vol. II, p. 170.
12. *L. & P.*, Vol. X, p. 461.
13. Ibid., p. 434.
14. Hall, *Chronicle*, p. 819.
15. *L. & P.*, Vol. X, p. 382.
16. Thomson, *Sir Thomas Wyatt and His Background*, p. 41.
17. *L. & P.*, Vol. X, p. 428.
18. Bell, *Notices of Burials in the Tower*, p. 108.
19. Friedmann, *Anne Boleyn*, Vol. II, p. 291.
20. *Spanish Chronicle*, p. 71.
21. Wriothesley, *Chronicle*, Vol. I, p. 42.
22. Hall, op. cit., p. 819.
23. *L. & P.*, Vol. X, p. 382.
24. *Archaeologia*, Vol. XXIII, p. 66; Burnet, *History*, Vol. I, p. 197; Godwin, *Annales*, p. 81; Nicolas, *Excerpta Historica*, p. 265; Thomson, op. cit., p. 41.

Epilogue

DURING the latter part of the twentieth century certain oculists were able to provide their patients with what came to be known as bifocal spectacles. The divided lens of this invention contained two types of vision, and those using them soon became accustomed to changing their sights from one to the other.

Towards the end of his reign, Henry VIII acquired a pair of gold-rimmed glasses, presumably for reading;[1] his mental and moral sights had always been bifocally organized; for he automatically eliminated one aspect of a situation in order to concentrate on another, while unaware that he was doing so. Therein lay much of his strength, enhanced by the persuasive powers which operated as effectively on his subjects as on himself. This process was specifically demonstrated on June 8th, 1536, when Parliament was summoned to hear his new arrangements for the succession.

Eighteen days had passed since the three hours' delay over the execution of Anne Boleyn, which resulted in Henry breaking his promise to Jane Seymour that he would have 'good news' for her by nine o'clock in the morning.[2] He made up for this by formally betrothing himself to her that same evening (he was then wearing the white mourning he retained for one day[3]) and arranging for their marriage to take place on June 2nd, when he remarked that he had 'come out of Hell into Heaven'.[4] She was proclaimed Queen of England on the 4th.

Henry then fell ill; and although he had recovered by the 8th, he was more than usually anxious about the establishment of a legitimate — and popular — succession. At this meeting, Chancellor Audley opened the proceedings by pointing out that, on the morning of May 20th, the Privy Council had implored His Majesty to take another wife without delay; and he had graciously consented. The only legitimate male heir was his nephew, James V of Scotland; but in no circumstances could he succeed — national feeling forbade it — and both Henry's daughters were bastards. The King and his Council had now found a remedy for this desperate situation; before announcing it, his matrimonial history must be outlined to the representatives of his people.

Their Sovereign Lord, the Chancellor explained, had unwittingly been led into two illegal alliances, and was therefore married for the first time at the dangerously late age of forty-five. The 'sorrows' he had endured through his first 'unlawful' marriage were briefly touched on; then came a description of 'the Lady Anne's' guilt, when—'Your Majesty, not knowing of any lawful impediments, entered into the bonds of the said unlawful marriage, and advanced the same Lady Anne to the sovereign state ... Yet she, nevertheless, inflamed with pride, and carnal desires of her body ... confederated herself with ... her natural brother, [and with] Henry Norris, Francis Weston, William Brereton and Mark Smeaton ... to the utter loss, disherison and desolation of this realm ... for the which ... they were convict and attainted.' The 'excellent goodness' of Queen Jane having been described at some length, His Majesty was then asked to dispose of the Crown by will. Whomsoever he selected to succeed him, whether male or female, his humble and obedient subjects would 'accept, love, dread and only obey'.[5]

It has been observed that if Anne Boleyn had been an innocent victim, then, 'no King of England was ever in so terrible a position as Henry VIII,' when he approved these pronouncements.[6] In fact, he approved them because he firmly believed her to have been guilty; and so did the majority of his hearers.

As the blame for the destruction for which she herself was not responsible did not fall on Henry—in signing the death-warrant of an adulteress he was merely obeying the law—it might, by some, be attributed to Cromwell. But the Vicar-General, as the principal servant of the State, was in the position of a surgeon employed to cut away a malignant growth from the body politic. To object that he did so by means now considered hideously corrupt, is to apply twentieth-century standards to an age in which justice yielded to expediency. And Cromwell's witnesses subscribed to this concept when they collaborated with him by providing evidence against a person whose inability to bear a son had made her a danger to their country. Therefore, according to contemporary standards, those concurring in Anne's condemnation acted as patriots, putting the State first, last, and all the time. The question of blame did not then—and should not now, in the historical sense—arise.

Anne Boleyn's removal entailed the penalization of her father, who lost his estates, and that of the Princess Elizabeth, who was deprived, not only of her rank, but of certain necessities. When she grew out of the wardrobe her mother had chosen, some time passed before Lady Bryan could persuade Cromwell to provide her with new clothes. What may have more concerned the child herself, was the loss of two dolls, one dressed in red velvet, the other in white satin, packed in a wooden box and left in one of her father's palaces, when she was moved to Hunsdon House, near Hatfield, in the year of her mother's execution.[7] Others fared better. Sir Thomas Wyatt, sent back to Kent — 'Those bloody days have broke my heart,' he told his father — [8] was later restored to favour. The Princess Mary eventually became reconciled to Henry through the auspices of her second stepmother — 'Nobody durst speak to me whilst *that woman* lived,' she remarked — [9] and Lady Rochford managed to collect her husband's goods from Cromwell.[10] A free pardon was then issued to all those imprisoned for abusing Anne and describing her daughter as illegitimate.[11]

So Anne Boleyn's rise and fall became a memory — not a pleasant one, naturally. Henry's subjects could only try to forget it in their pleasure at the success of his third marriage, which ended in October 1537, with the death, after child-birth, of the wife who provided him with the son so longed and prayed for — and who himself was doomed to perish in his sixteenth year.

Although King Henry chose to ignore his younger daughter for some time after her mother's death, he did not trouble to obliterate three comparatively trivial reminders of his second marriage. The frontispiece of Coverdale's Bible still bears Anne Boleyn's initials; and these, encircled by his, also remain on the screen of King's College chapel. Finally, an unknown prisoner, confined in the Martin Tower, carved on one of its walls the word 'Boullen', the letter H, and a Tudor rose. This tribute was destroyed in the nineteenth century.[12]

In the rather grim pageant of Henry's queens Anne Boleyn became the most conspicuous; and her fame has been constantly renewed in a series of dramatic presentations. In the earliest of these, the voice of the man whose love brought about her destruction is faintly echoed.

> Sweetheart,
> I were unmannerly to take you out,
> And not to kiss you.

And a few minutes later—

Sweet partner,
I must not yet forsake you. Let's be merry ...

NOTES

1. Williams, *Henry VIII and His Court*, p. 249.
2. *L. & P.*, Vol. X, p. 374.
3. Hall, *Chronicle*, p. 819.
4. *L. & P.*, Vol. X, p. 434.
5. Froude, *History*, Vol. II, p. 176.
6. Ibid.
7. Williams, *Elizabeth I*, p. 25.
8. Thomson, *Sir Thomas Wyatt and His Background*, p. 43.
9. *L. & P.*, Vol. X, p. 402.
10. Ibid.
11. Elton, *Policy and Police*, p. 277.
12. Bell, *Notices of Burials in the Tower*, p. 108.

Bibliography

Archaeologia, Vol. XXIII, London, 1831.
Baldwin Smith, L. *Henry VIII: The Mask of Royalty*, London, 1971.
Bapst, E. *Deux Gentilhommes-poètes de la Cour de Henry VIII*, Paris, 1891.
Benger, A. B. *Anne Boleyn*, London, 1821.
Bell, D. C. *Notices of Burials in the Tower*, London, 1877.
Bindoff, S. T. *Tudor England*, Harmondsworth, 1950.
Bourgueville, C. de. *Recherches et Antiquités*, Caen, 1588.
Bowle, J. *Henry VIII*, London, 1964.
Burnet, G. *The History of the Reformation of the Church of England*, ed. N. Pocock, 7 vols, Oxford, 1865.
———. *Collectanea*, 1687.
Byrne, M. St C. *The Letters of Henry VIII*, London, 1936.
Calendar of Letters, Despatches, and State Papers relating to Negotiations between England and Spain preserved in the Archives at Simancas and elsewhere, ed. G. A. Bergenroth, *et al.*, 13 vols, London, 1862–1954; cited as *Span. Cal. P.*
Calendar of State Papers and Manuscripts relating to English Affairs, Preserved in the Archives of Venice and in other Libraries of Northern Italy, ed. R. Brown, *et al.*, 9 vols, London, 1864–98; cited as *Ven. Cal. P.*
Cavendish, G. *Life and Death of Cardinal Wolsey*, ed. R. S. Sylvester, E.E.T.S., London, 1959; and where specified, Singer's edition of 1827.
Chapman, H. W. *The Sisters of Henry VIII*, London, 1969.
Chronicle of the Grey Friars of London, ed. J. G. Nichols, Camden Soc., Vol. LIII, London, 1852.
Clifford, H. *The Life of Jane Dormer*, London, 1887.
Collins, A. *Peerage of England*, London, 1709.
Dickens, A. G. *Thomas Cromwell and the English Reformation*, London, 1959.
Ellis, H. *Original Letters Illustrative of English History*, 3 series in 11 vols, London, 1825, 1827, 1846.
Elton, G. R. *England under the Tudors*, London, 1955.
———. *Policy and Police: Enforcement of the Reformation in the Age of Thomas Cromwell*, Cambridge, 1972.
———. *The Revolution in Tudor Government*, Cambridge, 1953.
Fish, S. *A Supplication for the Beggars*, n.p., 1529.
Foxe, J. *Acts and Monuments*, ed. G. Townsend, 8 vols, London, 1843–9.

Friedmann, P. *Anne Boleyn*, 2 vols, London, 1884.
Froude, J. A. *The Divorce of Catherine of Aragon*, London, 1891.
——. *History of England*, Everyman's Library, London, n.d.
Genies et Réalités, ed. Hachette.
Godwin, F. *Annals of England containing the Reignes of Henry the Eighth, Edward the sixt, Queen Mary*, London, 1630.
Hall, E. *Henry VIII, from The Union of the Two Noble and Illustre Famelies of Lancastre & Yorke*, ed. C. Whibley, 2 vols, London, 1904; cited as *Chronicle*.
Halliwell, J. O. *Letters of the Kings of England*, 2 vols, London, 1846–8.
Harpsfield, N. *The Pretended Divorce between Henry VIII and Catherine of Aragon*, ed. N. Pocock, Camden Soc., new series, Vol. XXI, London, 1878.
Herbert, Lord Edward of Cherbury. *The Life and Raigne of King Henry the Eighth*, London, 1649.
Heylyn, P. *History of the Reformation of the Church of England*, London, 1661.
Holinshed, R. *Chronicles of England, Scotland, and Ireland*, 6 vols, London, 1807–8.
Hume, M. A. S. *Chronicle of King Henry VIII*, London, 1889; cited as *Spanish Chronicle*.
Huxley, Aldous. *The Devils of Loudun*, London, 1970.
Jenkins, E. *Elizabeth the Great*, London, 1958.
Knowles, D. *Religious Orders in England*, Vol. III, Cambridge, 1959.
Letters and Papers, Foreign and Domestic, of the Reign of Henry VIII, ed. J. Gairdner and R. H. Brodie, 21 vols, London, 1862–1910; cited as *L. & P.*
Loke, W. *An Account of Materials furnished for the Use of Queen Anne Boleyn*, Miscellanies of the Philobiblon Soc., Vol. VII, 1862–3; cited as *Materials*.
Mackie, J. D. *The Earlier Tudors, 1485–1558*, London, 1952.
Mathew, D. *The Courtiers of Henry VIII*, London, 1970.
Mattingly, G. *Catherine of Aragon*, London, 1942.
Merriman, R. B. *Life and Letters of Thomas Cromwell*, 2 vols, London, 1929.
Morris, C. *The Tudors*, Fontana, London, 1966.
Nichols, J. G. *Narratives of the Days of the Reformation*, Camden Soc., Westminster, 1859.
Nicolas, N. H. *Excerpta Historica*, London, 1831.
Parmiter, G. de C. *The King's Great Matter*, London, 1967.
Pocock, N. *Records of the Reformation*, Oxford, 1870.
Pollard, A. F. *Wolsey*, London, 1929.
——. *Henry VIII*, London, 1934.
Prescott, H. F. M. *Mary Tudor*, London, 1953.

Read, Conyers. *Bibliography of British History: Tudor Period, 1485–1603*, London, 1959.

Ridley, J. *Thomas Cranmer*, Oxford, 1962.

Roper, W. *Life of Sir Thomas More*, ed. E. V. Hitchcock, E.E.T.S., London, 1958.

Round, J. H. *Early Life of Anne Boleyn*, London, 1886.

Rowse, A. L. *The Tower of London*, London, 1972.

Rutland MSS. Historical MS. Commission.

Scarisbrick, J. J. *Henry VIII*, London, 1968.

Span. Cal. P., see *Calendar of Letters, Despatches, and State Papers*, etc.

Spanish Chronicle, see Hume, M. A. S., *Chronicle of King Henry VIII*.

Stow, J. *Annales, or A General Chronicle of England*, ed. E. Howes, London, 1631.

——. *The Survey of London*, Everyman's Library, London, n.d.

Strickland, A. *Lives of the Queens of England*, 8 vols, London, 1851–2.

Strype, J. *Ecclesiastical Memorials*, 3 vols in 6, Oxford, 1822.

——. *Memorials of Archbishop Cranmer*, 3 vols, Oxford, 1854.

Thomas, W. *The Pilgrim: A Dialogue on the Life and Actions of King Henry the Eighth*, ed. J. A. Froude, London, 1861.

Thomson, P. *Sir Thomas Wyatt and His Background*, London, 1964.

Tyndale, W. *Obedience of a Christian Man*, n.p., 1528.

——. *Practice of Prelates*, n.p., 1530.

Ven. Cal. P., see *Calendar of State Papers and Manuscripts*, etc.

Williams, N. *All the Queen's Men*, London, 1972.

——. *Henry VIII and His Court*, London, 1971.

——. *Elizabeth I, Queen of England*, London, 1967.

Williamson, J. A. *The Tudor Age*, London, 1965.

Wriothesley, C. A. *A Chronicle of England*, ed. W. D. Hamilton, Camden Soc., new series, London, 1875, 1877.

Wyatt, G. *Extracts from the Life of the Virtuous, Christian and Renowned Queen Anne Boleyn*, London, 1817; cited as *Anne Boleyn*.

Index

SEMPER EADEM

The DESCRIPTION of the
TOWER of LONDON,
with all the Buildings & the Remains of a
Royal Palace;
and the Outermost Limits thereof
together with all such Places adjoyning
as do confine and abound the said
Liberties, made by the Direction of
Sr. John Peyton Kt.

Earl Lumley's House, sometime
belonging to Crookshol Pryne

The New Brick Wall

Pikes Garden

AC

TOWER HILL

The Pools of
the Scaffold

Barkin Church

Tower Street

The Houses between the Outward Gate
and the Hill are to London way

AH

The Minories or
Philadelphus

AB

Thames Street

Petty Wales

The Lyons Tower

The Lyons Gate

A

B

THE WH

The Lieutenants
Lodgings

THE
OF

F

E

D

THE

C

RIVER   THAMS